KNOWLEDGE, POWER
AND LEARNING

Companion Volume

The companion volume in this series is:
Learning, Space and Identity
Edited by: Carrie Paechter, Richard Edwards, Roger Harrison and Peter Twining

Both of these readers are part of the second level Open University course E211
Learning Matters: challenges of the information age. This is an innovative course,
which looks at the impact of new technologies on learning throughout life and in a
wide range of learning situations. The course forms part of the Open University
undergraduate programme.

How to apply

If you would like to register for this course, or simply to find out more information
about available courses, details can be obtained from the Course Reservations
Centre, PO Box 724, The Open University, Walton Hall, Milton Keynes, MK7
6ZW, UK (Telephone 0 (0 44) 1908 653231). Details can also be viewed on our
web page http://www.open.ac.uk.

KNOWLEDGE, POWER AND LEARNING

edited by
Carrie Paechter, Margaret Preedy,
David Scott and Janet Soler

P·C·P
Paul Chapman
Publishing Ltd

in association with

The Open
University

Compilation, original and editorial material
© Copyright The Open University 2001

First published in 2001

Apart from any fair dealing for the purposes of research or
private study, or criticism or review, as permitted under the
Copyright, Designs and Patents Act, 1988, this publication
may be reproduced, stored or transmitted in any form or by
any means, only with the prior permission in writing of the
publishers, or in the case of reprographic reproduction, in
accordance with the terms of licences issued by the Copyright
Licensing Agency. Inquiries concerning reproduction outside
those terms should be sent to the publishers.

 Paul Chapman Publishing Ltd
A SAGE Publications Company
6 Bonhill Street
London EC2A 4PU

SAGE Publications Inc.
2455 Teller Road
Thousand Oaks, California 91320

SAGE Publications India Pvt Ltd
32, M-Block Market
Greater Kailash - I
New Delhi 110 048

British Cataloguing in Publication Data
A catalogue record for this book is available from the British
Library

ISBN 0 7619 6936 5
ISBN 0 7619 6937 3 (pbk)

Library of Congress catalog record available

Typeset by Dorwyn Ltd, Rowlands Castle, Hants
Printed in Great Britain by Athenaeum Press, Gateshead

Contents

Acknowledgements

The editors and publishers wish to thank the following for permission to use copyright material:

The National Institute of Adult Continuing Education for Richard Edwards (1991) 'The politics of meeting learner needs: power, subject, subjection', *Studies in the Education of Adults*, 23:1;

Open University Press for Carrie Paechter (2000) *Changing School Subjects: Power, Gender and Curriculum*, Chap. 2;

Royal Geographical Society for adapted material from Doreen Massey (1995) 'Masculinity, dualisms and high technology', *Transactions of the Institute of British Geographers*, 20, pp. 487–99;

Taylor & Francis Books Ltd for John Sloboda (1993) 'What is skill and how is it acquired?' in *Culture and Processors of Adult Learning*, eds. Mary Thorpe et al, Routledge, pp. 253–73; Peter Scrimshaw (1997) 'Computers and the teacher's role' in *Using Information Technology Effectively in Teaching and Learning*, eds. Bridget Somekh and Niki Davis, Routledge, pp. 100–113; Michael Eraut (1994) *Developing Professional Knowledge and Competence*, Falmer Press, pp. 123–57; adapted material from Robin Usher (1997) 'Telling a story about research and research as story-telling' in *Understanding Social Research: Perspectives on Methodology and Practice*, eds. George McKenzie, Jackie Powell and Robin Usher, Falmer Press, pp. 27–41; Doreen Massey (1998) 'Blurring the boundaries? High-tech in Cambridge' in *New Frontiers of Space, Bodies and Gender*, ed. Rosie Ainley, Routledge, pp. 157–75; and material from Jane Kenway (1996) 'The information superhighway and postmodernity: the social promise and the social price', *Comparative Education*, 32:2, pp. 217–31;

Thompson Educational Publishing, Inc for Tara Fenwick (1998) 'Questioning the concept of the learning organisation' in *Learning for Life: Canadian Readings in Adult Education*, eds. S. Scott, B Spencer and Alan Thomas, pp. 140–52;

Triangle Journals Ltd for David Guile and Michael Young (1998) 'Apprenticeship as a conceptual basis for a social theory of learning', *Journal of Vocational Education and Training*, 50:2, pp. 173–192; and Carrie Paechter (1988) 'Schooling and the ownership of knowledge', *Curriculum Studies*, 6:2, pp. 161–74;

Every effort has been made to trace the copyright holders but if any have been inadvertently overlooked the publishers will be pleased to make the necessary arrangement at the first opportunity.

Introduction

A number of developments in recent years have brought an increasing focus on the relationship between knowledge, power and learning. The move towards seeing learning as a lifelong activity, rather than as confined to a comparatively short period of school-based study or initial work-related training, has made more salient some of the issues about the importance or relevance of different forms or types of knowledge. It has also led to an increased interest in questions of how these are legitimated. This latter issue has been exacerbated by the information explosion that has arisen as a result of vastly increased use of the Internet in the West. Theoretical work, particularly that investigating knowledge from postmodernist or poststructuralist standpoints, has called into question our traditional reliance on the importance and immutability of absolute truths. This work implies that there are many knowledges, each implicated in a different and complex set of power relations. At the same time, in the UK in particular, there has been an increased public, media and political involvement in the school classroom, with the nature and value of particular curricula and pedagogic approaches being more and more subject to public debate.

The themes of this book are increasingly important as we enter the twenty-first century. The move to what has been described as the 'information age' calls into question assumptions about the ownership of knowledge, its trustworthiness, and our ability to sift through and evaluate a rising tide of information. Partly as a result of this, knowledge is increasingly seen as contingent and contested. The complex relationship between knowledge and power is highlighted in the West by an increased individual access to information. We might want to argue that this will lead to greater democracy as citizens become better informed. On the other hand, as new technologies allow governments and corporations to amass increasing amounts of information about us as individuals, we may see the 'information age' as threatening our freedom of action.

We can consider the relationship between knowledge, power and learning from three interrelated standpoints, all of which address issues of importance to those involved in teaching and learning. First, we can ask: how is it determined which of a range of possible knowledges are legitimated as part of the official curricula of educational institutions or workplace learning? Who is able to influence this decision, and what forces come into play? Whose voices are heard, and what happens to those knowledges that remain important to learners but which are not legitimated in this way? Does increased use of new technologies mean that learners have greater access to these? Second, we need to address questions about how the ideas we have about knowledge relate to ideas about learning and pedagogy. What are the implications for different teaching and learning styles of different approaches to knowledge, and how are these views of knowledge related to particular teaching and learning styles? Third, we can consider how the relationship between learners, learning and knowledge are mobilized in particular learning environments. How do learners interact with the knowledges they are asked, or ask themselves, to deal with? How does their interaction with that knowledge affect their views of knowledge, of learning and of themselves?

The increased availability of information and communications technologies (ICT) for learning throughout our lives raises issues about power and control in relation to that learning. New technologies have the potential to give increased power to learners to control when, how and what they learn. Learning need no longer be confined to classroom-type situations; learners can access information, advice and, in some cases, specifically-designed resources, in their own time and under their own control. Only some learners, however, are so privileged; it may be that developments in ICT will bring a widening divide between those learners with access to its power and those who are excluded.

In this book we address these debates by focusing on the relationship between knowledge, power and learning. We look at how this relationship is changing due to the increased use of ICT in learning situations. The chapters consider the relationship between power and knowledge and how this affects learning, in traditional, institution-based learning situations, in the workplace, and in the home. Drawing on a wide variety of sources and standpoints we examine how knowledge, power and learning are changing as we move into the twenty-first century.

We begin with a chapter by Carrie Paechter which explicitly focuses on the relationship between gender, power and knowledge. In this chapter, Foucault's concept of power/knowledge is extended to look at the gendered nature of knowledge. Power here is conceptualized as relational and distributed, with micro-powers and corresponding micro-resistances being seen as central. Spatial arrangements and the control of students' bodies are seen here as central aspects of the operation of power within the school context. The author points to the ways in which disembodied aspects of knowledge (such as mathematics) are given priority within school. She argues that decontextualized knowledge is both imbued with greater power and regarded as masculine, and discusses the implications of this for the ways in which curricula have been negotiated and developed.

Chapter 2 develops this discussion of the implications of a gendered dualism between mind and body, abstract and situated knowledges in a specific workplace context. In it, Doreen Massey explores how the dualisms of reason/non-reason and transcendence/immanence influence the structuring of social relations in and around high-technology sectors in Cambridge. The author explores the significance of the masculinity associated with one pole of each of these dualisms for how these sectors are characterized and male scientists relate to them. She also considers some of the associated tensions in the relationship between the spheres of 'home' and 'paid work' for people living in high-tech industries.

Learners in adult education and some of the power/knowledge relations involved in current practices in this sector are considered in Chapter 3. Richard Edwards, like Paechter, writes within a Foucaultian framework. He discusses the increasing focus on the individual in adult learning and explores what is understood by the 'individual' in this context. He considers how learning can be seen as a political act which involves changing people, and suggests that this focusing on the individual can have a fragmenting effect. Edwards suggests that there will have to be further exploration of the issues of learner needs, if learning is to be empowering and emancipating.

This is followed by a chapter by Robin Usher which looks at social research and how we can regard the knowledge involved. Usher takes a postmodernist approach to social research, conducting his argument through a discussion of two novels by Umberto Eco, *The Name of the Rose* and *Foucault's Pendulum*. He uses this to consider the dependence of knowledge on social practices and contexts and to challenge the modernist assumption that knowledge is founded in disciplines. Research is seen as a social practice which both includes and excludes. The author concludes with an example (taken from Patti Lather's work) of how data can be presented in a variety of forms. These each foreground different interpretations and voices rather than knowledge in an absolute sense, suggesting that research can better be understood as story-telling.

The next few chapters consider specific aspects of particular learning situations, from apprenticeship to ideas about organizational learning and the specific issues of one-to-one teaching in a highly specialized and skill-based profession. These ideas are supported by chapters on how skills are learned and on ways in which teacher learning can impact on teaching.

In Chapter 5, David Guile and Michael Young propose a new perspective on learning, based on the idea of apprenticeship, arguing that this concept can be reconceptualized to provide the basis for a more socially inclusive theory of learning. The chapter explores how far new pedagogic criteria will have to be developed that might constitute the basis for such a theory of 'reflexive learning'. The authors argue that this approach to learning has implications for a number of current concerns in vocational education and training, for example, lifelong learning, collaborative/transformative learning and knowledge production. The chapter which follows, by Tara Fenwick, considers and critiques the concept of the 'learning organization', looking at this concept in the context of the tradition of organizational development and organizational learning, and the shifts to globalization, de-regulation and information-based industry and Total Quality Management. The author presents a discourse of the worker as continually deficient, needing to learn more, that echoes that of the needy learner discussed by Edwards in Chapter 3. In this discourse, however, learners are not seen as individuals but as part of the organization without race, gender, class or personality. Fenwick argues that the practices of the learning organization ignore the significance of both workplace and teacher/learner power relations. They also have a limited view of knowledge as being concerned only with problem-solving and detecting error. She concludes by suggesting that 'until its premises become clear, efforts to implement the learning organization will continually be challenged by real human beings and their needs, which weave together to create an organization'.

The next three chapters consider work-based skills from very different perspectives. In Chapter 7, John Sloboda discusses the nature of skills and skill learning. He outlines the characteristics of skilled activities and the relationship between skills and knowledge. He focuses on the structure of skills, how skills are acquired, the concept of talent and the role of practice in skill acquisition. The chapter concludes with a brief case study of an exceptional talent. The ideas in this chapter have particular relevance for the two which follow it. In Chapter 8, Michael Eraut discusses theories of clinical decision-making among medical practitioners and examines a number of theories of how medical decisions come to be taken in the context of practice, where decisions have to be made rapidly in conditions of considerable uncertainty. This is followed by a chapter in which Pip Eastop describes his work as a teacher of highly skilled student musicians within the context of a UK Conservatoire. The author discusses his own aims in teaching his students to be independent musical practitioners, focusing on training them to be able to listen to themselves critically and think creatively about their own technique so that they can perform the function of 'being their own teacher'.

The next two chapters return specifically to one particular aspect of the 'information age', the increased importance of new technologies. In Chapter 10, Peter Scrimshaw considers the changes for teachers and teaching that result from increases in school computer use and discusses ways in which teachers in schools can use computers for teaching and learning. He argues that CD-ROM and computer mediated conferencing demand a radical rethink of the teacher's role, partly because they increase greatly the range of knowledge available to learners. In Chapter 11, Jane Kenway evaluates the arguments surrounding the implications for the developing use of the Internet. Arguing that equal access to new technologies and equal competence in working with them must be a basic concern for educators, she assesses utopian and dystopian perspectives on technology from the point of view of social justice, the quality of life and politics. Kenway points out that there is the potential for people to use the new technologies to move beyond mere passive consumption of the products of others and to become both the producers and distributors of cultural products. However, she argues, there is also the danger that domination and surveillance will be extended through the spreading use of these technologies.

The final chapter in the book returns specifically to the issues of power and knowledge. In it, Carrie Paechter considers the relationship between 'school' knowledge and 'non-school' knowledge and the classroom power imbalances they represent. She critiques ways in which this distinction has been treated by earlier authors, arguing that 'non-school' or 'owned' knowledge has been defined simply as a negative of 'school knowledge', and that this does not aid our thinking in this area. Paechter suggests that a key aspect of 'owned knowledge' is that students should have access to the power it represents, but that power/knowledge relationships within and outside of school make this difficult to achieve.

The nature of knowledge is changing, as is our relationship to it. At the same time we have an increasingly complex understanding of the relationship between power, knowledge and learning, and of how this relationship impacts upon pedagogic situations. By bringing together these chapters, which individually focus on different aspects of these complexities and how they will be affected as we move further into the 'information age', we hope both to contribute to the understanding of knowledge, power and learning, and to affect the interactions of teachers and learners.

1

Power, Gender and Curriculum

Carrie Paechter

Perhaps, too, we should abandon a whole tradition that allows us to imagine that knowledge can exist only where the power relations are suspended and that knowledge can develop only outside its injunctions, its demands and its interests. Perhaps we should abandon the belief that power makes mad and that, by the same token the renunciation of power is one of the conditions of knowledge. We should admit rather that power produces knowledge (and not simply by encouraging it because it serves power or by applying it because it is useful); that power and knowledge directly imply one another; that there is no power relation without the correlative constitution of a field of knowledge, nor any knowledge that does not presuppose and constitute at the same time power relations.

(Foucault, 1977: 27)

This chapter considers the relationship between power, gender and knowledge and how this relationship translates into the school curriculum. In it I look at how networks of power, gender and knowledge intersect to determine how school knowledge is constructed, what knowledge is made available to which students, who is permitted to supply that knowledge and how they are allowed to do so.

One always has to start with some assumptions, with a basis beyond which one does not go in tracing back causes and connections. The starting point for this chapter is the idea, originating in the work of Foucault, that power and knowledge are so intertwined that there can be no knowledge without power, no power without knowledge. This goes alongside a belief that the gendered nature of both power and knowledge is fundamental to our understanding of the relationship among all three. Furthermore, although education presents itself as being about the communication and transfer of (disembodied) knowledge, it is at the same time about (embodied) gendered relations of power and issues in the transfer of that power. What this involves, if and how that transfer comes about, and how it is resisted, are therefore issues to be addressed if we are to gain an understanding of the relationship between power and knowledge as they operate in schools and other educational institutions (Marshall, 1990). It is also essential for an understanding of how the education system is used to support power relations within the wider society, both through differentiations in the kinds of knowledge offered to different cohorts of students, and, in elite schools, through the initiation of a particular group of children into a discourse which privileges ruling-class values and mores.

1

All social arenas are threaded through with multiple power relations, and educational institutions are no exception. These power relations are composed of and organized by the relationships between individuals and social groups on the basis of many interweaving factors: age, race, gender, social position, etc. In this context, the relationship between the participants in the social structures of education and the knowledge that is the commodity and currency of schooling is also important. Some students, for example, are not given access to some forms of curriculum, and some teachers are not permitted to teach some student groups or some curriculum areas; different groups and forms of knowledge are protected from cross-contamination. While in some cases this cultural quarantine is overt, in others the segregation between individuals and groups is embedded in the structure of institutions, more difficult to perceive and hence to resist.

My aim in this chapter is to show how the gendered power/knowledge relation operates in the formation of curriculum structures. Many proposed curriculum changes have included attempts to alter prevailing power/ knowledge relations, and have often failed due to insufficient understanding of the complexity of such relations and to the gender-blindness of those leading the innovation (Datnow, 1998). Examples include the UK government's assault, in the early 1990s, on the low status of design and technology (D&T) education, through changes in the content and composition of the subject and its position in the core of the new national curriculum. This largely failed because of a lack of understanding of the investment of teachers, both within and outside the D&T subjects, in the prevailing power/knowledge relations. Attempts, at the beginning of the twentieth century, to establish domestic science as an alternative, 'female' science, were also doomed to fail because the power/knowledge relations supported other, more 'masculine' forms of science education in a position of seniority, ensuring that girls aiming at high level qualifications would always have to study these forms (Manthorpe, 1986). The introduction, in the late 1980s, of a significant coursework element into the GCSE[1] examination in England and Wales, while having some success in challenging a situation in which boys tended to outperform girls in examinations, came under fire precisely because this effect challenged public and political assumptions about the relative ability of young men and women (Weiner, 1993; Younger and Warrington, 1996).

Gender, Power and Knowledge

The nature of power

A society without power relations can only be an abstraction. Which, it be said in passing, makes all the more necessary the analysis of power relations in a given society, their historical formation, the source of their strength or fragility, the conditions which are necessary to transform some or abolish others. For to say

that there cannot be a society without power relations is not to say either that
those which are established are necessary, or, in any case, that power constitutes
a fatality at the heart of societies, such that it cannot be undermined.

(Foucault, 1982: 222)

Central to Foucault's conception of the relationship between power and
knowledge is the idea that power is to be found throughout society in a
complex network of micro-powers, with corresponding micro-resistances.
Power, in this formulation, becomes distributed, built into the minutiae of
human relations, the assumptions of our discourses, the development of
our bodies and the fabric of our buildings. This view of power undermines
traditional liberal views of power relations and of the relationship between
knowledge and power (Blacker, 1998; Ingólfur Ásegir Jóhannesson, 1998).
First, power, rather than being located in a few individuals and institutions,
is seen as existing everywhere, as inhering in the multiple and complex
relations between all individuals, groups, institutions and even spaces in a
given society. Power, in this conception, 'means relations, a more-or-less
organized, hierarchical, co-ordinated cluster of relations' (Foucault, 1980:
198).

In suggesting that there can be no society without power relations,
Foucault is explicitly claiming that the liberal juridical view of power is
inadequate. Instead of seeing power as emanating from a conception of
state power derived from that of the sovereign, he offers an alternative. In
this, power does not derive from a single source, but instead is everywhere,
constituted by a complex network of relations between people and
institutions:

> the classical liberal normative contrast between legitimate and illegitimate power
> is not adequate to the nature of modern power. The liberal framework under-
> stands power as emanating from the sovereign and imposing itself upon the
> subjects. It tries to define a power-free zone of rights, the penetration of which is
> illegitimate.
>
> (Fraser, 1989: 26)

Such a 'power-free zone of rights' may be found, for example, in Rawls'
(1972) 'original position', in which individuals are invited to debate the
rules by which a society is to be governed, from behind a 'veil of ignorance'
concerning their position within that society. It sets up a moral and judicial
framework in which moral questions become 'like a math problem with
humans' (Gilligan, 1982: 26) and in which actual human relations are not
seen to play a role. Such a framework has been challenged, both by
Gilligan and her collaborators (Gilligan, 1982; Gilligan and Attanucci,
1988) working in the field of moral development, and by the philosophical
writing of Hekman (1995), who develops Gilligan's psychological work to
suggest alternative approaches to moral theory. These writers suggest that
we are able to use a variety of different moral voices, and that the dominance of judicially based paradigms is gender related. Males have been
found to use justice-based judgements more readily than females, who tend
to prefer to think in terms of the effects of their actions on others to whom

they are connected. This 'caring perspective' (Gilligan, 1982) has only recently been worked through philosophically, and its historically low and
unformulated status is an important example of the way the gendering of
power/knowledge relations relates to the androcentric nature of Western
thought.

Second, if there is no society without power relations, there is also no
knowledge without them either, which again has implications for the traditional liberal view of the power/knowledge relationship. Concomitant to
the idea of a power-free zone of rights, the liberal view of knowledge also
takes for granted that it is possible to have knowledge (for example, that of
pure mathematics) that is independent of power configurations. As we
shall see later, such knowledges are not only imbued with power relations,
but also deeply gendered.

Foucault's view of power has a number of implications both for analyses
of power and for strategies of resistance (Blacker, 1998; Gore, 1998; Ingólfur Ásegir Jóhannesson, 1998; Sheridan, 1980). In the first place, because power is not a unified force, a separate entity, it cannot be held or
accumulated.

> Power is not something that is acquired, seized or shared, something that one
> holds on to or allows to slip away; power is exercised from innumerable points, in
> the interplay of nonegalitarian and mobile relations.
>
> (Foucault, 1978: 94)

Power is not something that is held solely by the state or by a dominant
social group; it is something that is exercised (though not equally) by all.
Power is conceived of as coming from below; it is exercised in micro-
situations, in relations between individuals. Foucault sees power as beginning in small interactions and spreading to the wider social arena, rather
than the other way round. This in turn has implications for our approach to
the analysis of power, which has to start from the small and local and work
outwards to the global, rather than in the reverse direction; Foucault talks
about 'an *ascending* analysis of power' (1980: 99). Such a conception of
power has effects both on how we analyse its operation and on how we
think of resistance. Resistance is not only within, rather than opposed to,
power: it is also powerful in itself. Seeing power as a local, multiply networked phenomenon highlights the importance of micro-studies, of the
detailed examination of the power relations between small groups of individuals. At the same time it makes clear that even small resistances are
important: 'each localized struggle induces effects on the whole network'
(Sheridan, 1980: 139). Furthermore, by focusing on the *exercise* of power
Foucault is laying stress on the mechanisms through which this exercise
takes place, rather than on who, in particular, is wielding power at any one
time. What we have to consider, he argues, is the process, not who is
benefiting from it at any one moment.

> Of course we have to show who those in charge are ... But this is not the
> important issue, for we know perfectly well that even if we reach the point of

designating exactly all those people, all those 'decision-makers,' we will still not really know why and how the decision was made, how it came to be accepted by everybody, and how it is that it hurts a particular category of person, etc.

(Foucault, 1988: 103–4)

This emphasis on processes allows us to see that power can be inherent in structural mechanisms to the extent that it does not matter who operates them. For example, the design of Bentham's Panopticon, a prison constructed in such a way that its inmates are kept under constant, unobserved, surveillance, assures the application of power independently of who is operating the mechanism. Because the central observation tower is in darkness, while the cells on the perimeter are illuminated, the prisoners cannot tell when they are being watched. Since their freedom depends on them being seen to have reformed, they therefore have continually to police their own behaviour. The power relations are created by the way the Panoptic space is arranged, irrespective of the persons involved.

> It is an important mechanism, for it automatizes and disindividualizes power. Power has its principle not so much in a person as in a certain concerted distribution of bodies, surfaces, lights, gazes; in an arrangement whose internal mechanisms produce the relation in which individuals are caught up . . . There is a machinery that assures dissymmetry, disequilibrium, difference. Consequently, it does not matter who exercises power. Any individual, taken almost at random, can operate the machine.
>
> (Foucault, 1977: 202)

In the Panopticon, the power relations inhere and are enacted in and through the literal space of the building and the symbolic space of the prison. This is also the case in schools, where power relations are deeply bound up with the disciplining of students' bodies (Corrigan, 1988; Gore, 1998). In the early nineteenth century, school architecture followed an explicitly Panoptic pattern. Under the monitorial systems devised by Bell and Lancaster, large groups of children, subdivided into smaller clusters instructed by monitors, were observed and controlled by a single teacher (Hamilton, 1989). Children, both as individuals and in groups, moved within the instructional space according to fixed hierarchies, and the practice of 'place-capturing', whereby one's position in class was literally marked by one's physical location in the schoolroom, spatialized pupil and teacher hierarchies while translating pupil learning directly into spatial terms. Later, this was combined with the introduction of 'simultaneous teaching', of a class of children selected for their equal attainment, spatializing achievement still further as classes were taught in separate rooms. Within these separate classrooms, fixed, forward-facing desks allowed the teacher overtly to control pupils through constant surveillance. This move, from the single schoolroom to separate, smaller classrooms, both formed the class group into a more cohesive whole, and enhanced the status and privacy of the individual teacher; while students became more controlled and homogeneous, teachers became more individualized and independent. The playground, also invented during the same period, allowed for a more covert and thus more fully Panoptic surveillance (from the master's window) of supposedly free play (Markus, 1996).

The fixed-desk, formal classroom went almost unchallenged in state schooling for a 150 years. It was only in the 1960s that alternative school designs were proposed, in the context of attempts to change primary-school pedagogy (Palmer, 1971). The reaction against whole-class teaching that took place during this period brought with it a reaction against more formal uses of school space. Walkerdine (1984), for example, quotes two representations of classrooms from the Nuffield Mathematics project, one of a 'conventional junior classroom' showing desks in rows with the teacher at the front, and another of a classroom 'rearranged to make better provision for active learning' (pp. 156–7). In this latter classroom the desks have been replaced by tables, different areas of the room are available for different activities, and the space is, on the face of it, more flexible. That flexibility does not, however, include the possibility of whole-class teaching without significant rearrangement, and the pupils have lost the one piece of personal space they could previously lay claim to, their individual desk. The importance of personal desks to children, who are otherwise without ownership of classroom space, is highlighted by Nespor:

> Desks were one of the few spaces kids could claim as their own within the classroom, although the claim was not absolute: One of the worst humiliations a teacher could inflict was to force a kid to empty his or her desk. At Thurber, the desks were moveable tables with metal legs, plastic tops, and little cubbyholes underneath, which kids filled with enormous amounts of clutter.
>
> (Nespor, 1997: 132)

Moreover, with the move to less formal seating arrangements, the teacher's surveillance of the classroom has changed from being overt (sitting at the front and clearly seen by all) to being, by comparison, covert, as she or he moves around the room from one group to another. This more covert observation represents an increase in its Panoptic nature, as the student, no longer always able to perceive the direction of the teacher's gaze, has (as in the nineteenth-century playground) to be continually aware of its possibility and therefore to keep a check on her or his actions at all times. School science laboratories still present a sort of compromise between these two spatial arrangements. Although the layout of the furniture is more-or-less fixed and formal (it is often possible to rearrange the benches, but seldom done in practice), and there may be a raised demonstration/surveillance bench at the front, the teacher moves from group to group, while observing the whole.

This way of looking at power, as residing in relations, including spatial relations, rather than in persons or institutions, brings with it a complementary view of resistance, which is seen by Foucault as being within power. Power and resistance become mutually dependent.

> Their existence depends on a multiplicity of points of resistance: these play the role of adversary, target, support, or handle in power relations. These points of resistance are present everywhere in the power network. Hence there is no single

locus of great Refusal, no soul or revolt, source of all rebellions, or pure law of the revolutionary. Instead there is a plurality of resistances, each of them a special case

(Foucault, 1978: 95–6)

Resistance does not depend, therefore, principally on the existence and action of large revolutionary movements, and it is not necessary, or even possible, to aim at the overthrow of a whole power/knowledge matrix at once (Blacker, 1998; Ingólfur Ásegir Jóhannesson, 1998; Sheridan, 1980). Resistance can and does take place in micro-situations; there are innumerable, local points at which power chains can be broken. As there are 'local centres' of power/knowledge (Foucault, 1978: 98), so there can be local centres of resistance to the way that power/knowledge is exercised in a particular case. This opens up the possibility not only of considering in detail the ways in which power/knowledge relations are exercised in classrooms and staffrooms, but also of working out resistances to these. By rejecting a unified conception of the school as a repressive state institution (Bowles and Gintis, 1976; Harris, 1979) we have a way of resisting some of its more oppressive features without waiting for widespread social revolution (Whitty, 1985). It remains open to teachers and groups of teachers to work with their students to alter the operation of the power/knowledge matrix within their own situations.

Power/knowledge

Although I take as given the mutual implication of knowledge and power, this should not be seen as simple or straightforward. It is not enough to say that power is knowledge and knowledge is power and leave it at that (Hoskin, 1990). In fact Foucault himself takes too simplistic a view when he talks of abandoning a tradition in which 'knowledge can exist only where the power relations are suspended'. This tradition has not only dominated Western thought at least since the Enlightenment, it is also deeply embedded in our 'thinking-as-usual' (Schutz, 1964), a fundamental part of the language of knowledge and of truth-claims (Hekman, 1995). Walkerdine (1988) notes that in the case of the paradigmatic form of decontextualized knowledge, that of pure mathematics, it is precisely that decontextualization that renders the 'possessor' of such knowledge so powerful. Reason is seen as lying outside power relations and thus as having access to ultimate and unassailable truths, and it is this that confers power on those who are seen to have 'mastered' it. Although on one level it is an illusion that absolute, decontextualized knowledge will bring with it absolute and impartial power and control, this illusion in itself confers power. While power emanating solely from reason remains a chimera, the discourse surrounding it still confers on those that are seen as possessing knowledge a real (in the sense of exercisable) power that comes from its possession, rather than from the knowledge directly. Walkerdine refers to this belief in the power of reason as 'reason's dream', describing it as a

> fantasy of a discourse and practice in which the world becomes what is wanted: regular, ordered, controllable. The imposition of this discourse onto the world therefore renders to the mathematician, scientist, psychologist, linguist or whatever an incredibly powerful position. For s/he produces statements which are taken to be true. The result of a fantasy is lived as a fact.
>
> (Walkerdine, 1988: 188)

This view of the power of mathematical discourse is echoed by that of Chalmers with regard to science:

> The naming of some claim or line of reasoning or piece of research 'scientific' is done in a way that is intended to imply some kind of merit or special kind of reliability.
>
> (Chalmers, 1982: xv)

Walkerdine points out that although this power to control the world is in itself illusory, the discourse of the power of reason results in a situation in which those claiming such knowledge are given the power anyway. While the belief that pure, decontextualized knowledge brings power over an ultimately comprehensible universe is itself a fantasy, we nevertheless use it explicitly to open up routes to power within the wider society. Because we believe that those who have attained the 'mastery of reason' that comes with 'real understanding' (Walkerdine, 1988) already possess knowledge-related power, we allow them to develop this further, for example by giving them preferential access to higher level certification. Walden and Walkerdine document how girls in one school were directed towards lower level mathematics examinations, on the grounds that the girls' performance arose from 'rote-learning' rather than from 'real understanding', even though their attainment was equal to or better than that of boys who were given the opportunity to obtain higher status qualifications (Walden and Walkerdine, 1985). Such practices, if repeated nationally, can have the effect of restricting girls' access to certain areas of higher level study, as has been noted by Gipps and Murphy, again with regard to mathematics:

> there is evidence that some 1 percent of students (about 5000) who were entered for the intermediate grade tier [at GCSE] could have achieved a higher grade and that this affects more girls than boys. This 'misclassification' restricts their ability to continue their study of mathematics to A level.[2]
>
> (Gipps and Murphy, 1994: 224–5)

The difference in perceived power between contextualized and decontextualized knowledges is also apparent, in the UK at least, in the academic/practical divide that lies behind the low status of traditional technology education; the ability to build and maintain working machines is considered to be of lesser value than the understanding of the scientific principles according to which such machines operate (Goodson, 1992). Thus the fantasy of power and control vested in the understanding of the 'truths' of mathematics and science is translated into actual power within the wider social system. Connell *et al.* (1982) note that the emphases of what they refer to as the 'hegemonic curriculum', whose key features are 'hierarchically-organized bodies of academic knowledge appropriated in individual competition' (p. 122), parallels, and thus reinforces, the practices of the middle-class professional and business world. At the same time, hegemonic processes operating on subject disciplines also affect the sort of knowledge that is permitted to count and that which is not. The curriculum consists of both what students have the opportunity to learn and what is forbidden them (Cherryholmes, 1988; Popkewitz, 1997), and it is the operation of power that governs this knowledge distribution. This involves not only the restriction of certain subjects (or aspects of subjects) to certain students, but also what is permitted to count as knowledge within a subject (Harding, 1990), and the severity of the penalties for breaching these boundaries (Bernstein, 1971). For example:

> It is not enough to say that science is a set of procedures by which propositions may be falsified, errors demonstrated, myths demystified, etc. Science also exercises power: it is, literally, a power that forces you to say certain things, if you are not to be disqualified not only as being wrong, but, more seriously than that, as being a charlatan.

> (Foucault, 1988: 107)

The fantasy of the power of decontextualized knowledge also pervades relations within schools, affecting in particular the balance of 'knowledge possession' between teacher and taught. This is not to suggest that students are ignorant; it is rather that the knowledge that they have tends not to be that which is legitimated by the schooling system, largely because it is not of the form that is traditionally associated with power. Informal, everyday knowledge is not concerned with transcendent truths, but it is the latter that are regarded as power-bearing and are thus more highly valued. Furthermore, Marshall (1990) has pointed out that there is a further aspect of teacher-student power/knowledge relations, the imbalance in the knowledge each has of the other. He notes that within such institutions as the prison, the hospital and the school,

> knowledge has been developed about people, and their behaviour, attitudes, and self-knowledge have been developed, refined, and used to shape individuals. These discourses and practices have not only been used to change us in various ways but are also used to legitimate such changes, as the knowledge gained is deemed to be 'true'. Foucault identifies this knowledge, developed by the exercise of power and used in turn to legitimate further exercises of power, as power-knowledge.

> (p. 15)

Although I think that Foucault's use of the term is wider than this, such a definition is useful in pointing to the way that 'pastoral power', a concept found in Foucault's later work, is used within schools and other institutions to discipline its objects in the name of working for their well-being (better health, literacy, access to jobs, etc.). For one of the main features of pastoral power is that it

cannot be exercised without knowing the inside of people's minds, without exploring their souls, without making them reveal their innermost secrets.
(Foucault, 1982: 214)

The idea that pastoral power is used to justify and reinforce other power/ knowledge relations is important in pointing up the way that such relations can contain both a positive and a negative side. Within schools, the interaction between power and knowledge is thus not only concerned with the imbalances between teacher and taught in the amount and importance of the knowledge that they have. It is also about the power invested in the teacher by virtue of his or her knowledge of the student, a knowledge that is further stressed as an important pedagogic, as well as a disciplinary, tool (Walkerdine, 1984).

Power/knowledge and gender

It has often been argued that Foucault ignores gender in his analysis of power, and more specifically, that his analysis of power is androcentric (Hartsock, 1990; Morris, 1979; Soper, 1993). My own view is that this is an incorrect reading of his ideas, though it is only in his later work that he seems to acknowledge that the power/knowledge relation has a gender dimension (Foucault, 1978; 1984). Foucault's approach to power, however, is a fertile starting-point for the examination of the connection between power, knowledge and gender. His genealogical unpicking of power relations at the micro level not only allows us to make sense of the injunction to make the personal political but also to undercut power/knowledge structures by considering both their positive and their negative facets.

One area in which this is important is in looking at the pleasurable side of what Foucault terms our 'will to knowledge' (Foucault, 1978) and Walkerdine (1988) refers to as 'Reason's dream', the pleasure that comes from the illusory power of pure reason. While liberal theories of power have regarded it simply as repressive, Foucault points out not only that power is pleasurable, but that this pleasure is an important factor in the successful operation of power relations; we are held in power networks in part precisely because of this positive aspect:

> power would be a fragile thing, if its only function were to repress, if it worked only through the mode of censorship, exclusion, blockage and repression, in the manner of a great Superego, exercising itself only in a negative way. If, on the contrary, power is strong this is because, as we are beginning to realize, it produces effects at the level of desire – and also at the level of knowledge.
> (Foucault, 1980: 59)

Power is not simply repressive, but is bound up with our desire, the desire to know and to understand.

> power is pleasurable. It is the power of the triumph of reason over emotion, the fictional power over the practices of everyday life.
> (Walkerdine, 1988: 186)

Consequently, in considering the relationship between power and knowledge, we cannot conceive of power as simply a great negative, only to be resisted, but must also see it as emancipatory, as producing pleasure and a sense of mastery which, even if based on an illusion, allows us a glimpse of freedom. And it is this positive aspect to power which goes some way towards explaining our 'will to knowledge' (Foucault, 1978), our desire to understand, and our attempts to pass this knowledge on to succeeding generations, even as such attempts are constantly frustrated by power's negative aspects.

At the same time, however, this pleasure, as well as the power it accompanies, is gendered, and often, especially for women, comes at a price. Although what is seen as 'pure' knowledge, worth knowing for its own sake, has varied over time, whatever has this label has generally been given a masculine[3] marker and concomitant higher status. Currently the paradigms of knowledge particularly associated with 'the fantasy of possession of total power and control' (Walkerdine, 1988: 207) are those of pure mathematics, and, to a lesser degree, science.[4] Such decontexualized knowledges have been constructed to exclude women (and, until relatively recently, working-class men (Goodson, 1992)) in a number of ways. In the early twentieth century, for example, girls spent less time on mathematics and science than did boys, making their entry into the higher reaches of these subjects extremely difficult. At the same time, this exclusion has meant that the subjects themselves have had their stereotypically masculine characteristics reinforced; non-objectivist science, for example, has not made much headway in the academy (Harding, 1990). This dominance of masculine-labelled forms of thought is not confined to these areas. As indicated above, for example, the dominant paradigm of moral reasoning, derived from Kant and Rawls, is a rationalist one which tries to operate independently of the particularities of human relationships. This paradigm has been used by Kohlberg to set up a developmental progression from bounded and particular to abstract and generalizable moral decisions. Women and non-white or -Western males, however, have been found to score only at the lower and intermediate levels of this sequence. Gilligan (1982) has challenged this model on empirical grounds, arguing that any theory of moral development that excludes females from the higher levels must be built on an androcentric model of ethical thought (Hekman, 1995). She produces evidence to suggest that women in practice tend to favour alternative models when making moral decisions although both genders, when prompted, are able to use a variety of 'moral voices' (Gilligan, 1982; Gilligan and Attanucci, 1988).

Because powerful forms of knowledge are those which are decontextualized, in order to have access to the pleasure associated with them both women and men have to relinquish the personalized, contextual aspect of the self. The paradigm of decontextualized knowledge requires the suspension of subjectivity and a denial of the body. Both of these are problematic for females. First, emphasis on human interconnectedness and the contingencies of human relationships makes women and girls take more account of context in a variety of situations (Gilligan, 1982; Gilligan and Attanucci, 1988; Gipps and Murphy, 1994; Murphy and Elwood, 1997; Murphy, 1990). Second, femininity is produced in Western society as fundamentally embodied, so that to ignore or deny the body is to disregard a fundamental aspect of the self.[5] At the same time, those disciplines in which the power-pleasure relationship is particularly strong are constructed as masculine against a femininity which is constructed as unable to access them. Thus, for women and girls to become involved with such disciplines, to engage with them successfully, requires a denial of femininity, of part of one's (albeit socially constructed) identity. This, in turn, undercuts one's sense of personal power. Furthermore, Brown and Gilligan (1993) suggest that adolescent girls experience a period of crisis which stems from conflicts between speaking out about their knowledge of themselves and others (and thus demonstrating their pastoral power) and preserving the quality of their relationships. Here the pleasurable aspect of power, the sense of connection through intimate knowledge of oneself and others, is undercut by the realization that to speak out about what one knows goes against accepted norms for female behaviour and threatens the girls' relationships with those close to them. If human connectedness is, as Gilligan (1982; 1988) suggests, more central to female thinking than to that of males, this is an important, and gendered, limitation on women's ability to use pastoral power/knowledge.

Gender, Power/Knowledge and Curriculum

We have seen, then, that knowledge is gendered in a number of ways. Furthermore, because powerful knowledges are generally gendered masculine, power/knowledge is gendered in its turn. What bearing does this have on the school curriculum?

What ends up as part of the curriculum arises from gendered power/knowledge relations. It is the product of negotiation, some of which itself has a gender dimension (Paechter and Head, 1995). Decisions about both what is taught and what is not (Cherryholmes, 1988) are taken within gendered power/knowledge relations; they reflect the levels and types of power accorded to different forms of knowledge and different actors in the decision-making process. Monaghan and Saul (1987) note, for example, that in the USA the continued predominance of the teaching of reading over the teaching of writing is partly due to social control issues in settler times. At this period, reading, especially of the Bible, was seen as an important way of transmitting social mores to young children. Writing, on the other hand, was not only regarded as less socially necessary, but also brought with it the freedom to write for and of oneself; it was accordingly played down.

What is taught, and how, can also be governed more directly by power/knowledge relations. In the UK, the founders of the nineteenth-century Mechanics Institutes saw scientific education as a means to the control of dissent among skilled (male) artisans. These institutions provided a limited scientific curriculum in which all conflicts and questions were removed and the provisional nature of scientific knowledge was played down or excluded. The emphasis was on practical demonstrations of the wonders of science, the desired result being moral improvement and a law-abiding artisan class, their time spent reading scientific literature rather than radical tracts. Furthermore, it was hoped that by giving skilled artisans further schooling opportunities this would distance them further from the labouring classes and make them less likely to join with the latter in social revolution (Shapin and Barnes, 1977). By permitting a potentially rebellious group some sense of power acquired through knowledge, the possibility of a bid for greater power, through rebellion, was avoided.

As well as being governed by power/knowledge relations related to class and gender in wider society, the curriculum is also gendered as a result of its application to teachers and students as embodied beings, and bodies are overtly gendered. Some aspects of the curriculum (physical education most especially, of course) apply directly to the body, and it is noteworthy that these can be the most gendered (Bryson, 1987; Fletcher, 1984; Paechter and Head, 1996; Scraton, 1993; Sherlock, 1987; Talbot, 1993). However, this is not the only way in which bodies are disciplined by the school curriculum (Corrigan, 1988). In my own study of interdisciplinary initiatives in secondary schools, students repeatedly characterized the differences between subjects in terms of physical freedom or constraint; subjects were marked as those in which one could talk or move around or, conversely, in which one had to stay still at one's desk (Paechter, 2000). In this way, the (subject) discipline disciplines the embodied subject; the gendered nature of the latter has its effect upon the former.

Finally, those areas of knowledge perceived to be more powerful are able to augment their power through greater access to curriculum time and institutional space. Pre-eminent among these are mathematics, science and information technology, though (in English-speaking countries) English can command time (but not so easily space), partly due to its legacy of equipping the nation's youth with the skills to read improving literature (Monaghan and Saul, 1987). Science, pre-eminently, is able to make powerful bids for both time and space; for example, when the English and Welsh National Curriculum was first introduced in 1989 most 14–16-year-olds were expected to take 'double science', meaning that they would have to cover twice as much ground as they would in subjects like geography or modern foreign languages. The amount of curriculum time, the number of teachers required combined with the use of specialist rooms means that science departments, often male-dominated, take up large areas of school space and can resemble semi-independent fiefdoms, with the staff remaining in the preparatory rooms during breaks rather than mingling with their colleagues in the common staffroom, again emphasizing the 'separateness' of this powerful domain.

Gender, power, knowledge and curriculum are therefore intimately interrelated. Gendered access to positions of power arises, through the curriculum offered or denied to particular groups, from differential access to knowledges which are themselves marked differentially with relation to power. At the same time, and partly because of this, some forms of knowledge are quite clearly labelled by gender, and, of these, those signified as masculine are usually the more powerful. Women and girls have traditionally been excluded from such forms, initially simply through curriculum exclusion, and, more recently, by their being marked in ways that adolescents in particular find difficult to reconcile with their sense of self. Boys are also excluded from some areas of knowledge in this way, but the domains to which they have less access also confer less power, so they do not lose so much, at least in this respect. Meanwhile, curriculum decisions, taken as a result of micropolitical struggles that are themselves located in gendered power/knowledge networks, perpetuate an inequality which stretches right through schooling and from teacher to student.

Notes

This is an edited version of a chapter in *Changing School Subjects: Power, gender and curriculum* (2000) Buckingham, Open University Press.

1. General Certificate of Secondary Education, the main school leaving examination, usually taken at age 16+.
2. A level is the most prestigious university entrance level examination in England and Wales.
3. By 'masculine' I mean commonly and stereotypically associated with the male gender. I do not wish to imply any essentialism in my use of the term or of its conventional opposite, 'feminine'.
4. This has not always been the case. In the nineteenth century in the UK classics dominated the curriculum for men; women were expected to study science, then of lower status (Delamont, 1994).
5. I am not suggesting here that women and girls are 'naturally' like this, or that embodiment and giving emphasis to human interconnectedness are essential attributes of those gendered female. Rather, I would argue that the ways in which females are constructed by the discourses of Western society lead them to think and act in these ways (Paechter, 1998).

References

Bernstein, B. (1971) 'On the classification and framing of educational knowledge', in M. F. D. Young (ed), *Knowledge and Control* (West Drayton: Macmillan) pp. 47–69.
Blacker, D. (1998) 'Intellectuals at work in power: toward a Foucaultian research ethic', in T. S. Popkewitz and M. Brennan (eds) *Foucault's Challenge: discourse, power and knowledge in education* (Columbia: Teachers College Press) pp. 348–367.

Bowles, S. and Gintis, H. (1976) *Schooling in Capitalist America* (London: Routledge and Kegan Paul).

Brown, L. M. and Gilligan, C. (1993) 'Meeting at the crossroads: women's psychology and girls' development', *Feminism and Psychology*, 3(1): 11–35.

Bryson, L. (1987) 'Sport and the maintenance of masculine hegemony', *Women's Studies International Forum*, 10(4): 349–360.

Chalmers, A. F. (1982) *What is this Thing Called Science?*, 2nd edition (Milton Keynes: Open University Press).

Cherryholmes, C. H. (1988) *Power and Criticism: Poststructural Investigations in Education* (New York: Teachers College Press).

Connell, R. W., Ashenden, D. J., Kessler, S. and Dowsett, G. W. (1982) *Making the Difference: Schools, Families and Social Division* (London: George Allen and Unwin).

Corrigan, P. D. R. (1988) 'The making of the boy: meditations on what grammar school did with my body', *Journal of Education*, 170(3): 142–161.

Datnow, A. (1998) *The Gender Politics of Educational Change* (London: Falmer Press).

Delamont, S. (1994) 'Accentuating the positive: refocusing the research on girls and science', *Studies in Science Education*, 23: 59–74.

Fletcher, S. (1984) *Women First* (London: The Athlone Press).

Foucault, M. (1977) *Discipline and Punish* (London: Penguin).

Foucault, M. (1978) *The History of Sexuality Volume One* (London: Penguin).

Foucault, M. (1980) *Power/Knowledge: selected interviews and other writings 1972–1977* (Hemel Hempstead, Herts: Harvester Press).

Foucault, M. (1982) 'The subject and power', in H. L. Dreyfus and P. Rabinov (eds) *Michel Foucault: Beyond Structuralism and Hermeneutics* (Brighton: Harvester Press) pp. 208–226.

Foucault, M. (1984) *The Use of Pleasure: The History of Sexuality Volume Two* (London: Penguin).

Foucault, M. (1988) *Politics, Philosophy, Culture: Interviews and other writings 1977–1984*, Kritzman, L.D. Edition (London: Routledge).

Fraser, N. (1989) *Unruly Practices: Power, Discourse and Gender in Contemporary Social Theory* (Cambridge: Polity Press).

Gilligan, C. (1982) *In a Different Voice: psychological theory and women's development* (Cambridge, Mass.: Harvard University Press).

Gilligan, C. and Attanucci, J. (1988) 'Two moral orientations: gender differences and similarities', *Merrill-Palmer Quarterly*, 34(3): 223–237.

Gipps, C. and Murphy, P. (1994) *A Fair Test? Assessment, Achievement and Equity* (Buckingham: Open University Press).

Goodson, I. F. (1992) 'On curriculum form: notes towards a theory of curriculum', *Sociology of Education*, 65: 66–75.

Gore, J. (1998) 'Disciplining bodies: on the continuity of power relations in pedagogy', in T. S. Popkewitz and M. Brennan (eds) *Foucault's Challenge: discourse, power and knowledge in education* (Columbia: Teachers College Press) pp. 231–251.

Hamilton, D. (1989) *Towards a Theory of Schooling* (Lewes: The Farmer Press).

Harding, S. (1990) 'Feminism, science and the anti-Enlightenment critique', in L. J. Nicholson (ed) *Feminism/Postmodernism* (London: Routledge) pp. 83–106.

Harris, K. (1979) *Education and Knowledge* (London: Routledge and Kegan Paul).

Hartsock, N. (1990) 'Foucault on power: a theory for women?', in L. J. Nicholson (ed) *Feminism/Postmodernism* (London: Routledge) pp. 157–175.

Hekman, S. J. (1995) *Moral Voices, Moral Selves: Carol Gilligan and feminist moral theory* (Cambridge: Polity Press).

Hoskin, K. (1990) 'Foucault under Examination: the crypto-educationalist revealed', in S. J. Ball (ed) *Foucault and Education* (London: Routledge) pp. 29–53.

Ingólfur Ásegir Jóhannesson (1998) 'Genealogy and progressive politics: reflections on the notion of usefulness', in T. S. Popkewitz and M. Brennan (eds) *Foucault's Challenge: discourse, power and knowledge in education* (Columbia: Teachers College Press) pp. 297–315.

Manthorpe, C. (1986) 'Science or domestic science? The struggle to define an appropriate science education for girls in early twentieth-century England', *History of Education*, 15(3): 195–213.

Markus, T. A. (1996) 'Early nineteenth century school space and ideology', *Pedagogic History*, 32(1): 9–50.

Marshall, J. D. (1990) 'Foucault and Educational Research', in S. J. Ball (ed) *Foucault and Education* (London: Routledge) pp. 11–28.

Monaghan, E. J. and Saul, E. W. (1987) 'The reader, the scribe, the thinker: a critical look at the history of American reading and writing instruction', in T. S. Popkewitz (ed) *The Formation of School Subjects* (London: Falmer Press) pp. 85–122.

Morris, M. (1979) 'The pirate's fiancee', in M. Morris and P. Patton (eds) *Michel Foucault, Power, Truth, Strategy* (Sydney: Feral Publications) pp. 148–168.

Murphy, P. and Elwood, J. (1997) 'Gendered experiences, choices and achievement – exploring the links' *Equity Issues in Gender and Assessment. 23rd Annual Conference of the International Association for Educational Assessment, June 1997* (Durban, South Africa)

Murphy, P. F. (1990) 'Gender difference: implications for assessment and curriculum planning', *British Educational Research Association* (London)

Nespor, J. (1997) *Tangled up in School* (Mahwah, New Jersey: Lawrence Erlbaum Associates).

Paechter, C. F. (2000) *Changing School Subjects: Power, Gender and Curriculum* (Buckingham: Open University Press).

Paechter, C. F. and Head, J. O. (1995) 'Power and gender influences on curriculum implementation', *American Educational Research Association Annual Meeting* (San Francisco).

Paechter, C. F. and Head, J. O. (1996) 'Gender, identity, status and the body: life in a marginal subject', *Gender and Education*, 8(1): 21–30.

Palmer, R. (1971) *Space, Time and Grouping* (Basingstoke: Macmillan).

Popkewitz, T. S. (1997) 'The production of reason and power: curriculum history and intellectual traditions', *Journal of Curriculum Studies*, 29(2): 131–164.

Rawls, J. (1972) *A Theory of Justice* (Oxford: Oxford University Press).

Schutz, A. (1964) 'The stranger', in B. R. Cosin, I. R. Dale, G. M. Esland, D. MacKinnon and D. F. Swift (eds) *School and Society* (London: Routledge and Kegan Paul) pp. 27–33.

Scraton, S. (1993) 'Equality, coeducation and physical education', in J. Evans (ed) *Equality, Education and Physical Education* (London: Falmer Press) pp. 139–153.

Shapin, S. and Barnes, B. (1977) 'Science, nature and control: interpreting mechanics' institutes', *Social Studies of Science*, 7: 31–74.

Sheridan, A. (1980) *Michel Foucault: The Will to Truth* (London: Tavistock Publications).

Sherlock, J. (1987) 'Issues of masculinity and femininity in British physical education', *Women's Studies International Forum* 10(4): 443–451.

Soper, K. (1993) 'Productive contradictions', in C. Ramazanoglu (ed) *Up Against Foucault* (London: Routledge) pp. 29–50.

Talbot, M. (1993) 'A gendered physical education: equality and sexism', in J. Evans (ed) *Equality, Education and Physical Education* (London: Falmer Press) pp. 74–89.

Walden, R. and Walkerdine, V. (1985) *Girls and Mathematics: From Primary to Secondary Schooling* (London: Heinemann).

Walkerdine, V. (1984) 'Developmental psychology and the child-centred pedagogy: the insertion of Piaget into early education', in J. Henriques, W. Hollway, C. Urwin, C. Venn and V. Walkerdine (eds) *Changing the Subject* (London: Methuen) pp. 153–202.

Walkerdine, V. (1988) *The Mastery of Reason* (Cambridge: Routledge and Kegan Paul).

Weiner, G. (1993) 'The gendered curriculum – producing the text: developing a poststructural feminist analysis', *Annual Conference of the Australian Association for Research in Education* (Perth, December 1993).

Whitty, G. 1985 *Sociology and School Knowledge* (London: Methuen).

Younger, M. and Warrington, M. (1996) 'Differential achievement of girls and boys at GCSE: some observations from the perspective of one school', *British Journal of Sociology of Education* 17(3): 299–313.

2

Blurring the Binaries?
High-Tech in Cambridge

Doreen Massey

An important element in recent feminist analyses of gender has been the investigation and deconstruction of dualistic thinking. This chapter takes up one aspect of this issue of dualisms and the construction of gender. It examines the interplay between two particular dualisms in the context of daily life in and around high-technology industry in the Cambridge area of England. The focus on dualisms as *lived*, as an element of daily practice, is important (see Bourdieu, 1977; Moore, 1986), for philosophical frameworks do not 'only' exist as theoretical propositions or in the form of the written word. They are both reproduced and, at least potentially, struggled with and rebelled against, in the practice of living life. The focus here is on how particular dualisms may both support and problematize certain forms of social organization around British high-technology industry.

High-technology industry in various guises is seen across the political spectrum as the hope for the future of national, regional and local economies (Hall, 1985) and it is important therefore to be aware of the societal relations, including those around gender, which it supports and encourages in its current form of organization.[1] In the United Kingdom 'high tech' has been sought after by local areas across the country and has been the centrepiece of some of the most spectacular local-economic success stories of recent years. In particular, it is the foundation of what has become known as the Cambridge Phenomenon (Segal Quince & Partners, 1985). The investigation reported on here is of those highly qualified scientists and engineers, working in the private sector in a range of companies from the tiny to the multinational, who form the core of this new growth. These are people primarily involved in research and in the design of new products. They are at the high-status end of high tech. And there are two things we need to know about them here: first, that the overwhelming majority of them are male; and second, that they work extremely long hours and on a basis which demands from them very high degrees of both temporal and spatial flexibility (see Henry and Massey, 1995). It was the conjunction of these two things which led to the train of enquiry reported here.

Reasons for the Long Hours of Work

There are three bundles of reasons for the long hours worked by employees in these parts of the economy.[2]

The first bundle of reasons revolves around the nature of competition between companies in these high-technology activities. It is the kind of competition which has frequently been characterized as classically 'post-Fordist': production frequently takes place on a one-off basis, as the result of specifically negotiated, and competitive, tenders. High up among the criteria on which tenders are judged is the time within which the contract will be completed. Moreover, both during and after production there is a strong emphasis on responsiveness to the customer: in answering enquiries, in solving problems which emerge during and after installation/delivery of a product, in being there when needed – even if the telephone call comes through from California in the middle of the night. It is not so much the inherent unpredictability of R & D as the way in which it is compressed into the spatio-temporal dimensions required by this particular social construction of competition which is the issue. 'Time' is important to successful competition. The results of the investigation should give pause for thought. For these are high-status core workers in what is frequently heralded as a promising flexible future. The demands which this flexibility places even on these workers are considerable.

Moreover, these pressures for long hours are added to by a second bundle of reasons: those which revolve around the nature of competition within the labour market. There are a number of strands to this, but the most significant derives from the market's general character as knowledge-based. It is a market in individualized labour power, valued for its specific learning, experience and knowledge. In order to compete in this labour market (and others like it) employees must, beyond the necessity of working the already-long hours required by their companies, continue to reproduce and enhance the value of their own labour power. They must keep up with the literature, go to conferences, maintain the performance of networking and of talking to the right people, and so forth. This is additional labour which is put in outside of the hours required by the company and its success, but it is equally necessary for the success of the individual employee. Within the workplaces, too, the interaction between employees can produce a culture which glorifies long hours of work. Again, this may derive from competition between individuals, but it may also result from various peer-group pressures – the need 'not to let the team down', for instance, can become a form of social compulsion (Halford and Savage, 1995).

But the third reason that the employees in these parts of the economy work such very long hours is completely different. It is, quite simply, that they love their work. Figure 2.1 illustrates some aspects of this; the first four quotations are from scientists themselves, the last two from company representatives. These scientists and engineers become absorbed by their

We don't *need* to work longer – I think people choose to because they enjoy their work, because they own the project . . . and there's also ownership of the client.

The clock doesn't matter at all. The only restriction for me is I don't like to get home too late. The landlady's given me a key, but I don't like to arrive much after midnight.

I've got so much holiday I don't know what to do with it.

. . . because I enjoy it . . . I enjoy the work . . . I enjoy computers . . . I often wonder what I would have done if I'd had to get a job in the days before computing.

One person was sent abroad to a conference because they would not take time off.

But the thing we have discovered over the years is that people who work here, and get into it, become addicted . . . we find the problem of getting some people to leave; they do get very engrossed in the thing . . . This circuit of people working on the system here, the difficulties are extracting them, for some other thing that may be necessary, like they haven't had any sleep for the last 40 years!

Figure 2.1   *Enthusiasm for work leading to longer hours*

work, caught up by the interest of it; they don't like to leave an element of a problem unsolved before they break off for the evening. The way this is interpreted, or presented, by different groups varies. Thus, company representatives speak of the kinds of people they seek to employ as committed and flexible, as 'motivated', as 'able to take pressure', as not being the kind to watch the clock, and they not infrequently acknowledge that this characteristic may derive from pure interest in the work itself. Some company representatives were quite clear that their search for employees was directed towards finding these characteristics. The scientists themselves often talk of their delight in the nature of the work, of its intrinsic interest. Where these male scientists have partners, however (and all the partners we identified were women), the partner's view of it was often more cynical, more tinged with the observation of obsessiveness, or of workaholism.[3]

A couple of points are worth making at this juncture. First, one's immediate response to the working lives of these employees may well be critical. Certainly, as we carried out the research, ours was so, in principle at least. Yet all of the reasons for this perhaps excessive duration of work also have their other side: thoroughly ambiguous though each is in a different way. In terms of competition, 'putting the customer first' is no bad thing (especially if you are the customer). Yet the demands it places on employees can be enormous. In terms of the labour market, it is usually interpreted as an advance that one's value is based on knowledge and experience rather than, for example, on lack of unionization, or the lowness of the wages one is prepared to accept. Again, the individualization of the labour market must in some senses be an advance, certainly over the treatment of workers as a mass, as an undifferentiated pool of nameless labour power. The idea that we are heading towards an economy and society which are based on knowledge, however unlikely in fact, has always been treated as a change for the better. Finally, the fact that people enjoy their work, and that they enjoy it in part precisely because it is knowledge-producing (in the employees themselves), can only be seen as an improvement over the kinds of jobs which are characterized above all by mind-numbing monotony and a desire to get to the end of the day. After years of exposing the fact and the effects of de-skilling I find it hard to criticize jobs because they are too absorbing and demand too much in the way of skill-enhancement! (Yet this very dilemma may point to the fact that the problem has been wrongly posed. Maybe it is the polarization between de-skilled and super-skilled which should be the focus of our attention. . . .)

A further point worth noting is that the second and third of these reasons for long hours (the nature of the labour market and the love of the work) – though perhaps less so in its particular articulation, the first (the nature of competition in the sector) – are shared by many other occupations and parts of the economy, especially professional sectors and perhaps most particularly academe. Some of the issues which arise are therefore of much more general relevance, beyond the relatively small sectors of high technology in Cambridge. Certainly, they posed questions to us personally, as we did the research. Yet in other ways, the particular manner in which these pressures function, and the kinds of social characteristics with which they are associated, are quite specific to individual parts of the economy.

Dualisms and Masculinities

One of the specificities of these high-technology sectors is closely linked to the *reasons why* the employees are so attached to their jobs and how these are interpreted. The dynamics in play here are bound up with elements of masculinity, *and of a very specific form of masculinity*. Above all, the attachment to these jobs is bound up with their character as scientific, as being dependent upon (and, perhaps equally importantly, confined to) the exercise of rationality and of logic. Within the structure of the economy, these jobs represent an apex of the domination of reason and science. It is this which lends them much of their status and which in part accounts for the triumphalist descriptions they are so often accorded in journalistic accounts. What is demanded here is the ability to think logically.[4] It is, in other words, a sector of the economy whose prime characteristics, for employees at this level, are structured around one of the oldest dualisms in Western thought – that between Reason and non-Reason; and it is identified with that pole – Reason – which has been socially constructed, and validated, as masculine (see, especially, Lloyd, 1984).

Moreover, in this dualistic formulation science is seen as being on the side of History (capital H). It makes breakthroughs; it is involved in change, in progress. And it is here that it links up to the second dualism which emerged as this research proceeded: that between transcendence and immanence. In its aspect of transcendence, science is deeply opposed to that supposed opposite, the static realm of living-in-the-present, of simple reproduction, which has been termed immanence. This opposition between transcendence and immanence is also a dualism with a long history in western thought. And again it is transcendence which has been identified as masculine (he who gets out and makes history) as against a feminine who 'merely' lives and reproduces. As Lloyd argues, 'Transcendence', in its origins, is a transcendence *of* the feminine. In its Hegelian version, it is associated with a repudiation of what is supposedly signified by the female body, the 'holes' and 'slime' which threaten to engulf free subjecthood (see Sartre, 1943: 613–4). . . . In both cases, of course, it is only from a male perspective that the feminine can be seen as what must be transcended. But the male perspective has left its marks on the very concepts of 'transcendence' and 'immanence' (Lloyd, 1984: 101). The two dualisms (Reason/non-Reason, and Transcendence/Immanence) are thus not the same, though there are interrelations between them.

The reasons for these characterizations, and for the construction of these dichotomies in the first place, and their relationship to gender, have been much investigated (see, for instance, Dinnerstein, 1987; Keller, 1982 and 1985; Easlea, 1981; Wajcman, 1991; O'Brien, 1981; Hartsock, 1985). There has been a close relation between the constitution of science on the one hand and of gender on the other. David Noble's (1992) history of 'a world without women' tells the long story of the capturing by enclosed masculine societies of the kind of knowledge production which was to receive the highest social valuation.

Such dualist thinking, as has already been said, has been subject to much criticism. However, the nature of the criticism has changed and been disputed. In *The Second Sex* Simone de Beauvoir famously urged women to enter the sphere of transcendence. In recent years, however, it has rather been the fact of thinking dualistically which has been objected to. Dualistic thinking has been criticized both in general as a mode of conceptualizing the world and in particular in its relation to gender and sexual politics. In general terms, dualistic thinking leads to the closing-off of options, and to the structuring of the world in terms of either/or. In relation to gender and sexuality it leads, likewise, to the construction of heterosexual opposites and to the reduction of genders and sexualities to two counterposed possibilities. Moreover, even when at first sight they may seem to have little to do with gender, many such dualisms are in fact thoroughly imbued with gender connotations, one side being socially characterized as masculine, the other as feminine, and the former being accordingly socially valorized. The power of these connotational structures is immense, and it is apparently not much lessened – indeed it is possibly only rendered more flexible – by the existence among them of inconsistencies and contradictions.

It was only gradually, though, in the course of considering the interview material and the nature of work in the scientific sectors of the economy, that the issue of dualisms emerged as significant in this research. What people said, the way life was organized and conceptualized, the unspoken assumptions which repeatedly emerged: these pushed the enquiry in this direction.

Thus, for example, it was evident that in Cambridge these scientific employees were specifically attached to those aspects of their work which embody 'reason' and 'transcendence'. What they really enjoy is its logical and scientific nature. They themselves when talking may glory in the scientificity of their work, and frequently exhibit delight in the puzzle-solving, logical-game nature of it all.[5] Their partners comment upon their obsession with their computers, and both partners and company representatives talk of boys with toys (one representative candidly pointing out that these guys like their jobs because the company can buy far more expensive toys than the men themselves could ever afford):

> We have toys which they can't afford. You know engineers, big kids really; buy them a computer, you know you've got them . . . you know [they are] quite happy if you can give them the toys to play with.

This attachment to computers may be seen in this context as reflecting two rather different things, both of which are distinct from the more technologically oriented love of 'fiddling about with machines'. On the one hand these machines, and what can be done with them, embody the science in which the employees are involved. They are aids and stimuli to logical thought. On the other hand their relative predictability (and thus controllability) as machines insulates them from the uncertainties, and possibly the emotional demands, of the social sphere.

The aspect of transcendence comes through in the frequent characterization of these jobs in terms of 'struggling' with problems, as 'making breakthroughs'; as being up against a scientific-technical 'frontier'. One scientist, reflecting on the reasons for his long hours of work, talked of being 'driven by success' and the fact that he was 'always reaching higher'. Another scientist in the same company, but who was quite critical of the hours worked by others, argued that for some people crisis is part of the job culture: 'It's a sort of badge of courage.' Other words, too, reflect the effort and the struggle of it all: 'If I stagger out of here at 11 o'clock at night I really don't feel like going home and cooking.' There's the quest: 'As a parent I try to spend as much time as I can with [the child] but in my quest for whatever it is I tend to work very hard.' There's the compulsion: 'If you've gotta do it then you've gotta do it.' And, hopefully, there's the triumph:

> his wife is much more even-tempered than my wife who says sort of 'what the hell, Friday night we have got to go out and don't you forget it', but [my wife] accepts the fact that if there is nothing on specifically and nothing to be done . . . [then] the chances are that I will disappear, and reappear looking cross-eyed and what not, with a slightly triumphant smile or look downcast.

That quotation illustrates also a further phenomenon: that the self-conception of many of these employees is built around this work that they do and around this work specifically as scientific activity: 'the machine in front of them is their home', 'It is their science which dominates their lives and interests'.

Moreover, this glorification of their scientific/research and development capabilities on the part of the scientists can go along with a quite contrasting deprecation of their ability to do other things, especially (in the context of our interviews) their incompetence in the face of domestic labour. This is work which it is quite acceptable not to be good at. Thus:

> Laundry? '*I shove it in the machine.*' Cleaning? '*I do it when it gets too much.*' Shopping? '*Tesco's, Friday or Saturday.*' Cooking? '*I put something in the microwave. Nothing special. As long as it's quick and easy that's good enough for me.*' Gardening then? '*When necessary.*'

There is here none of the pleasurable elaboration on the nature of the tasks which typifies descriptions of the paid scientific work. The answers are short and dismissive.

Such attitudes are important in indicating what is considered acceptable as part of this scientist's own presentation of himself. Not only is the identification with scientific research very strong and positive, but it seems equally important for him to establish what is *not* part of his picture of himself. Domestic labour and caring for his daily needs and living environment are definitely out. It is not just that scientific activity is positively rated but that it is sharply cut off from other aspects of life. This is precisely the old dualism showing its head in personal self-identification and daily life. What was going on was a real rejection of the possibility of being good at *both* science *and* domestic labour. A framing of life in terms of 'either/or'.

In this case, and in some others, such downplaying of the rest of life extended to all non-work/scientific activities. But such extreme positions were not common and seem to be more evident among single men than those with partners, and, even more markedly, than among those with children. Some men were clearly aware of the issue. For one scientist, a new baby had 'completely changed his life' (what this meant was that he went home early almost every other night), and yet the difficulty of balancing or integrating the sides of life was evident:

> I feel frustrated . . . when . . . after this baby that's changed my life . . . I go home early every other day (almost) and pick her up at 4.35, take her home, play with her until bedtime, and . . . I find that sometimes that's quite frustrating, and keeps me away from work. I mean – it's fulfilling in its own right, but it's . . . I'm conscious of the fact that . . . I call it a half-day, you know. I find it frustrating.

Finally, some of the comments made about the scientists by (some of) the partners were particularly sharp and revealing. They were:

> Not very socially adequate.
> Better with things than with people.
> Work gets the best of him.
> Work is the centre of his life.

One of the very few female company representatives (that is, a member of management, not of the scientific team) reflected:

> Well, when I first joined the company there were twelve people here and they stuck me in an office with the development team and it was a nightmare. I really hated it. They didn't talk, they didn't know how to talk to a woman, they really didn't.

What appears to be going on, in and around these jobs, is the construction/ reinforcement of a particular kind of masculinity (that is, of characteristics that are socially coded masculine) around reason and scientificity, abstract thought and transcendence. It is a process that relates to some of the dualisms of western thought and that, as we shall see, has concrete effects in people's lives.

Such characteristics of the employees, it must be stressed, relate to the more general nature of their jobs. These are jobs which derive their prestige precisely from their abstract and theoretical nature, the very construction and content of which are the result of a long process of separation of conception from execution (and of the further reinforcement of this distinction through social and spatial distancing). Jobs, in other words, which enable and encourage the flourishing of these kinds of social characteristics. The long hours which, for the various reasons discussed above, are worked in them enforce both their centrality within the employees' lives and a passing on of the bulk of the work of reproduction to others. In Cynthia Cockburn's words: 'Family commitments must come second. Such work is clearly predicated on not having responsibility for childcare, indeed on having no one to look after, and ideally someone to look after you' (Cockburn, 1985: 181). The implication of all this is not only that these jobs are an embodiment in working life of science and transcendence but also that in their very construction and the importance in life which they thereby come to attain, they enforce a separation of these things from other possible sides of life (the Other sides of Reason and of Transcendence) and thus embody these characteristics *as part of a dualism*. By expelling the other poles of these dualisms into the peripheral margins of life, and frequently on to other people (whether unpaid partner or paid services), they establish the dualisms as a social division of labour. The pressure is for someone else to carry the other side of life.

If there is indeed a form of masculinity bound up with all this, then the companies in these parts of the economy let it have its head; they trade on it and benefit from it, and – most significantly from the point of view of the argument in this chapter – they thereby reinforce it. Furthermore, the possession of these characteristics, which are socially coded masculine and which are related to *forms* of codification that resonate with dichotomous distinctions between two genders, makes people more easily exploitable by these forms of capital. There is here a convergence of desires/interests between a certain sort of masculinity and a certain sort of capital.

This is not to say that what is at issue here is simple 'sexism'. Our interviews did not reveal the explicit sexism found in some other studies, including Cockburn's (1985). We did not encounter much in the way of strong statements about the unsuitability of women for these jobs. There were a few such statements but they were infrequent in the overall context of our interviews. Nor was it clear that the male scientists who displayed the characteristics which have been described always recognized them explicitly as masculine (although further probing may well have unearthed more evidence on this score). What is at issue here is not so much overt discrimination or sexism as deeply internalized dualisms which structure personal identities and daily lives, which have effects upon the lives of others through structuring the operation of social relations and social dynamics, and which derive their masculine/feminine coding from the deep socio-philosophical underpinnings of western society.

The Work/Home Boundary

The boundary between work and 'home' has often been seen, and in this case can be seen, as an instantiation of the dualism between transcendence and immanence.[6] At work the frontiers of history are pushed forward; at home (or so the formulation would have us believe) there is a world of feelings, emotions and (simple) reproduction. Lloyd, once again, summarizes the complex arguments which have evolved:

> We owe to Descartes an influential and pervasive theory of mind, which provides support for a powerful version of the sexual division of mental labour. Women have been assigned responsibility for that realm of the sensuous which the Cartesian Man of Reason must transcend, if he is to have true knowledge of things. He must move on to the exercise of disciplined imagination, in most of scientific activity; and to the rigours of pure intellect, if he would grasp the ultimate foundations of science. Woman's task is to preserve the sphere of the intermingling of mind and body, to which the Man of Reason will repair for solace, warmth and relaxation. If he is to exercise the most exalted form of Reason, he must leave soft emotions and sensuousness behind; woman will keep them intact for him.
>
> (Lloyd, 1984: 50)

The fact that all this can be, and has been, severely criticized in terms simply of its descriptive accuracy, most particularly from a feminist perspective, has not destroyed its power as a connotational system. What is at issue in the ideological power of these dualisms is not only the material facts to which they (often only very imperfectly) relate (many women don't like housework either, many female paid employees negotiate a work/home boundary, etc.), but the complex connotational systems to which they refer. The negotiation of this boundary has emerged in our research as a crucial element in the construction of these men's attitude to their work, and in their construction of themselves.

One of the avenues of enquiry which originally sparked my interest in designing this research derived from statements made in interviews in a previous project (Massey *et al.*, 1992). That project also was concerned with investigating high-tech firms, in this case specifically those located on science parks, and one of the recurring themes in a number of the interviews concerned the blurring of boundaries. 'The boundary between work and play disappears' was a formulation which stuck in my mind. What absorbed me at that point was the characterization of everything outside of paid work as 'play' and, especially given the very long hours worked in the companies we were investigating, it prompted me to wonder who it was that performed the domestic labour which was necessary to keep these guys fed and watered and able to turn up for work each morning. [. . .] But what the interviewee had in mind was the fact that work itself had many of the characteristics of play: that you get paid for doing things you enjoy, you have flexible working arrangements, you take work home, you are provided with expensive toys. In this formulation, there really is no boundary between paid work and play. In this way of understanding things, 'the home' in the sense of the domestic, of reproduction, of the sphere of emotions, sensuality and feelings, or of immanence, does not enter the picture at all.

How then do we interpret what actually happens to the boundary between work and home in the case of these scientists in Cambridge? There are two stages to the argument.

First, there is indeed a dislocation of the boundary between work and home. Most particularly, this is true in a temporal and spatial sense. Indeed it is a dislocation which primarily takes the form of an invasion of the space and time of one sphere (the home) by the priorities and preoccupations of the other (paid work). This can be illustrated in a whole range of ways. The high degree of temporal flexibility in terms of numbers of hours worked turns out in practice to be a flexibility far more in one direction than in the other. While the demands, and attractions, of work are responded to by working evenings, weekends, bank holidays and so forth – and it is expected that this will be so, this 'commitment', and 'flexibility' are required to be an accepted member of this part of the economy – the 'time-in-lieu' thereby in principle accrued is far less often taken and indeed has to be more formally negotiated, and the demands of home intrude into work far less than vice versa. Or again, spatially, work is very frequently taken home. A high proportion of these employees have machines, modems, and/ or studies, in the space of the domestic sphere, but there is no equivalent presence of the concerns of home within the central space of paid work (at the most obvious level, for example, not one of the companies we investigated had a crèche). One of the company representatives we interviewed spoke of the employees being 'virtually here' (in the workplace) even when working at home, because of the telecommunications links installed between the two places. Moreover this raises a third and very significant aspect of this one-way invasion. A lot of our interviewees spoke of the scientists' difficulty in turning off thoughts about work, of not thinking about the problem they were puzzling over, even when physically doing something quite different. The men wondered if they should charge to the company time spent thinking in the bath. A few, both men and partners, spoke of episodes when the man would get up in the middle of the night to go and fiddle with some puzzle:

> He is thinking about it most of the time. He might be digging the garden but he is thinking about it. If he gets back at two in the morning he can go to sleep and just wake up in the middle of the night . . . and he has solved a problem in his sleep, or he will . . . have to go and look at textbooks and things.

Men, partners, and sometimes children, commented on minds being elsewhere while officially this was time for playing with the children or driving the car on a day out. Here there is a real 'spatial' split between mind and body. Here there really is a capsule of 'virtual' time-space of work within the material place of the home. While the body performs the rituals of the domestic sphere the mind is preoccupied with the interests and worries of work.

> I am well aware of the fact that in many areas, that you are better having the 9–5pm and everything like that, but I have never found it at all compatible with trying to work or trying to pursue a bit of research or a bit of development, to have to give up at the magic hour or whatever . . . and I mean you can't say to somebody you will think between 9 and 5pm and you will not think between 5.05pm and 8.55am.

This is eminently understandable, and in many ways an attractive situation – it is good to have paid employment which is interesting, and it is a challenge to resist the compartmentalization of life into mutually sealed-off time-spaces. But what is important is that once again this works only one way. While domestic time is in this sense porous, work time is not. Indeed, and this is the significant point, in its present construction it *cannot* be so. While it is assumed that one may think about work while playing with the children or while out for the day with the partner, the reverse is not the case. Indeed a reason quite frequently given for working late nights and weekends at the office is that the time-space is less disturbed then – even if other people are doing the same thing there is less in the way of incoming telephone calls and so forth. One of the dominant characteristics of this kind of work is that it demands, and induces, total concentration. The above quotation is interesting in its implication that 'thought' is involved only in paid work. Moreover it is the kind of thought which requires a lack of intrusion; it is totally absorbing. Even the reservations to this 'all-work' atmosphere of the workplace in a sense reinforce its truth. Thus one or two workplaces had a gym and elaborate catering facilities on site, the aim being to aid rather than detract from the overall ability to concentrate. And in one company, partners – seemingly in despair at ever seeing their men – came into the office:

> they have children and wives and they are always retailing the complaints from their wives. . . . This is a constant complaint . . . there is a perennial complaint that the partner never sees them and they are always in here. In fact, partners tend to come in here and work in the evenings because that's where the other one is; they have different kinds of jobs but they can bring their work with them and do it here.

In fact, it is hardly an invasion: she is conforming to the norms of the workplace; what she has brought in with her is her 'work', not the sphere of the domestic, and he can carry on with what he has to do.

This does not mean that levels of concentration within the workplace do not vary, or that time-out cannot be taken. Indeed time-in-lieu, trips to the shops, etc., provide occasional windows in the working day. But within the workplace, everything, even the exercise of the body, is geared to the productivity of the intellect:

> I was amazed when I went there – I'd been working at [major corporation]. This huge factory . . . had shut and I came down here to the interview with [smaller company, Cambridge-based] and I walked up the stairway and on every floor there was a series of little offices and ramps around the edge and the middle of each floor was open and there was a ping-pong table or a snooker table and everybody seemed to be playing games and I thought that this is supposed to be a place of work – and then when I saw all the things they were doing – a chap put his bat down and [would] go off and design an IC in a little room in the corner.

What we have here, then, is the workplace constructed as a highly specialized envelope of space-time, into which the intrusion of other activities and interests is unwanted and limited.[7] 'The home', however, for most of these scientists, is constructed entirely differently. Both temporally and spatially it is porous, and in particular it is invaded by the sphere of paid work.

There is, in other words, a great asymmetry of power between these two spaces, home and work. The latter can both protect its own inviolability and invade the former. One element in this differential power is simply the force of the wage relation. The workplace and its activities are associated with market/commercial relations which, as in so many other instances, simply override the affective and non-market relations through which the home is constructed. The inequality in power is also attributable to the ongoing, daily relations between already established genders. Many of the scientists' partners gave up the struggle to defend the space-time of domesticity: 'It's just not worth having a row about it. In the end, I put up with it.'

Yet there are also deeper reasons for this asymmetry of power between the spaces of home and work. Once again they are bound up with the dualisms of gender and of science and their intimate relation to spatiality.[8] These men's jobs are devoted to thought, to R & D, to the production of 'knowledge'. And in western society the production of knowledge has for long been associated with abstraction from the real world: with the classic separation of mind from body. The men's workplaces reflect that deep-rooted philosophy: they are designed to isolate the activities of the mind and they are designed to celebrate those activities. The activities of the mind need a space abstracted from the rest of the world and in turn such spaces become elite because they are of the mind. Their status gives them power.

And yet this explanation needs a further twist. Not all places of intellectual work have to be like this. One or two of the female partners we spoke to also worked in intellectual environments, but spoke differently about their workplaces: '[Children] come in all over the place, and make a mess with my computer, and there are also [other] people with children around, and also colleagues will invite children to see different things.'

What seems to be distinct about the culture of high technology which is the focus of this investigation is its (particular form of) masculinity. And the particular spatiality of the places of this work both is a product of long-established intersecting dualisms and, in its construction, helps to reinforce those dualisms. These are not merely spaces where knowledge-production may happen but spaces which in the nature of their construction (as specialized, as closed-off from intrusion, and in the nature of the things in which they are specialized) themselves have effects – in the structuring of the daily lives and the identities of the scientists who work within them. Most particularly, in their boundedness and in their dedication to abstract thought to the exclusion of other things, these workplaces both reflect and provide a material basis for the particular form of masculinity which hegemonizes this form of employment. Not only the nature of the work and the culture of the workplace but also the construction of the space of work itself, therefore, contributes to the moulding and reinforcement of this masculinity.

Yet what has been discussed so far is an alteration in the boundary between home and work which consists of nothing more than the spatio-temporal transgression by one sphere (one side of the dualism) into the other. The second stage of the argument, however, is that in whatever manner one interprets this 'blurring' of boundaries it does not entail any kind of overcoming of the dualism itself. Yet it is the fact of dichotomy itself (reason/non-reason; transcendence/immanence) which has been criticized as being part of that same mode of thinking which also polarizes genders and the characteristics so frequently ascribed to them. What, then, can be learned about the possibility of unification from this study of Cambridge scientists?

Resistance

The characteristics which have been described above are traits of *masculinity*, not of men. As already implied there is no simple homogeneity among the men we studied. However, these characteristics are strongly embedded within the culture of this part of the economy (with some variation in detail between different types of jobs). Moreover, the strength of this embeddedness means that these characteristics 'pull' all its participants towards them. Individual men have relations to these characteristics which are more or less celebratory or painful. Many of them recognize the need to negotiate the very different personas they inhabit at home and at work – the scientist with the new baby (quoted earlier) was doing just that. And what he was confronting there was precisely the difficulty of preventing his dominant self-conception as a scientist from completely overriding those other potential sides of himself. Other men actively try to resist this potential domination. Their number is small and their reasons varied. Most commonly resistance is a response to stress or to strongly articulated objections from the partner, or to a genuine sensitivity to the men's felt need to live a more varied life, not to miss out on the children growing up, and so forth.

However, the resistance takes a particular form. It is almost entirely to do with working hours, and with the time and space which work occupies, rather than with wider characteristics of the job. It also takes place almost entirely at the individual level. These workplaces are not unionized. Moreover, at a more general social level, while there are trade-union campaigns and feminist arguments for a shorter working day and week, they have as yet made very little progress. Certainly there seems to have been no thoroughgoing cultural shift, in spite of the increasing proportion of employment which is part-time, in favour of shorter working hours. Indeed, since in these parts of the economy at least some of the compulsion to work long days comes from the interest in and commitment to the work itself, it is not clear how such jobs and others like them relate to the wider arguments about working time. Given all this, it is the scientists individually who decide how they are going to respond to the pressures and attractions of their jobs, and how they will negotiate the work/home boundary and the distinct identities the different spaces may imply.

In this context it is deeply ironic that one of the important mechanisms of resistance, and one adopted by a number of the men, is precisely to insist on the necessity for and the impermeability of the boundary between work and home. Given the fact that the tendency is for work to invade home life one obvious mechanism for resistance is to protect home life from intrusion. This happens in a number of ways. Some men (a few only, but then the resisters in total are not a high proportion of the whole) have decided not to take work home, thereby preserving the space of home and the time spent in it from the intrusion of the demands of paid work. Sometimes this will involve an intrusion in time terms, maybe involving staying longer at the workplace in order to finish a task there rather than take it home. It is here the *space* of home which is seen as being the most important not to violate. Other men, though again only a few, have made themselves rules about *time* and insist on keeping to a regular daily routine and on arriving and leaving the workplace at set times. Over the long term it is possible that this will be detrimental to their careers, but the men are aware of this and indeed in some cases have adopted the strategy because of other problems (personal stress, problems with health or personal relationships) which had been produced by a previous commitment to the high pressure and long hours more typical of these companies in general. It must be emphasized that this is not the only way of coping with the pressures of this work where they are experienced as a problem. Other scientists, and couples, have found other ways of dealing with the demands and compulsions of this kind of work but what is significant about this one is its irony. The 'problem', as we have argued above, has been posed through the working-out in everyday life of some of the major dualisms of western ways of thinking. Yet, in the absence of collective resistance, legislative action of wider cultural shifts, individual attempts to deal with some of the conflicts thus provoked may result in a reinforcement of the expression of those very dualisms. The dichotomies are rigidified in order to protect one sphere (the home, the 'rest of life') from invasion by the other (scientific abstraction, transcendence). The problems posed by the dualisms result in their reinforcement.

The last section concluded on an irony: that those who were attempting to resist the domination of their lives by one side of a dualistic separation most often found themselves reinforcing the divide between the two poles of the dualism. This was one among a number of ironies in the situation analysed here. What such Catch-22 situations indicate is that the way out of the conundrums does not lie at that level. The 'solution' must be sought in a deeper challenge to the situation.

Similarly, the empirical material discussed here raises a number of confusions and complexities around the politics of campaigns for a shorter working day/week. They are issues, too, which relate as much to academe, especially in its present increasingly intensified and individually competitive form, as they do to the high-tech work discussed in the chapter. They are issues which touched me personally as an academic and which made me think about my own life as I did the research. It is a privilege to have work which we find interesting. At a meeting of feminist academics, where we discussed an early version of this chapter, *none* of us wanted our 'work' to be restricted to thirty-five specified hours in each week. While all of us wanted to resist the current pressures on hours produced by the reinforcement of competitive structures, we did not want to lose either the feeling of autonomous commitment or the possibility of temporal flexibility. But neither did we like the actual way in which this 'flexibility' currently works – the pressure towards what can only be called a competitive workaholism and the inability to keep things under control. These are things which we as academics, as well as those in the high-technology sectors discussed here, need to confront. For when an important element of the pressure on time results from personal commitment on the one hand and individualized competition on the other, as well as from sectoral and workplace cultures, how can any form of collective resistance be organized?

In the longer term the aim must be to push the questioning further, to try to find those solutions which may involve questioning the dualisms themselves. That is, instead of endlessly trying to juggle incompatibilities, and to resolve ambiguities which in reality point to contradictions, it is important to undermine and disrupt the polarizations which are producing the problem in the first place. In philosophy, and in particular in feminist critical philosophy, this position is by now well established. The aim in general is not now only to valorize the previously deprioritized pole of a dualism (as Simone de Beauvoir did) but to undermine the dualistic structure altogether.

Such more fundamental critiques may be carried into other areas. Thus, in the early part of this chapter I wrote of the difficulty I had encountered, after years of criticizing de-skilling within industry, when finding myself criticizing jobs for being too absorbing. Another irony indeed. However, as was hinted there, it may be that the very dilemma points to the fact that the issue would be better posed in another way. Rather than being critical of de-skilling or super-skilling as such, it is the polarization between them which should be the focus of critical attention. What is at issue here – and it is an issue which again involves us as academics – is the *social division* between conception and execution, between intellectuals and the rest.

What I find more problematical as a political issue is the division of the lives of the scientists described in this chapter between abstract and completely 'mental' labour on the one hand, and the 'rest of life' on the other. In the version of this chapter that was sent to referees I had unreservedly applauded those few attempts which we had come across to resist the compartmentalization of life into mutually sealed-off time-spaces. At least one referee questioned this, asking simply: '*Why* is it good to resist compartmentalization?' And I know for myself that one thing I thoroughly enjoy is to sit down in the secluded and excluding space of the Reading Room at the British Museum and devote myself entirely to thinking and writing. And yet . . . do we want lives sectioned-off into compartments, into exclusive time-spaces (Lefebvre's abstract spaces): for the intellect, for leisure, for shopping . . .?

This dilemma might relate to, and be partially addressed by, considering the major dualism discussed in this chapter – that in which 'Science' itself is involved. It is perhaps that the problem lies most fundamentally in the postulated separation-off of the isolated intellect from the rest of one's being, and calling the product of the working of that (supposedly) isolated intellect: knowledge. That process of the separation-off of spaces of the mind is one with a long history in the West and which, arguably, is also a history of the production of this form of scientific masculinity. David Noble (1992) has documented the long struggle to create a priesthood (more lately, an academe) through which society's knowledge was seen to be produced and legitimized. What he clearly demonstrates is both the long historical continuities which exist between certain early-Christian forms, all-male monasteries, early European universities, and today's academy. The sphere of the production and legitimization of knowledge was, he shows, and in the words of his title, a world without women. But it was not created so without a struggle: it was constantly challenged by those with other ideas about how knowledge should be organized, who could have access to it and who could legitimately be thought to produce it. Moreover, it was also challenged by those who had other ideas about the construction of gender. From early Christian sects, through the Cathars of southern

France, through the radical dissenters of the sixteenth and seventeenth centuries, to the arguments of today's feminists, a challenge has been mounted not only to the exclusive possession of this knowledge (and the spaces of this knowledge) by men, but to the nature of the construction both of 'knowledge' itself and of its attendant form of masculinity and of dichotomized male and female. And in this long historical engagement spatiality has been a crucial term: the struggle to construct elite and excluding spaces celebrating and augmenting the separateness and the status of the activities of the (scientific/masculine) mind (see Massey, 1997). The spaces of high-technology R & D which have been investigated in this chapter are thus part of a long line of spaces integral to the hegemony of particular sorts of knowledge and particular sorts of masculinity.

If we were to challenge that idea of knowledge which is founded upon the separation of mind from body we should need not only that feminists invade the spaces of its production, but also that we challenge the construction of the spaces themselves. Among many others Ho has argued for an alternative:

> This manner of knowing – with one's entire being, rather than just the isolated intellect – is foreign to the scientific tradition of the west. But . . . it is the only authentic way of knowing, if we [are] to follow to logical conclusion the implications of the development of western scientific ideas since the beginning of the present century. We have come full circle to validating the participatory framework that is universal to all indigenous knowledge systems the world over. I find this very agreeable and quite exciting.

(Ho, 1993: 168)

The real irony, then, may be that the long-standing western (though not only western) dualism between abstract thought and materiality the body may lead through its own logic to its own undermining. And it is on that dualism that much of the separation within the economy between conception and execution – and thus these 'high-tech' jobs themselves – has been founded.

Notes

I would particularly like to thank Nick Henry, with whom much of the empirical work for this chapter was done, for much discussion and comment. A first version of this chapter, titled 'Masculinity, dualisms and high technology', was presented in a seminar series at Syracuse University. I should like to thank Nancy Duncan for her invitation. She has collected the seminar papers into a book: *Bodyspace*, published by Routledge.

1. Only one aspect of these relations is explored in this chapter. The work forms part of a wider project on high technology and the social relations which surround it. This research was funded by the ESRC: R000233004: 'High-status growth? Aspects of home and work around high-technology sectors' and [was] carried out with Nick Henry, now at the Department of Geography, University of Birmingham.

The project forms part of a wider programme of five pieces of research on the nature and consequences of growth in the south-east of England in the 1980s. The programme was based in the Geography Discipline, Faculty of Social Sciences, the Open University, from where further information, and a series of Occasional Papers are available.

2. The first two of these reasons are explored in more detail in Henry and Massey (1995). As part of the research we interviewed representatives of nineteen companies, sixty male scientists and thirty-eight partners, all of whom were female. 'Partnership' was defined in terms of cohabitation. About one third of the scientists were not cohabiting. The quotations from interviews which are cited in this chapter have been selected as *symptomatic*. They capture, or express with precision, points or attitudes which were typical or widely prevalent or, if indicated so in the text, which characterized attitudes held by some among the interviewees.

3. One result of this absorption in their work is of course that these men have less time over than they might otherwise have for life in the domestic sphere. [. . .] In discussions on the present chapter, Cynthia Cockburn wondered 'whether the time stolen by these men to sustain their addictive habit may actually not be stolen from the home (other men don't spend more time than they have to in the home), but rather stolen from pub, club and trade union' (personal communication). There is probably a lot in this. The point in the present chapter is precisely to emphasize that what characterizes these sectors is a *particular form* of masculinity.

4. Cynthia Cockburn has pointed to some of the inconsistencies and contradictions even here – see her treatment of the concept of 'intuition', and of the scientists' ambiguous relation to it (Cockburn, 1985). Indeed, the very fact that the men 'really love' their work, are 'obsessive' and so forth, touches on realms outside that of pure Reason (see Massey, 1996). The attempt to purify the spaces of science is never really successful. But as pointed out in the opening paragraph, consistency has never been the outstanding attribute of the functioning of these dualisms, nor has *in*consistency seemed much impediment to their social power.

5. Similar worlds have been described by Tracey Kidder (1982) and Sherry Turkle (1984).

6. While the home/work distinction may validly be read as an instantiation of this dichotomy it must be stressed that there is far more to the possibilities of 'immanence' than having children and doing the housework.

7. This is broadly true of most workplaces, though to different degrees. The windowless boxes of so many modern factories precisely demonstrate the desire not to let the eye/mind wander 'outside' during working hours. But in the kinds of employment under discussion here, together with some others, it is especially marked.

8. This argument is explored further in Massey (1996).

References

Bourdieu, P. (1977) *Outline of a Theory of Practice*, Cambridge Studies in Social Anthropology, Cambridge: Cambridge University Press.

Cockburn, C. (1985) *Machinery of Dominance: Women, Men and Technical Know-how*, London: Pluto Press.

Dinnerstein, D. (1987) *The Rocking of the Cradle and the Ruling of the World*, London: Women's Press.

Easlea, B. (1981) *Science and Sexual Oppression: Patriarchy's Confrontation with Woman and Nature*, London: Weidenfeld & Nicolson.

Halford, S. and Savage, M. (1995) 'Restructuring organisations, changing people: gender and restructuring in banking and local government', *Work, Employment and Society* 9(1): 97–122.

Hall, P. (1985) 'The geography of the fifth Kondratieff', in P. Hall and A. Markusen (eds) *Silicon Landscapes*, London: Allen & Unwin, pp. 1–19.

Hartsock, N. (1985) *Money, Sex and Power*, Boston: Northeastern University Press.

Henry, N. and Massey, D. (1995) 'Competitive times in high tech', *Geoforum* 26(1): 49–64.

Ho, M.-W. (1993) *The Rainbow and the Worm: the Physics of Organisms*, London: World Scientific.

Keller, E. F. (1982) 'Feminism and science', *Signs: Journal of Women in Culture and Society* 7(3): 589–602.

——(1985) *Reflections on Gender and Science*, New Haven, CT: Yale University Press.

Kidder, T. (1982) *The Soul of a New Machine*, Harmondsworth: Penguin.

Lefebvre, H. (1991) *The Production of Space*, trans. D. Nicholson-Smith, Oxford: Blackwell.

Lloyd, G. (1984) *The Man of Reason: 'Male' and 'Female' in Western Philosophy*, London: Methuen.

Massey, D. (1996) 'Politicising space and place', *Scottish Geographical Magazine* 112(2): 117–23.

—— (1997) 'Economic/non-economic', in R. Lee and J. Wills (eds) *Geographies of Economies*, London: Arnold.

—— Quintas, P. and Wield, D. (1992) *High-tech Fantasies: Science Parks in Society, Science and Space*, London: Routledge.

Moore, H. (1986) *Space, Text and Gender*, Cambridge: Cambridge University Press.

Noble, D. (1992) *A World without Women: the Christian Clerical Culture of Western Science*, New York: Alfred A. Knopf.

O'Brien, M. (1981) *The Politics of Reproduction*, London: Routledge & Kegan Paul.

Sartre, J.-P. (1943) *Being and Nothingness*, trans. H. E. Barnes, London: Methuen.

Segal Quince & Partners (1985) *The Cambridge Phenomenon*, Cambridge: Segal Quince & Partners.

Turkle, S. (1984) *The Second Self: Computers and the Human Spirit*, London: Granada.

Wajcman, J. (1991) *Feminism Confront Technology*, Cambridge: Polity Press.

3

Meeting Individual Learner Needs: Power, Subject, Subjection

Richard Edwards

> Truth is a thing of this world: it is produced only by virtue of multiple forms of constraint. And it induces regular effects of power. Each society has its own regime of truth, its 'general politics' of truth: that is, the type of discourse which it accepts and makes function as true; the mechanisms and instances which enable one to distinguish true and false statements, the means by which each is sanctioned; the techniques and procedures accorded value in the acquisition of truth; the status of those who are charged with saying what counts as true.
>
> (Foucault, 1980: 131)

In Britain, 'learner-centred', 'student-centred' and 'client-centred' have largely become the currency of educational discourses about adults. Whether it is the Department for Education and Employment, practitioners in the field, staff developers or learners themselves, the meeting of learning needs has become a largely unquestioned orthodoxy. Placing learners at the heart of the learning process, assessing and meeting their needs, is taken to be a progressive step in which learner-centred approaches mean that persons are able to learn what is relevant for them in ways that are appropriate. Waste in human and educational resources is reduced as it is suggested learners no longer have to learn what they already know or can do, nor what they are uninterested in.

These developments have taken place within the context of a growing interest in lifelong learning and the extension of educational and training opportunities available to adults. However, it would be naïve to suggest that this is due simply to the strength of long-standing arguments in favour of developing more opportunities for adults. Demographic, economic, technological and political priorities have created the necessary conditions for these developments. While the needs of the economy and those of the learner and potential learner may not appear to be simply or readily reconcilable, the fact that learner-centred approaches are advocated within an alleged context of economic requirement for greater lifelong learning is the background for this chapter.

Most practitioners in the arena of the education and training of adults have rightly welcomed the greater status given to their work and have sought to exploit current conditions as far as is possible. This is understandable. As an activity, relatively marginalized due to the focus on schooling children, the possibility of intervening to extend learning opportunities for

adults is not something to be missed. However, this concentration on ex-
ploiting the current conditions has meant that there has been little detailed
critical engagement with the outcomes of these changes and their relationship to the wider spheres of economic and political change in Britain. It is
the latter which is the focus of this chapter.

The acceptance and developments of learner-centred approaches has
spawned a large literature and wide variety of practices. Three possible
reasons can be used to explain this variety:

(1) learners' needs are different and demand different responses;
(2) the ideas of learner-centred education and training are being appropri-
    ated to mask and mystify learning processes and experiences in which
    the needs of learners are secondary to other needs – of institutions,
    government, employers, customers, professional groups, and so on;
(3) there are different concepts of the learner implicit in the discourses
    about meeting learners' needs.

While it is certainly true that (1) and (2) are significant aspects in learner-
centred practices, it is (3) on which I wish to concentrate, as I believe it to
be more fundamental in shaping learning opportunities for adults and implicit in much that is manifested in (1) and (2).

The point I wish to pursue is that different conceptions of the learner
produce practices that reflect and reproduce positions that are part of the
wider processes of social development and reproduction. As practitioners,
we assume certain things about the learner, which are, in fact, the product
of our own and other practices in the socio-cultural context. These assumptions and practices are not politically neutral. They are the manifestations
of struggles within the exercises of power that shape human existence and
social development. I want to suggest that assumptions about the learner in
learner-centred discourses and practices are part of the struggle to transform economic, social and political practices in Britain which often reinforce pre-existing relations of inequality.

Historically, this piece expands on the nineteenth-century debates on the
value of state education for the working class and the issues of state-
provided education as an aspect of social control, an ideological state apparatus of benefit to the minority capitalist class (Johnson, 1988). It also
attempts to develop and explore issues raised by Thompson (1983) and
Tait (1989) among others (Welton, 1987; Cowburn, 1986). However, the
issues explored here and the way they are elaborated are more fundamentally influenced by the work of the French philosopher and historian of
ideas Michel Foucault and his analyses of the way power is manifested in
social settings, of which state power is only one instance (Marshall, 1989;
Usher and Edwards, 1994). Foucault's central argument is that power pervades every aspect of the social and notions that there is a politically
neutral 'reality' separate from power are ill-conceived. Knowledge, our
understandings of the world and ourselves, is thus both an outcome and
part of the exercise of power in societies.

> Power and knowledge directly imply one another: that there is no power relation without the correlative constitution of a field of knowledge, nor any knowledge that does not presuppose and constitute at the same time power relations.
>
> (Foucault, 1977: 27)

In this analysis, power is not conceived simply as a constraint upon persons, thereby ruling out possibilities. It also makes things possible, it is enabling.

> We must cease once and for all to describe the effects of power in negative terms: it 'excludes', it 'represses', it 'censors', it 'abstracts', it 'masks' it 'conceals'. In fact power produces; it produces realities; it produces domains of objects and rituals of truth.
>
> (Foucault, 1977: 174)

The outcome is to make problematic what is perceived as unproblematic, to examine the ways in which power is manifested in our understandings of ourselves, our practices and the world.

In the context of this chapter, this involves problematizing the notion of the person who is articulated as having learning needs and the notion of needs itself. Who is the person at the centre of learning processes? What assumptions are being made about that person? What values underpin those assumptions? How does this affect the view of learning needs, the ways they are determined and met? What is the outcome for the learner of particular needs being met in particular ways? What is the relationship to political processes, the political impact and context of the practices developed? In developing learner-centred approaches, the assumption is that practitioners are becoming more responsive to the needs of learners. What is overlooked is that discourses about learning needs construct learners in particular ways with particular consequences, and are implicated in particular exercises of power.

It is beyond the scope of this chapter to explore and elaborate the whole range of discourses on learning needs. What I wish to do is concentrate on the notion that the person at the heart of the learning process should be conceived as an individual. Even where it is recognized explicitly that persons are social constructs, (Jarvis, 1987) it is nonetheless argued that each person has a particularity, an individuality which is the focus for practitioners. I wish to explore some of the ways in which this notion reflects and reproduces the political project of reorganizing consent and sustaining the legitimacy of liberal capitalism and other inequalities of the social formation – the practices of 'governing at a distance' (Rose, 1996). This is not an unambiguous set of processes without contradictions and sites of opposition. Power is not monolithic. However, I wish to outline the broad thrust of the argument rather than elaborate its intricate details.

The notion of the learner as an individual with needs is manifested in a range of practices. For example, programmes for the adult unemployed focus on tailoring training to individual needs. Adults entering programmes are 'counselled' about their areas of occupational interest. Their past achievements are assessed and an individual action plan developed around their needs – the deficits in themselves that they have been 'encouraged' to confess (Metcalfe, 1992). In theory, this charts their individual course through the programme. The programme meets the learning needs of the individual unemployed adult. I leave aside whether this does describe the practice within such programmes and the assumptions in the notion of the unemployed.

Many other initiatives in education and training are an attempt to develop practices that respond more effectively to individual learning needs. Modularization, open learning and the increasing use of information and communications technologies, for example, seek to extend the range of choice available to learners and provide the means for charting routes that meet their individual needs, interests and circumstances. We also have developments in the assessment of prior learning and credit accumulation and transfer. The increased possibilities for diversifying provision and making it more flexible in some ways enable greater individualization. Learners are being actively targeted and identified as individual consumers to whom practitioners will respond. These assumptions are manifested in developing practices and are part of the ways in which

> subjects are gradually, progressively, really and materially constituted through a multiplicity of organisms, forces, energies, materials, desires, thoughts etc.
>
> (Foucault, 1980: 97)

Learning is linked to our identity and needs as individuals and reinforced through diverse pedagogic practices.

The dominant impression surrounding practices to meet individual learning needs is that the provision of education and training is being opened up to adults. Greater choice and flexibility are available to learners as we become responsive to the needs of individuals. However, before we become too accepting of this view about the expanding and changing faces of lifelong learning, increasing choice and autonomy, let us pause to examine some of the contradictions that lie at the heart of current developments.

Learning has always been a political act, a contested notion and practice, the control and outcome of which is an aspect of the wider power struggles. How we view ourselves and the world shapes what we view as possible and the forms of activity in which we engage. In various dimensions – personal, educational, vocational, social, recreational – learning is about transforming a person in some way. Through learning, we change. However, the way in which we are transformed is specific to our experience of learning and the meanings we and others give to it. In this process, transformation cannot necessarily be equated with emancipation, as the nature and content of the transformation is situated in particular exercises of power and inequality, and is part of the dynamic reproduction of societies – local, regional, national, transnational. Specific assumptions about learners entail an implicit acceptance and rejection of particular relations of power. In assuming learners are individuals with needs we are also implicitly accepting and rejecting certain views of the social. The notion of the learner is constructed within a matrix which is itself a manifestation of power, conditional on and to certain exercises of power. In our practices and the concepts we use to describe, explain and justify them is a notion of the political and a particular form of the social that we reflect and reproduce.

This is as true for the notion of the individual, as it is for other concepts:

> the individual is not to be conceived as a sort of elementary nucleus, a primitive atom, a multiple and inert material on which power comes to fasten or against which it happens to strike, and in so doing subdues or crushes individuals. In fact it is already one of the prime effects of power that certain bodies, certain gestures, certain discourses, certain desires, come to be identified and constituted as individuals.
>
> (Foucault, 1980: 98)

In becoming a particular subject – an individual – we are subject to particular regimes of power. Thus, in meeting the needs of individual learners – particular needs met in particular ways – while making certain outcomes possible, we are also fundamentally restricting the possibilities for personal and social development within certain exercises of power. In meeting the needs of individuals, we are inevitably subordinating persons to the power relations that position the individual as the primary identity of persons in the social. Individual freedom requires specific forms of constraint. These are based on unequal exercises of power, of – for instance – class, gender and race. In meeting the needs of individuals, therefore, we are part of the practices that organize views of persons and the world that reflect and reproduce these unequal relations of power, and, most obviously, the relations of revitalized liberal capitalism. We are part of 'the production of regimented, isolated and self-policing subjects' (Dews, 1987: 150) assisting the maintenance of inequality without force.

This is not simply a question of political values being inherent in learning processes. It is more fundamentally about the construction of a learner's identity. In learning, we do not only learn content, we inscribe meaning to the world and to ourselves, we become who we are. I learn that I am a white, male, middle-class lecturer with a whole baggage of complex and contradictory values associated with these positions within which I articulate my identity as a person. In so far as individualism is the dominant organizing principle for these notions, I own each as an attribute and the social relations and conflicts which underpin them are lost. Individualism fragments my identity and social experience in particular ways. I become 'disciplined'. As Marshall (1989: 107) explains, Foucault

> uses discipline to identify a body of knowledge with a system of social control. A body of knowledge is a system of social control to the extent that discipline (knowledge) makes discipline (control) possible, and vice versa . . . As knowledge develops so also do the parallel practices of controlling the outcomes of behaviour.

The meanings we ascribe result from and in the exercises of power and the struggles within and between them. The outcome of who we learn to be is felt and is part of the wider realm of economic and social relations we inhabit. The learner at the centre of the learning process is assumed to have a particular identity and, in providing a particular form of learning programme, that identity is reproduced and reinforced. It may not be entirely surprising therefore that traditional adult education with its liberal view of learners and the values and assumptions underpinning that view should have largely attracted middle-class learners (Keddie, 1980).

Many are working to extend the availability of learning opportunities for adults and to have a far more accessible system. Learner-centred approaches are part of this process. However, if certain assumptions about the learner at the centre of this process presuppose and reproduce inequalities, what is the price being paid in terms of personal and social possibilities? Are learners even aware of the price being paid? Are practitioners? In problematizing assumptions about the learner I am questioning whether the expansion of learning opportunities for adults is simply a positive gain. Whose gain? And at what cost? For whom? When lifelong learning and individual self-improvement become almost compulsory as a buttress against social and economic exclusion, is being positioned as a needy individual a sound pedagogical stance? The contradictions at the heart of this process need to be highlighted before we become blinded by meeting individual learner needs and subordinating ourselves to exercises of power that truncate possibilities within certain boundaries of inequality.

What is the effect for learners of meeting their individual needs? 'Choice' and 'autonomy' are keywords in this process. Persons are able to make greater choices about their learning and this increases their capacity for autonomous choice and action in their own lives. We create practices which reflect and engender notions of individual equality of opportunity. While this provides a pyramid of opportunity for the individuals who are able to compete within the educational setting, it condemns us all to relations of power that reproduce certain forms of inequality. Individuals escape, but inequality and the subordination of groups continues. Unequal opportunity is perpetuated and legitimized within a discourse of equality of opportunity. Individual escape rather than social transformation is the learning project. It is we as individuals who adapt to changing contexts that are themselves constructed as inevitable.

Traditional courses are fragmenting into smaller sections from which individuals choose – or, perhaps more accurately, make decisions about – those most appropriate to them. These are no longer simply available from formal providers of learning opportunities. Workplaces, voluntary groups and open learning do and will play an increasing role in providing relevant opportunities. New technologies are being developed to disperse learning and learners even wider. Individual choice is engendering the diversification or fragmentation of learning. For the individual learner the net result of this process is a potential increase in a person's physical isolation from other learners. People meet when undertaking similar modules, but the possibility of building sustained and sustainable relationships or developing and exploring collective concerns is reduced by the lack of ongoing interaction and the emphasis on the individual development of the learner in those situations. This process may result in the development of 'the individual', but at the expense of greater alienation within the learning environment from other learners and the reproduction of the alienated relationships within the wider social formation. Of course, this is exaggerated and over bleak. Modularization can be seen as an opportunity to widen social networks, as can the more interactive uses of new technologies. If we have access to the web, we can engage in a range of interactions and communication practices unimaginable not so long ago. But these all entail different forms of interaction or sociality that in themselves require further investigation. And indeed individuality can have positive benefits, if we are to avoid being reduced to Borg-like drones – 'resistance **is** futile'! Exercises of power are empowering even as they constrain.

The practices that are being developed to meet the needs of individuals reinforce the identity of persons as separate from one another, engendering autonomy within inequality, autonomy as consumers of products, educational and/or otherwise, sustaining the economic activity essential to the restructuring of capitalism. This has been stated elsewhere in slightly more glowing, but critically unreflective terms:

> The theory and the practice of individual learning are founded on a set of values and assumptions which many of us will share, and which are vital to the health of our society. They are the values of western, Judeo-Christian society. They include a belief in the intrinsic and fundamental worth of every individual soul. They include the liberal view that the individual should be free to exercise choice, and to grow in an individual way, unimpeded by state control and direction . . . But individual learning is a mode of education which reflects, and also promotes, the very values which give our society its meaning, for ultimately it is the well-being and growth of each individual which is the purpose of, and justification for, the democratic state.
>
> (Moore, 1983: 153/169)

The view that individualism and liberal democracy are integrally linked is certainly true, that it is based on the emancipation of persons from oppressive social relations and freedom of choice in anything other than formal terms is patently false. This is not to deny the historical advantages of liberal democracy. However, the autonomy of the individual ignores the increased governmentality (Rose, 1996) or regulation of behaviour in the modern era, regulation unaddressed by 'self-policing' individuals. Individual learning and the values it reflects and reproduces are those which help to sustain inequality. They are part of what makes that continuation possible.

In an article examining the politics of open learning, Tait (1989) suggests that open learning schemes are popular with certain governments because they keep students isolated from one another, studying at home. Student communities, with their potential for opposition to governments, are not able to form, which, in turn, enables the continuation of established regimes of power. The needs of individuals may be met, but the hidden agenda is the reproduction of the status quo. Constructing the learner as an individual is part of the political project of fragmenting potential sites of collective opposition to current structural inequalities and building a consent in which alternatives to present practices are not articulated in ways which make them possible. More recently though, the development of open learning to bring isolated individuals together virtually has enabled possibilities for different forms of collective engagement, such as on land rights issues by the San in Southern Africa and the Aborigines in Australia. However, even these developments may be subject to a disciplinary gaze – just who is watching all this e-mail traffic?

As I have said, these changes are not without contradictions. It is no accident that social skills and personal effectiveness are key areas of development in current educational and training practice. When the focus is on the individual the social is reintroduced as a series of techniques to be used by individuals in their interactions with others, instrumental to their own self-interest or their need to be included. Having marginalized the social, social inclusion becomes a problem to be addressed. The political nature of social relationships is removed from the agenda of educational discourse and replaced by notions of key skills and core competences.

In focusing our practices on the individual, we are reproducing the fragmentation of collective experience and social relations that is part of the wider social, economic and political changes, often formulated as a situation of late modernity or postmodernity (Giddens, 1990). The collective nature of experience, its constitution in unequal relations of power, is not addressed in programmes to meet the needs of individuals. Persons learn to experience themselves as autonomous from others, as private consumers of goods. Meeting the learning needs of individuals can therefore be argued to contribute to the needs of the liberal capitalist state for a population which is disciplined to consent – actively or passively – to the inequalities or exclusions it produces. As such, it is not surprising that state funding is supporting initiatives in this area of development so fully.

The 1980s and 1990s increasingly saw the privatisation of social existence in many arenas. Consumption within the home in many ways has taken primacy over any public engagement. Engaging in struggle around unequal relations of power is articulated as of less importance than individual choice, autonomy and consumption. The rottweiler, satellite dish and the burglar alarm are emblematic of these changes. To influence this process is more than simply an educational question. We cannot change the world through education alone. However, our practices play a central part in the politics of identity. This is not a question of emancipation from the functioning of power, but of changing the ways in which power is manifested, changing what power makes possible.

> a society without power relations can only be an abstraction . . . [However,] to say that there cannot be a society without power relations is not to say either that those which are established are necessary, or in any case, that power constitutes a fatality at the heart of societies, such that it cannot be undermined. Instead I would say that the analysis, elaboration, and bringing into question of power

relations and the 'agonism' between power relations and the intransitivity of freedom is a permanent political task inherent in all social existence.

(Foucault, 1982: 222–3)

How far does the notion of needs reinforce or diverge from assumptions about individual learners and affect the construction of identities? Like the notion of the individual, needs are articulated within a range of discourses. Armstrong (1982) has argued that meeting learning needs is used to serve as an institutional rationale for the claiming of resources at a time of economic constraint. It is part of a welfare model of education supposedly making it more difficult to deny resources. Needs being met are constructed as more important than satisfying the wants and desires of persons. The latter are viewed as more gratuitous than needs, less important. This allows practitioners to argue that there is a wider range of learning needs at a time when there is increasing emphasis on vocational outcomes and consumer choice, when needs are being redefined as the sovereign choices of consumers. However, what are the consequences of framing a discourse of needs, seeking to go beyond the apparent choices of consumers, within a discourse of individualism?

If we argue that individuals have learning needs, we are suggesting the necessity of an uncovering process to discover what these needs are. In many ways, this is manifested in the developing practices of guidance and counselling as a central component of learner-centred approaches (Usher and Edwards, 1998). What this implies is that the needs are inherent in the person, that once we probe beyond the wants and desires we shall discover the learning needs which we can seek to meet. It is a stance that sees needs as embedded in individuals, the start of the learning process, rather than an outcome of previous learning and the very process of learning that takes place in the discovery of needs. It suggests a pathological view of the learner. We discover what is wrong with learners, what they need to learn to become better individuals, and then provide the relevant balms.

In working with persons to discover learning needs, we are encouraging them to name certain of their experiences as needs – i.e. learning requirements which are fundamental to them – and then to give names to those needs. More importantly, we are encouraging them to view their needs as belonging to them as individuals, decontextualized from the social relations that frame their life possibilities. We are helping persons to construct identities for themselves – to name the unnamed – and this is not a neutral process. It is both part of and an aspect of the prior assumption of the individualism inscribed in learner-centred approaches.

How we construct the notion of the learner at the centre of the learning process is a powerful act, reflecting political assumptions and with political consequences. What is surprising is the way in which the meeting of individual learning needs has been accepted with so little comment, as simply a positive development to extend access, choice and opportunity to adults. The question 'who are learners?' is not simply an empirical one. The consequences of the answers we give are not politically neutral. These issues require further exploration. We need to problematize and politicize notions of the learner and examine them as an outcome of power struggles and the ways in which practices reflect/reproduce/subvert pre-existing exercises of power. In the end, we need new 'regimes of truth'.

Note

This chapter is a revised version of an article, 'The politics of meeting learners' needs: power, subject, subjection', that appeared in *Studies in the Education of Adults* (1991) 23, 1: 85–97.

References

Armstrong, P. (1982) 'The myth of meeting needs in adult education and community development', *Critical Social Policy*, pp. 24–37.

Cowburn, W. (1986) *Class, Ideology and Community Education*, Croom Helm.

Dews, P. (1987) *Logic of Disintegration: Post-structuralist Thought and the Claims of Critical Theory*, Verso.

Foucault, M. (1977) *Discipline and Punish*, Harmondsworth: Peregrine Books.

Foucault, M. (1980) *Power/Knowledge: Selected Interviews and Other Writings 1972–1977*, Brighton: Harvester Press.

Foucault, M. (1982) 'The subject and power' in H. L. Dreyfus and P. Rabinow, *Michel Foucault: Beyond Structuralism and Hermeneutics*, Brighton: Harvester Press.

Giddens, A. (1990) *The Condition of Modernity*, Cambridge: Polity Press.

Jarvis, P. (1987) *Adult Learning in a Social Context*, Croom Helm.

Johnson, R. (1988) 'Really useful knowledge 1790–1850: memories for education in the 1980s' in T. Lovett (ed.), *Radical Approaches to Adult Education: A Reader*, Routledge.

Keddie, N. (1980) 'Adult education: an ideology of individualism' in J. Thompson, (ed.) *Adult Education for a change*, London: Hutchinson.

Marshall, J. (1989) 'Foucault and education', *Australian Journal of Education*, 33: 99–113.

Metcalfe, A. (1992) 'The curriculum vitae: confessions of a wage-labourer', *Work, Employment and Society*, 6(4): 619–641.

Moore, M. (1983) 'The individual adult learner' in M. Tight (ed.), *Adult Learning and Education*, Croom Helm.

Rose, N. (1996) *Inventing Ourselves,* Oxford: Basil Blackwell.

Tait, A. (1989) 'The politics of open learning', *Adult Education*, 61: 308–313.

Thompson, J. (1983) *Learning Liberation: Women's Responses to Men's Education*, Croom Helm.

Usher, R. and Edwards, R. (1994) *Postmodernism and Education*, London: Routledge.

Usher, R. and Edwards, R. (1998) 'Confessing all? A "postmodern guide" to the guidance and counselling of adult learners', in R. Edwards, R. Harrison and A. Tait (eds) *Telling Tales: Perspectives on Guidance and Counselling in Learning*, London: Routledge.

Welton, M. (1987) '"Vivisecting the nightingale": reflections on adult education as an object of study', *Studies in the Education of Adults*, 19: 46–68.

4

Telling a Story about Research and Research as Story-telling: Postmodern Approaches to Social Research

Robin Usher

We are so used to thinking of research as providing a special kind of methodologically validated knowledge about society that it's not easy to accept the notion of research as story-telling. We think of story-telling as 'unserious', as fictional, whereas the dominant image of research is that it is about finding the 'truth' and therefore an altogether more serious business. Equally, it's not easy to accept that any account of research is itself an example of telling a story since explicating the 'nature' of research through the notion of a story does not somehow seem appropriate.

However, my starting point is that the task of understanding or finding out about something is best approached indirectly and obliquely. In the light of this, I want to present postmodern approaches to research, initially at least, through a reading of Umberto Eco's novels – *The Name of the Rose* (Eco, 1984) and *Foucault's Pendulum* (Eco, 1990). Whilst it is clear that this is a rather indirect and oblique way of proceeding, my argument is that a postmodern understanding of social research is best secured in this way. Thus I will try to exemplify through this approach something important about the postmodern. In this way, I will show the textuality, 'fictionality', and narrativity or story-telling dimensions of research. I will present research as story-telling by first telling a story (Eco's) which although not about research can nonetheless help us to understand research from a postmodern perspective.

The stories that unfold in Eco's novels have often been seen as a metaphor for the fundamental quest of the modernist project, a quest for knowledge of the deep underlying causes of events, for unitary meaning and the total explanation of phenomena. In *Foucault's Pendulum*, the three protagonists through their work as publishers of esoterica become intrigued by conspiracy theory writings that purport to explain history in terms of a grand 'plan' cleverly hidden by its mysterious and unknown authors. Here, the quest for knowledge is taken to its ultimate (and irrational) end. On the assumption that the more unlikely the connections made the more convincing the plot which ensues, they set out to devise a plan of their own using random computer-generated associations. When a group committed to a conspiracy theory of history hears of the plan it proceeds to hunt them down for their hidden 'knowledge'. The more they protest that there is no 'plan' in reality, the more the group believes that there is. Our protagonists end up meeting bizarre deaths at the hands of this group for a knowledge which does not 'exist'.

At one level, *Foucault's Pendulum* is questioning the modernist separation of knowledge from power. For its authors, the plan is nonsense, the knowledge it purveys fictional and 'harmless'. Yet in the event it proves to be a knowledge which is powerful in its effects and in ways not obvious to those concocting it. The message then is that knowledge which purports to 'explain' reality in terms of its deep underlying meanings is always implicated with power, is dangerous because of that, and must be treated with caution lest it overwhelm those who create it and those who become subject to it.

More generally, *Foucault's Pendulum* can also be read as a cautionary tale to all those in the social sciences whose objective, in line with their commitment to the modernist project (the search for deep underlying 'realities'), has been the development of explanatory 'grand designs'. The story of the 'plan' can be read as an allegory of all the grand designs that have sought to erect structures, systems and overarching theories – designs which fabricate the world to the extent that this is what the world ends up becoming. The thinking that lies behind this is that if only the jigsaw can be constructed from the pieces of data randomly strewn around we can have the 'big picture' which will explain and give a final and definitive meaning to the disorder and contingency of the world. Armed with this deep knowledge, the world can then be controlled and changed and we, through this, can become empowered. This is the totalizing dream of the modernist project, a dream which in the end has nothing to do with reason but everything to do with desire – the desire for mastery and ultimately control – and hence is itself totalitarian.

In *The Name of the Rose* a monk, William of Baskerville, is called in to solve a number of inexplicable murders at a monastery with a library which contains the most extensive collection of books and manuscripts in the Christian world. This quest then becomes entangled with a quest for the book whose identity is unknown yet whose possession is the motive for the murders. The plot of the novel is centred on the library – a library which is itself a labyrinth with many hidden secrets, the foremost being the mysterious book around which the action revolves. The library is where all knowledge is to be found, if you know how to find it; and only someone like a detective, with deeply penetrating observation and highly developed powers of reasoning, can unlock the secrets of the library-labyrinth and thereby know the 'truth' (the identity of both the murderer and the book).

As McHale (1992) points out the essence of the modernist project which shapes our dominant conception of the nature of research is encapsulated in the question 'how can the world be truthfully known'? The detective is therefore an apt metaphor for the modernist social researcher. He (and Eco deliberately makes him a 'he') seeks the truth usually in the form of a quest for a missing or hidden item of knowledge and does not rest until this item is found and the truth discovered. The problem, then, which both the detective and the researcher contend with is the accessibility and circulation of knowledge where the individual mind, aided only by its power of reasoning, has to grapple with an elusive, hidden reality in order to find the deep hidden meaning that underlies chaotic and disordered events.

Yet William of Baskerville, the prototype detective-scientist, ultimately fails in his quest. He discovers the 'truth' (or rather *a* truth because the library contains many truths) but only by stumbling upon it rather than by a successful chain of reasoning. As he himself finally admits, there was no mastermind, no plot, and no pattern underlying the murders. Thus the champion of reason only 'solves' the mystery through constant misinterpretation of the evidence and even then only through irrational associational leaps prompted by a dream and a grammatical error. This element of the irrational (or the non-rational) in William's detective work can be read as a challenge to the very adequacy of and faith in systematic reason and scientific method. In the novel, it subverts the detective story's knowledge structure and in the parallel world of the modernist project it subverts the quest for knowledge at the very heart of that project. What takes its place is another, alternative strategy which displaces the modernist concern with how the world is to be truly known with the question – what is this world and what is to be done in it?

It is this notion of 'constructed worlds' which marks Eco's novels as postmodern. In *Foucault's Pendulum*, the three protagonists by putting together a story construct a world which becomes real. In *The Name of the Rose* there is a plurality of largely incommensurable worlds created at a variety of different levels which confront each other. Both texts embody the very postmodern notion that different languages, different registers of the same language, different discourses each construct the world differently; in effect, different worlds are 'knowledged' or 'languaged' into being.

At the same time, however, just as these worlds are created they are destabilized – in other words, their status as constructed worlds is laid bare and the very process and strategy of 'world-making' is thus foregrounded. In *The Name of the Rose* there is a doubling or mirroring of a world within a world. As McHale (1992) points out, the structure of the library for example is a scale model of the known world, its floor plan reproducing the map of the world. It is a labyrinth that represents a labyrinthine world. This doubling of worlds opens up an abyss of a potentially infinite regress which destabilizes the world constructed by the text and by so doing foregrounds the concern with 'world-making' and the role of language in the construction of worlds. The text becomes self-referential or self-reflexive by drawing attention to its own world-making through the use of textual strategies such as doubling.

In *The Name of the Rose* Eco projects, through the 'space' of the library, a reflection of the postmodern conception of the world. As readers, we experience it as both an interior and physical space of uncertainty, complexity and disorientation. In Eco's texts there are spaces where worlds are both made and subverted, making us aware in the process of complexity and plunging us into uncertainty and disorientation. Yet this, whilst bewildering and troubling, is also productive because it draws our attention to the process of world-making and directs us towards a reflexive stance.

Jameson (1991) suggests that postmodern spaces should be read as allegories of the contemporary condition, the almost unthinkably complex, interrelated and interactive, global system of multinational capitalism, the information superhighway and the condition of 'hyper-reality' where the signs and symbols of reality have become more 'real' than reality itself. Postmodernist 'space' points to the ungraspable of this world and thus it can be seen as standing for the futility of our attempts to master it through totalizing knowledge and the discovery of deep underlying meanings. This is the 'lesson' that both William of Baskerville and the protagonists of *Foucault's Pendulum* come to learn.

Social Research in a Postmodern Mode

Postmodernism therefore rejects the idea that there is a privileged scientific method which acts as the methodological guarantee of a true and certain knowledge. This method seeks to formulate universal rules as to what can be counted as scientific knowledge, a set of universal characteristics that qualifies a practice as scientific, a theory or explanation as adequate. Postmodernism questions the dominant positivist/empiricist conception of scientific knowledge which traditionally sets the standard and provides the model for all knowledge claiming to be scientific. In particular, it challenges the leading assumptions of the positivist/empiricist research tradition that:

- observation is value-neutral and atheoretical;
- experience is a 'given';
- a univocal and transparent language is possible;
- data is independent of its interpretations;
- there exist universal conditions of knowledge and criteria for deciding between theories.

In the postmodern, there is a questioning of whether knowledge is established through systematic empirical observation and experiment, or whether a necessary first step requires a shifting of the way the world is seen and the construction of a new world to investigate.

On the other hand, a postmodern approach does not simply embrace the alternative hermeneutic/interpretive research tradition since it sees this as still implicitly operating within the parameters of the positivist/empiricist tradition – in other words, the emphasis on the 'subjective' instead of the 'objective' is merely a reversal which still works within a framework of 'objective-subjective' as polar opposites. Instead, a postmodern approach seeks to subvert this dichotomy and suggest alternatives which radically challenge and critique the dominant view in all its various forms.

All of this has implications for the researcher as knowing subject considered to be endowed with a universal and essential human nature – unitary, rational, consciousness- or mind-centred. This essential nature is conceived as endowing researchers with the capacity to stand outside the world they are researching and to transcend their own subjectivity, history and sociocultural location. Postmodernism argues instead that subjects and hence researchers cannot be separated from their subjectivity, history and sociocultural location. In the postmodern there is always decentring; we are always enmeshed in the 'text' of the world, and we become what we are through intersubjectivity, discourse and language. Equally, the separation of subject and object, objectivity and subjectivity, is itself a position maintainable only so long as the knower (the researcher) is understood as decontextualized and the object known (the researched) is understood as the 'other' unable to reflect back on and affect the knower (Acker *et al.*, 1991).

The need to take account of the status of knowers-researchers and their sociocultural contexts, the intimate inseparability of knower and known, the known and the means of knowing, the impossibility of separating the subjects and objects of research – all this challenges the assumption of an 'objective' world and the foundational systems of thought which secure, legitimate and privilege 'objective' ways of knowing that world.

As a result, I want to argue that all social research is located in knowledge-producing communities. Although these are not exactly communities in the Kuhnian sense with a single and settled research perspective and a single disciplinary matrix (Kuhn, 1970), the production of any kind of systematic theoretical or 'scientific' knowledge (as against informal or craft knowledge) always takes place and indeed requires a knowledge-producing community of some sort, no matter how flexible and loosely structured it may be.

One consequence of this is that it is never a matter of researchers 'doing their own thing', although this individualistic conception is a powerful one. Even though it is not always carried out collectively, research is always collective in two important senses. First, in the sense that it is intertextual. Intertextuality refers to the inhabiting of any particular text by 'the structure of the trace . . . the interlacings and resonances with other texts' (Wood, 1990: 47) which works both at the conscious and unconscious levels. In effect, intertextuality points to the place of history in textual production – the way in which history is inserted into the text and particular texts into history. Second, that it is a delimited set of activities legitimated by a relevant community where certain activities are judged appropriate and function as criteria for validating knowledge outcomes, whilst others are ruled out of order and excluded. Communities define rules of exclusion, set boundaries and impose closures. This narrows what can be done and what will count as legitimate research, valid knowledge outcomes and 'truth'.

In particular research activities, the existence of a knowledge-producing community is a taken-for-granted 'background', implicit yet largely un-acknowledged. As researchers, our awareness of the activity of research is normally in terms of a 'process' systems metaphor, e.g. that research is a process or system, usually with the following stages – literature search, hypothesis generation, generation of field data, analysis of data (usually by quantitative means), validation of hypothesis, conclusions and recom-mendations. Of course, the notion that research is a 'system' does have a certain heuristic value but it is also very limiting because it makes research seem mechanistic, a step-by-step linear and finite activity. Most signifi-cantly, it projects a model of research as both disembedded – an ahistorical, apolitical and technical activity, a decontextualized set of procedures and methods – and disembodied in the sense of being carried out by abstracted, asocial, genderless individuals without a history or culture.

If instead we see research as a social practice we are better able to recognize that it is not a universal process of applying a set of general methods or of following a set procedure. Rather methods and procedures are themselves a function of the knowledge-producing community's prac-tice, its 'culture', its networks of implicit beliefs and pre-suppositions, whose rules, boundaries and exclusions, no matter how flexible, legitimate and sanction certain kinds of activity and exclude others.

Consider for a moment one of the effects of a practice's exclusions. Let's take as an example the fact that social and educational research cannot be presented in the form of a literary text. Now, of course, literature (or 'fictioning') is also a social practice where worlds are created. We have seen examples of this earlier in considering Eco's texts. Research is also about constructing worlds so in this sense research is just as 'fictional' as literature even though both are equally 'real'. Presenting research in the form of a literary text is just as much creating a world, albeit a very different one, as presenting research in terms of the linear process model. I'm not arguing that social research is the same as literature but I am saying that both are 'world-making' social practices. More specifically, both are textual prac-tices, examples of world-making through particular ways of 'reading' and 'writing', interpreting and understanding the world. Social research is therefore a textual practice but it cannot be presented in the form of a literary text because that is outside the boundaries of what is constituted as acceptable by the knowledge-producing communities of social science.

A Postmodern Approach to Research: an Example

I shall now try to show what it means to do research in the postmodern mode by presenting an example drawn from Patti Lather's research into student resistance to liberatory curriculum (Lather, 1991). The research was a three-year enquiry into student resistance to a liberatory curriculum in an introductory women's study course. Here she explores what it means to do research differently although on the face of it the research is conventionally empiricist in the sense that she collects data from interviews, research reports and entries from her own reflective diary.

Her aims were to:

- create a space from which the voices of those not normally heard could be heard;
- move outside conventional research texts, and the unacknowledged textual devices found in 'scientific' research;
- ask questions about the way she as researcher constructed her research text and organized meaning;
- challenge the myth of a found world in research and its effective communication outside the intrusion of language and an embodied researcher;
- explore a complex and heterogeneous reality which does not fit neatly into pre-established categories;
- be concerned with the politics of research by recognizing that categorizing is an act of power which always marginalizes;
- put the researcher back into the picture. The researcher is a social subject in relation with others. The specificity of the researcher, for example Patti Lather's interest in emancipatory pedagogy, shapes the process and product of her enquiry.

What is particularly interesting about this research is that Patti Lather analysed and presented her data not simply in a conventional form but in the form of four tales:

- A realist tale – a tale based on the assumption of a found world knowable through adequate method and theory; in other words, a conventional account.
- A critical tale – a tale based on the assumption that there are powerful determining structures underlying the world which are invisible to everyday understandings. The researcher's job is to bring these out into the open and and by so doing challenge their dominance.
- A reconstructive tale – a tale that attempts to undermine powerful tales, such as the two above, that appear to, as it were, tell themselves. This tale discloses the constructed nature of other tales (that the story they tell is not simply a reflection of the world 'as it really is') and in this way foregrounds its own constructed nature.
- A reflexive tale – a tale which brings the teller of the tale (the researcher) back into the narrative. Here the idea is to show that the author/researcher does not exist in a transcendental realm but is embodied, desiring, and herself invested in contradictory privileges and struggles.

Taking this example, I want to set out some of the implications of a postmodern approach to social research. I present this in the form of a number of questions rather than a list of certainties:

- Is it more useful to see research as a practice rather than a process? What follows from seeing research this way?
- If we do see research as a practice, then what would it mean to see it specifically as a textual practice, a practice of writing?
- As a practice of this kind, is it not then akin to a 'fictional' text in the sense that it too, like the latter, is in the business of constructing a world or worlds? If this is the case, then doesn't research always raise questions of reflexivity?
- Does the existence of reflexivity suggest that all research, whatever else it may be, is autobiographical? But what is 'autobiography' and what is its relation to the self who researchs?
- Does being reflexive also mean taking account of the effects of the 'situatedness' of research – in other words, asking where is it 'coming from'?
- What about the part played by language, textual strategies and conventions in achieving 'objectivity' and 'truth'?
- Do we need to be careful about what is 'underneath', the operation of power and its effects through particular discourses?
- If research is textual, then are research texts arguing against other texts rather than reflecting the world?
- If our concern is that research contributes to domination and oppression, should research be aimed explicitly at emancipation? But do we then need to be careful that our desire for this might merely lead to another form of oppression, of 'speaking for others'?

Post-text

In the text that has unfolded I have tried to tell a story about social research and one of my ways of doing this has been to recount Eco's story – a story which on the face of it is not about research. Yet as we have seen, by reading Eco in a particular way we can gain an understanding (a 'different' understanding?) of research which might otherwise not have been possible. This is one way of following a deconstructive strategy – a strategy with which postmodernism is commonly associated.

The lesson here (and Patti Lather's research shows this very clearly) is that such a strategy is not an alternative perspective on research, let alone a new method for doing research. What it is, if it is anything at all, is an injunction to be constantly vigilant, to take nothing for granted in doing research. By being vigilant we are reminded to always ask not only – what is my research finding out? – but also – where is it coming from? what is it doing? and with what is it implicated? In this way, we become aware that research is not a transcendental activity or merely the application of an invariant technical process. Most of all, we become aware that research is both a 'constructed' and a 'constructing' activity.

Furthermore, in telling this, a postmodern story, about research we can better understand research as story-telling – as 'constructed' and 'constructing'. What is also revealed, as Eco shows only too clearly, is that story-telling can also be powerful, oppressive and dangerous. There are always two sides to the text of social research.

Note

This is an edited version of a chapter in G. McKenzie, J. Powell and R. Usher (eds.), *Understanding Social Research: Perspectives on Methodology and Practice*, London and Washington, D.C., Falmer Press.

References

Acker, J., Barry, K. and Esseveld, J. (1991) 'Objectivity and truth: problems in doing feminist research', in Fonow, M. and Cook, J. (eds) *Beyond Methodology*, Bloomington, Indiana University Press.

Eco, U. (1984) *The Name of the Rose*, London, Picador.

Eco, U. (1990) *Foucault's Pendulum*, London, Picador.

Jameson, F. (1991) *Postmodernism: The Cultural Logic of Late Capitalism*, Durham, NC, Duke University Press.

Kuhn, T.S. (1970) *The Structure of Scientific Revolutions*, Chicago, University of Chicago Press.

Lather, P. (1991) *Getting Smart: Feminist Research and Pedagogy With/In the Postmodern*, London, Routledge.

McHale, B. (1992) *Constructing Postmodernism*, London, Routledge.

Wood, D. (1990) *Philosophy at the Limit*, London, Unwin Hyman.

5

Apprenticeship as a Conceptual Basis for a Social Theory of Learning

David Guile and Michael Young

Introduction

There are a number of reasons for the renewed interest in the institution of apprenticeship.[1] The most obvious one is that a growing number of governments (e.g. the USA and many countries in the European Union) are trying to strengthen the skill base of their future workforce by establishing a new form of apprenticeship that fulfils some of the functions of traditional craft apprenticeships, but takes into account their weaknesses and the new demands of the late twentieth century economies (Fennell, 1994). The second reason is the emergence of a literature on learning organizations, and, more generally, the idea that if societies of the future are to be economically competitive, they have to become learning societies and individuals have to become lifelong learners. The concept of apprenticeship, although not associated with lifelong learning as it is currently used, is particularly attractive in this new context. Not only does it focus attention upon an active role for individuals in organizing their own learning, it also implies that individuals have prime responsibility for putting themselves in a position to learn. However, in the learning organization, learning society and lifelong learning literature, very little attention has been given to the process of learning itself (Young, 1995; Young & Guile, 1996). Nor for that matter has the literature that heralded the introduction of the UK's Modern Apprenticeship programme accorded the process of learning much consideration (Fuller, 1996).

We share an interest in the modern forms of apprenticeship that are being developed in the UK and other countries. However, our focus here is not on apprenticeship as a social institution. The concern of this chapter is, conceptual rather than substantive. Following cultural anthropologists such as Jean Lave (Lave, 1993, 1995; Lave & Wenger, 1991), we are interested in the potential of the concept of apprenticeship as the basis for a social theory of learning. Existing approaches to learning tend to rely on behaviourist and individualist assumptions; they are dependent on transmission pedagogies and the concept of the transfer of decontextualized knowledge to vocationally specific contexts, and are frequently associated with cognitive science accounts of expertise as the stable individual mastery of well-defined tasks. Our particular interest is in how far the reconceptual-

56

ization of apprenticeship along the lines we propose will lead to the development of new pedagogic criteria that might constitute the basis for a theory of 'reflexive learning'.[2]

This chapter has five sections. Section 1 is a brief discussion of the main sociological approaches to work and learning at work in order to make clear how they differ from the approach developed here. In Section 2, we analyse the concept of apprenticeship and highlight several critical issues which neither the traditional assumptions of concept itself, nor subsequent attempts to modify it, have considered. Section 3 is a brief examination of previous attempts to reformulate the concept of apprenticeship[3] as a basis for a broader-based theory of learning within formal education. In response to the issues raised in the previous sections, Section 4 considers recent developments in what is known as activity theory (Vygotsky, 1978; Scribner & Cole, 1971; Wertsch, 1981). In particular, we consider the ideas of 'zones of proximal development' and 'learning as social practice', and assess their potential as a basis for a more comprehensive social theory of learning. The chapter concludes with brief comments on the possible implications of the approach to learning that is developed in this chapter for a number of current concerns in vocational education and training; we give particular consideration to the issues of 'lifelong learning', 'collaborative'/'transformative' learning and 'knowledge production'.

Learning at Work: Some Sociological Perspectives

Sociologists and political economists have attempted to identify the effects of changes in work upon human consciousness and activity since the beginning of the industrial revolution (Smith, 1974; Marx, 1844). The main macro-sociological debate about work within industrial and organizational sociology, sometimes dubbed the labour-process debate (Wood, 1982, 1989), was originally concerned with the effects of automation upon the skill levels of workers and their collective sense of social identity (Blauner, 1964) and the nature of workplace socialization (Braverman, 1974; Noble, 1991). However, during the 1980s and early 1990s the focus of these debates shifted significantly, concentrating on such new production concepts as 'post-Fordism', 'flexible production' and 'lean production' (Warner *et al.*, 1990; Womack *et al.*, 1991).

In reviewing this body of work, Casey comments that it has long been recognized that:

> work is an educational site in which pedagogical and learning practices have always taken place.
>
> (Casey, 1995: 74)

Casey identifies the existence of two alternative sociological perspectives on work and learning. One originates from industial sociology and labour education and adopts a macro-sociological analysis. Research within this tradition has endorsed the link between formal training and development programmes and economic success. It explicitly argues that the quality of workplaces ought to be evaluated in terms of the educational opportunities and the learning environments that they provide for workers, and stresses that responsibility for planning learning opportunities ought to be a manifest function of senior management in all workplaces (Leymann & Kornbluh, 1989; Keep & Mayhew, 1995; Pipan, 1989; Streek, 1989, 1994). On the other hand, as Casey points out, researchers who have been influenced by the ethnographic studies of the 'Chicago School' have adopted a very different perspective. One of the underlying premises of the 'Chicago School' has always been that work serves as a primary site of socialization. However, the main focus of their research was to explore the 'hidden' or inintentional outcomes of workplace socialization rather than analysing the purpose and structure of formal training and development programmes (Becker *et al.*, 1961; Geer, 1972; Hughes, 1958, 1971).

Despite the fact that much of the research which has emanated from these two sociological perspectives recognizes the different ways that work can serve educational purposes, neither has systematically addressed the nature of workplace learning, nor identified which pedagogical practices actually support it. Even Streek's highly sophisticated analysis of changing workplace skill needs and the 'institutional preconditions'[4] required to support their development, falls short of articulating any pedagogic strategy to successfully accomplish skill development within modern production. It goes little beyond endorsing the value of integrating formal and informal learning (Streek, 1994). Streek does not even acknowledge the existence of a debate as to which approaches to learning might be more valuable for assisting individuals and teams to develop the workplace capabilities that he argues are required in 'diversified quality production' (ibid.). Where research has focused directly upon apprenticeship within different occupational groups, it has mainly adopted a sub-culture perspective. Thus, apprenticeship has been viewed as a process of socialization into official or unofficial workplace cultures and not explicitly as an approach to learning.

The Concept of Apprenticeship

The view of learning implicit in the traditional concept of apprenticeship involves four main elements – the apprentice as learner, the idea of trade or craft knowledge as fixed and unproblematic, the master as teacher and the idea that learning in workplaces is a form of context-bound understanding not conducive to transfer (Pratt, 1992). Moreover, in both classic cognitive psychology and the anthropology of education, apprenticeship is portrayed as lacking an explicit theory of instruction and not dependent upon formal teaching (Scribner & Cole, 1971; Collins *et al.*, 1989; Coy, 1989). Learning is seen as a natural process that occurs via observation, assimilation and emulation which happens over time without any substantial intervention from more experienced others. Research from other branches of social science,[5] however, has identified models of apprenticeship that embrace formal and informal learning within structured on- and off-the job training provided by employers (Brown *et al.*, 1994; Fuller, 1996). Nevertheless, one of the overriding conclusions of these studies is that apprentices and employers are still inclined to accord primary importance to the acquisition of craft knowledge or skills. In other words, they are concerned with the implicit rather than the explicit dimensions of learning.

The focus on apprenticeship in developing a theory of learning, therefore, is valuable in that it directs us away from the idea of learning as transmission towards learning as a process in which the apprentice is involved in 'learning by doing' with the 'master' as the major role model. Moreover, the idea of apprenticeship creates the overriding impression that expertise is developed through the gradual accumulation of experience under the guidance of an established master.[6] The model of knowledge within apprenticeship tends to be a combination of trade or craft knowledge handed down by the master and the implicit knowledge (similar to Zuboff's, 1988, 'action oriented skills') that is part of all activity.[7]

The traditional concept of apprenticeship tends to be generalized to any craft, profession or process in which people acquire forms of expertise or skill (Fennell, 1994). Such generalization assumes that the process of learning is invariant and the same for all types of apprenticeship. However, in practice, work contexts vary widely. In some cases they are relatively routine and require little explicit knowledge, whereas in others they are highly knowledge-intensive. Also work contexts vary according to whether the knowledge involved is a 'traditional' craft or constantly developing body of 'theory' (Gott, 1995). As a consequence, theories of learning not only need to take account of differences in the degree of expertise needed within specific occupations, but also in differences in the content and quality of such expertise (Engestrom, 1997). Moreover, the nature of workplace practices and the demands they make on apprentice learners are likely to be quite different when different forms of knowledge or work are involved. This is apparent from studies of both workplaces and classrooms. Studies of work teams who repair state of the art war planes (Gott, 1995), accounts of collective learning amongst a group of service technicians (Orr, 1990), as well as studies of 'cognitive apprenticeship' in education (Collins *et al.*, 1989) and 'apprenticeship in thinking' (Brown, 1993) have all highlighted how collaborative practices mediate opportunities for learning. It is hardly surprising, therefore, that such studies frequently imply the need for further analysis of the complex interrelationship between cognition and context, and a review of the model of learning associated with traditional apprenticeships.

Conceptualizing apprenticeship as a social theory of learning

A growing body of research on learning and cognition has introduced a new focus into the debates about the interrelationship between cognition, context and practice. Such studies have begun to draw attention to how the process of learning always involves changes in knowledge and action, and how such changes are central to learning and the development of new forms of practice (Chaiklen & Lave, 1993; Engestrom & Middleton, 1996). These studies have highlighted a number of the weaknesses of the traditional understanding of apprenticeship.

First, they stress the importance of how knowledge is socially constructed and how the new apprentice becomes part of a work-based 'community of practice' (Lave & Wenger, 1991). Second, they emphasize learning as a process of 'boundary crossing' mediated by access to different 'communities of practice' (Lave, 1993; Engestrom *et al.*, 1995). Third, they show how learners increasingly need to relate scientific and everyday concepts in making sense of workplace practices or problems (Gott, 1995). Fourth, they point to how resources external to 'communities of practice' may be needed to overcome internal contradictions (Engestrom *et al.*, 1997). Fifth, they indicate how 'learning' technologies can be seen as 'resources' for learning and that to do so involves rethinking some of our assumptions about intelligence, learning and workplace activity (Tikhomirov, 1981; Pea, 1993).

Apprenticeship, formal education and the zone of proximal development

As noted earlier in this chapter, it has traditionally been assumed that formal education and apprenticeship involve quite different modes of learning, quite different teaching strategies and result in different capacities to transfer knowledge and skill from one context to another (Scribner & Cole, 1973). However, we take the view with Lave (1996) and other recent work (Billett, 1996; Engestrom *et al.*, 1995; Ghererdi *et al.*, 1997) that it is more useful to assume that there are common processes underlying both learning in school and work-based learning. Vygotsky's concept of the zone of proximal development (Vygotsky, 1978) in particular, provides a useful way of exploring this assumption.

Many educationalists have acknowledged the critical importance to our understanding of pedagogy and the design of learning programmes of Vygotsky's concept of the 'zone of proximal development' (Britton, 1987). The concept is central to Vygotsky's theory and it has been modified and developed by Cole in the USA (Cole, 1985), and given a broader interpretation within 'activity theory' (Wertsch, 1981; Griffen & Cole, 1985), and in the soviet tradition of psychology by Leontiev via his notion of 'cultural practices' (Leontiev, 1981).

Vygotsky defined the 'zone of proximal development' as:

the distance between the actual development level as determined by independent problem solving and the level of potential development as determined through problem solving under adult guidance or in collaboration with more able peers.

(Vygotsky, 1978: 85)

The concept was central to Vygotsky's programme of trying to identify the pedagogic structure(s) needed to assist learners move beyond the stage of mastery that they were capable of on their own. One consequence of the various reconstructions of Vygotsky's original ideas has been the development of a series of pedagogic strategies such as 'scaffolding', 'modelling' and 'fading' which have been designed to assist teachers to help children to participate in activities slightly beyond their current competence (Brown *et al.*, 1989).

Over the years neo-Vygotskian and other cognitive psychologists have offered many different interpretations of the concept of the 'zone of proximal development'. Some have restricted the use of the concept to child development. For example, Rogoff has argued that the 'zone' is a dynamic region of sensitivity to learning the skills of a culture in which children develop through 'guided participation' in problem solving with more experienced members of the culture (Rogoff, 1990). Rogoff was therefore able to extend Vygotsky's focus on the basic teacher/student relationship and include the interrelations between children, their caregivers and other companions. She was thus able to understand how children learn to participate in the skilled activities of a culture.

Davydov on the other hand argues that the 'zone' refers to a 'cultural region' where children close the distance between the extent of known scientific knowledge and their particular knowledge (Davydov & Radzikhovski, 1985). One consequence of this insight has been that Brown and Collins and their colleagues have been able to show that formal learning can be enhanced if the skills and knowledge that students learn are embedded in a social and functional context. They proposed students should be given ill-defined tasks and real-world problems in order to explicitly enculturate them into the ways of knowing, the cultural practices and the belief systems of the school subject in question (Collins *et al.*, 1989; Brown, 1993). Cole, on the other hand, broadened the use of the concept by suggesting that culture and cognition create each other within the 'zone' via a dynamic interrelationship between people and social worlds as expressed through language, art and understanding. Accordingly, Cole laid the conceptual foundations for the concept to be applied to human development in general, rather than being restricted to analyses of child development (Cole, 1985).

The zone of proximal development and apprenticeship

As we stated at the beginning of this chapter, one of the main attractions of Lave's proposal that a reconceptualization of apprenticeship could be the basis for a social theory of learning was that it provides an approach that does not rely on behaviourist and individualist assumptions about the learner or on a transmission model of teaching. Lave built upon Cole's original argument that culture and cognition create each other within the 'zone of proximal development'. Her concept of apprenticeship emphasizes the dynamic interrelationship between social, cultural, technological and linguistic practices. Furthermore, she identifies how such practices afford individuals and groups opportunities to learn, over a period of time. In this way she highlights the collective nature of learning (Lave & Wenger, 1991; Lave, 1996).

By adopting a social and cultural perspective on the zone of proximal development, Lave is able to reveal greater commonality between formal education and apprenticeship than has usually been accepted. By this observation we do not mean to imply that she is simply rejecting the work of those who have addressed the differences between apprenticeship and formal education; of course there are differences. It is a question of a shift in perspective and can be illustrated by reference to recent studies of technical and professional apprenticeships.[8] These studies develop (at least implicitly) their own conception of the zone of proximal development as applied to the different forms of apprenticeship they are analysing. They assume that learning occurs through such well established processes as observation, assimilation and emulation. Accordingly, 'apprentice learners' are assisted to extend their capabilities beyond their current levels of performance. The underlying pedagogic practices are implicit, rather than explicit. However, the studies also reveal how apprentices generate new knowledge, an outcome that has previously been assumed to be only associated with formal learning.

Despite this recognition, these studies still retain a conception of the 'zone of proximal development' that sees apprentices as largely learning from experts. This has a number of implications. First, it continues to limit the focus to an individualistic approach to learning at the expense of acknowledging the importance of the social and cultural processes that shape learning (Guile & Young, 1996). Secondly, it fails to differentiate between the 'official' conceptions of knowledge offered to apprentices within their formal training programmes and apprentices' own skills of acquiring, within a community of practice, the forms of tacit knowledge relevant to their emerging job-related needs (Orr, 1990; Ghererdi et al., 1997). Third, it maintains a focus upon learning existing work practices and skills, rather than pointing to how new forms of capability needed by many forms of advanced production can be encouraged (Prospect Centre, 1991). Finally, these studies assume, by inplication, that the traditional features of apprenticeship as a learning context – for example, strong hierarchical divisions of labour, an emphasis on task-specific skills and the close proximity of craft or professional 'experts' – will remain constant. On the other hand, there is growing evidence that as the organization of work changes,[9] demands for more generic problem solving abilities and of greater levels of collaboration and devolved responsibility are emerging. These changes clearly emphasize the need for an approach to learning that links the way employee identities are formed to the increasingly collective character of work and supports a greater emphasis on self-reliance so that learners are able to cope with the changes in work that are taking place.

Extending the Uses of the Zone of Proximal Development

The appeal of Vygotsky's theory lies in the emphasis it places on the idea of mind in society (Vygotsky, 1978), and its associated focus of cognitive development in specific contexts. As Rogoff has argued:

> from a socio-cultural perspective the basis unit of analysis is no longer the (properties of the) individual, but the (processes of) socio-cultural activity, involving participation in socially constituted practices.
>
> (Rogoff, 1991: 14)

This perspective has offered contemporary researchers a way of escaping from the hegemony that behavioural, and, more recently, constructivist, theories of cognitive development have held on learning (Lave, 1993, 1995; Engestrom, 1995; Wertsch, 1985). Over the last few years neo-Vygotskians and other cognitive psychologists have started to examine the processes through which cognition is developed among individuals and groups in different types of situation. As Starr has argued, this focus on the relationship between context, cognition and pedagogy has been particularly fuelled by:

> the failure of rationalism to account for or to prescribe people's behaviour (which is not new) and what is new, a large interdisciplinary movement in the academy and in the sciences that is documenting this state of affairs.
>
> (Starr, 1996: 320)

Dissatisfaction with 'rationalist' explanations of human behaviour has led researchers to begin to critique those approaches to pedagogy that involve presenting conceptual knowledge that is abstracted from the situations in which it is to be learned and used (Billett, 1997; Layton, 1991; Lave, 1996; Starr, 1997).

This shift from a 'mentalist' to a 'culturalist' perspective on the process of cognitive development has been accompanied by the development of alternative conceptions of the zone of proximal development. Two examples of such alternative conceptions are to be found in Lave's work on identity formation and skill development among West African apprentices (Lave and Wenger, 1991), and Engestrom's work on the social transformation of the organization of work (Engestrom & Cole, 1994; Engestrom, 1993, 1997). It is through this reconceptualization of the 'zone of proximal development' that we shall suggest the concept of apprenticeship may provide the basis of a social theory of learning. One consequence is likely to be a shift from understanding apprenticeship as a 'social institution' inextricably bound up with traditional craft activities and technical skills, to seeing it as a basis for conceptualising the process of learning that is more broadly applicable to a variety of modern work contexts.

The zone of proximal development: a societal perspective

Lave and Wenger identify what they define as a 'societal' perspective on 'zones of proximal development':

> we place more emphasis upon connecting issues of sociocultural transformation with the changing relations between newcomers and old-timers in the context of a changing shared practice.
>
> (Lave & Wenger, 1991: 49)

In contrast to the more normative interpretations of the zone of proximal development referred to earlier, the 'societal' perspective highlights the historical and social dimensions of learning. First, it directs attention to the distance between individuals' everyday activities and the historically new forms of social practice that need to be collectively generated as solutions to everyday problems. Secondly, it identifies learning as a social process and acknowledges the contribution that technological and other external 'resources' can make in support of such learning processes.

Lave and Wenger are interested in (i) identifying how social structures and social relationships influence the process of learning over time, (ii) the importance of relationships between one context of learning (or 'community of practice' to use their term) and another, and (iii) the opportunities available for learning within such communities, and the human and technological resources that support them. They conceive of learning:

> in terms of participation (since it) focuses attention on ways in which it is an evolving, continuously renewed set of relations.
>
> (Lave & Wenger, 1991: 51)

Furthermore, they argue that participation:

> can be neither fully internalized as knowledge structures (within individual minds) nor fully externalized as instrumental artefacts or overarching activity structures. Participation is always based on situated negotiation and re-negotiation of meanings in the world. This implies that understanding and experience are in constant interaction – indeed, are mutually constitutive.
>
> (Ibid.: 51)

Viewing the relationship between learning, activity and sociocultural contexts as a mutually constitutive process within 'communities of practice' leads Lave and Wenger to challenge the idea that expertise in a given field is invariant and consists of mastery of discrete tasks and skills. They are therefore able to reconceptualize intelligence as a distributed process rather than as an attribute of individuals. Their argument suggests that 'zones of proximal development' are populated by such resources as physical and cultural tools, as well as other people, and that these resources are used, or come together to be used to shape and direct human activity. It follows that, from their perspective, intelligence and expertise are acquired through a process of accomplishment, rather than being a matter of self-possession. As Lave comments:

> People in activity are skilful at, and are more often than not engaged in, helping each other to participate in changing their ways in a changing world.
>
> (Lave, 1993: 5)

This is not to deny that individuals develop particular forms of 'knowledgeability' (i.e. forms of knowledge and skill). However, Lave and Wenger, emphasize the collective basis through which individuals develop a social identity, learn new forms of social practice, and become 'knowledgeable'. By 'knowledgeability' they mean the combination of knowledge and skill required to successfully operate within a 'community of practice'.

Lave and Wenger's 'societal' conception of the zone of proximal development introduces a radically different approach to three issues that are central to any understanding of learning in modern societies. First, they emphasize that activity, meaning, cognition, learning and knowing must be seen in relation to each other (Lave, 1991). Second, they indicate the importance of studying how people develop their social identities through participation within different 'communities' and in more than one 'community'. Third, they highlight the importance of examining how individuals maintain their identities and sense of meaning while moving across organizational and cultural boundaries.

As already noted, Lave and Wenger argue that learning is not a special mental process, rather it is:

> a relational matter, generated in social living, historically, in social formations whose participants engage with each other as a condition and precondition for existence.
>
> (Lave & Wenger, 1991: 95)

Thus, learning becomes a matter of developing social relationships and hence identities within different 'communities of practice'. Such a perspective offers a fresh perspective on the question of transfer of skills and knowledge. For most research, 'skill transfer' as evidence of learning, refers to whether students are able to take ideas into workplaces that have been learnt within a formal educational process. As a result there is a tendency to ascribe 'failure to learn' to factors concerning the social pathology of individuals or of the teachers. This diverts attention away from the importance of providing opportunities for individuals to participate in workplaces and other 'communities of practice'. By contrast, Lave and Wenger's approach highlights how providing an extended range of opportunities in workplaces can enhance personal and group learning and encourage students to try out ideas learned in school or college. It follows that increasing access and participation, within and between different 'communities of practice', will increase individual and collective 'knowledgeability'.

Lave and Wenger's analysis adds another dimension to reformulating existing ideas about skill transfer. Conventional approaches usually assume that contexts are invariant.[10] They also rely upon narrow transmission models of teaching and play down recognition of the meaning of any skill to learners. The assumption is that the message to be transferred is always understood, thus it is assumed that there is no need to address how new knowledge might be produced within the contexts between which the knowledge or skill is to be transferred. Nevertheless, as many studies have demonstrated, accomplishing the transfer of learning and crossing organizational boundaries is a complex and challenging process (Engestrom & Middleton, 1996). It involves people developing the capacity to think beyond the immediate situation that they find themselves in an understanding why it might be both possible and necessary to generate new knowledge.

The zone of proximal development: a transformatory perspective

In order to address how people learn to do things that they have not previously accomplished, Engestrom elaborates the idea that 'zones of proximal development' are collective and can be the basis for the transformation of contexts, cognition and practice. He concentrates upon identifying how collaboarative activity is needed to reconfigure workplace activity and knowledge (Engestrom, 1993, 1995). He recognizes that many existing approaches to learning assume that it involves the circulation of existing knowledge rather than the production of 'knowledgeability' (Guile & Young, 1997).

Engestrom also argues that considerable variation exists in the fundamental imprint of the different groups with their different goals and circumstances, on what it might mean 'to know' on a particular occasion, in a particular context or within the culture of a particular organization. Consequently, he shifts the focus from a sole reliance upon the definitions of experts of what is to be learned and how it is to be learned. He emphasizes the importance of encouraging learners to identify contradictions or puzzles within existing knowledge or workplace practice as a way of developing new knowledge. It is these 'problems' which Engestrom sees as legitimate starting points for exploring and designing solutions and therefore for learning (Engestrom & Cole, 1994).

Engestrom's studies of the transformation of a Health Centre in Finland highlight, as we have argued elsewhere:

> the relationship between different modes of learning, the types of outcome arising from each mode, and the influence of context and conditions upon each mode of learning.

> (Guile & Young, 1997: 14)

Although he accepts Lave and Wenger's premise that learning is a social and reflexive process that leads 'communities' to change their identities over time, Engestrom argues that learning within 'communities of practice' is more consistent with the slow continuous evolution of practice. Nevertheless, as the Health Centre studies demonstrate, crisis points often occur because the 'communities of practice' end up confronting conflicts or problems that are not immediately resolvable (Cole & Engestrom, 1993). His research indicates that it only becomes possible for people to learn how to transform existing 'communities of practice' and reconfigure activity more effectively when two conditions are met. These are, first, the context of learning must be able to be expanded to include the existing organization, purpose and 'tools' of work, and its location in the wider community. This avoids adopting a narrow focus upon 'here-and-now' problems and 'quick-fixes'. It also enables new possibilities for the organization of work to be extensively debated and their likely implications for other related activities to be considered prior to any process of change (Engestrom, 1996). Second, concepts and ideas that are external to the community may have to be introduced as a basis for enabling the felt dilemmas and contradictions within the community of practice to be reconceptualized. As Engestrom's field studies indicate, this enables participants to construct a vision of the past and of possible futures (Engestrom *et al.*, 1996).

In contrast to Lave and Wenger, Engestrom retains a role for concepts and learning technologies that are external to an organization's existing culture and environment. Information technologies, as Pea's work makes clear, can be used to enhance individual learning within given parameters (Pea, 1993). The implication of Pea's research is that information technology can be used to create the possibility of 'communities of practice' being extended to become distributed 'communities of learning'. Such communities would enable their members to extend the sources of information to which they had access, expand their socio-cultural basis and develop new forms of 'knowledgeability'.

Furthermore, as Engestrom points out elsewhere (Engestrom, 1995), he advocates using a learning cycle that explicitly incorporates context, cognition and contradiction. Unlike Kolb's (1984) much better known approach, Engestrom's learning cycle enables individuals and groups to connect the current level of their understanding about practice to emerging ideas as to how to transform practice. At the same time, he indicates that new conceptual and technological resources must be used sensitively within 'communities of practice', if they are to complement the forms of learning already engaged in within communities. We have argued elsewhere that such activity can be described as a process of 'reflexive learning' (Guile & Young, 1997) and is the 'micro' expression of the 'macro' process of reflexive modernization (Beck *et al.*, 1994).

It follows therefore, that, contrary to the assumption of traditional approaches to apprenticeship that learning is implicit and informal and pedagogy is irrelevant, it becomes possible to identify how pedagogic structures are embedded within workplace activity. Lave and Wenger

(1991) stress the idea of situated learning which sensitizes us both to the negotiated character of learning as a social practice and to how opportunities to participate within workplace cultures influences whether and how we learn. Hence, their emphasis upon the social character of the 'zone of proximal development'. Engestrom, however, goes one stage further with his idea of 'transformative' learning, which, rather than only focusing upon the transmission of existing knowledge, acknowledges the importance of new knowledge being produced within workplace communities. The critical issue for Engestrom is that although transformative learning has to be designed, design focuses on more than formal teaching and has taken into account the context as a whole. He retains a role for a theory of instruction as well as a focus on the social processes, relationships and resources that are needed to support learning. Instruction in this sense involves ensuring that the goals of learning are clear and people are encouraged to think beyond the immediate circumstances. This ensures that the 'zone of proximal development' is collectively organized to facilitate the transformation of context, cognition and practice. As Lave has acknowledged (Chaiklen & Lave, 1993), this is the key issue in contemporary learning theory. It is of course no less applicable to learning in classrooms than it is to workplace learning and the links between the two.

Conclusion

We began this chapter by expressing our interest in the question of the relationship between learning and work and the scope of workplaces as sites of learning. We suggested that the concept of apprenticeship could be reformulated to approach these issues. We recognized that although the questions of learning and work are not new to the sociological or educational literature, much of the research which has emanated from both these fields has rarely given specific attention to the nature of workplace learning. Furthermore, it has done little to identify which pedagogical practices might support workplace learning, or to suggest how far the concept of apprenticeship might be more broadly applicable to it and other forms of learning. This led us to argue that the concept of apprenticeship should not be restricted to craft or professional activity, or, more broadly, limited to the historical forms it has taken and their uncritical acceptance of notions such as learning by doing and the master as the major role model.

We have argued that the growing body of research that has become known as activity theory has introduced a new focus and set of possibilities for building on apprenticeship as an approach to learning. Such studies have begun to draw attention to how the process of learning always involves changes in knowledge and action. Various re-interpretations of Vygotsky's concept of the 'zone of proximal development' have been central to this reformulation of ideas about learning. We identified the existence of three different conceptions of the 'zone of proximal development' – the 'normative', the 'social' and the 'transformational' – and argued that they provide an expanded view of the 'zone' that builds on ideas drawn from studies of apprenticeship and provide the beginning of a social theory of learning.

Specifically, we stressed the importance of the work of Lave and Wenger, and Engestrom, and how it enables the focus on learning within apprenticeship to be broadened away from its traditional reliance upon:

- an individualistic conception of the learning process;
- a transmission model of pedagogy; and
- the specialist knowledge of experts.

This has led them also to challenge (a) individualistic ideas of intelligence or 'mastery', (b) the idea that knowledge consists of representations within the mind and (c) the idea that skill is the property of individuals.

Both Engestrom's and Lave and Wenger's ideas, therefore, imply that any attempt to use the concept of apprenticeship as the basis of a social theory of learning has to confront and overcome two contradictions that are likely to arise in many different kinds of workplaces. First, there is the contradiction between continuity and displacement within workplace 'communities of practice'. Workplace learning, or 'legitimate peripheral participation' to use Lave and Wenger's expression, can be used (or not used) as a means to ensure the continuity of practice and to provide opportunities for the circulation of 'knowledgeability' amongst members. Second, the same process can be used to respond to learners' differing needs to have a stake in the development of new practices. They can thereby begin to establish their own future identities and develop the capacity for lifelong learning. Accordingly, lifelong learning becomes understood as a social, cultural and collective process, rather than as some mystical and abstract form of 'meta-learning' (Garrison, 1992). Whether the former or later tendency predominates will depend amongst other factors, such as funding, time and the goals of management.

The second contradiction is between the form of social organization involved in the production of the an existing 'commodity' and that involved in transforming it. Thus, as we have argued elsewhere, ideas about the continuous transformation of production imply that learning must be linked to the process of production and its attendant forms of social organization. This involves recognizing the importance of those 'institutional preconditions for learning' that either inhibit or facilitate learning within workplaces (Guile & Young, 1997).

It is our contention that these are the kind of learning demands that are increasingly being made, implicitly and explicitly, by new workplaces. Reconceptualizing the concept of apprenticeship as a social theory of learning along the lines we have described, offers, we would suggest, a basis for turning these demands into practical programmes.

Notes

1.   We define the institution of apprenticeship as the constellation of both legal and contractual rules and relations governing the status of employment, the associated workplace entitlements and the formal and informal educational processes that socialize a young worker into a workplace and occupational culture.

2.   The concept of 'reflexive learning' is derived from the work of Beck, Giddens & Lash (1994) and is discussed in more detail in Guile & Young (1997).

3.   We refer to the ideas of 'cognitive apprenticeship' (Collins *et al.*, 1989) and 'apprenticeship in thinking' (Rogoff, 1991).

4.   An alternative approach to how adults learn in the workplace can be found in the adult education literature: Brookefield (1987), Knowles (1980), Mezirow (1990) and Marswick (1987). Despite the theoretical differences within the literature, most writers adopt an individualistic and psychological preconception to learning. They do not address the social and cultural being of learning.

5.   We are referring to the different specialisms of educational research such as comparative and vocational education.

6.   These ideas have similarities with Dreyfuss's notion of moving from the status of a 'novice' to that of an 'expert' within a particular profession or craft (Dreyfuss & Dreyfuss, 1986).

7.   The term 'action-orientated' skills was first used by Zuboff to distinguish between the skills associated with traditional workplaces and the skill demands of workplaces transformed by the introduction of information technologies; these she referred to as 'intellective skills' (Zuboff, 1988).

8.   For example studies that have focused upon (i) the labour process and the 'meister' system (Ghererdi *et al.*, 1996); (ii) 'professional apprenticeship' and the role of the 'reflective practitioner' (Schön, 1987); and (iii) integrated models of work-based and in-company training (Raizen, 1990).

9.   For example Zuboff's study of paper manufacturing firms, banks and insurance companies (Zuboff, 1988).

10.   In other words, it is assumed that they are transparent and unproblematic and involve mechanistic conceptions of the 'skills of transfer' as the mastery of, and re-application of, discrete skills or domains of knowledge (Bridges, 1993).

References

Beck, U., Giddens, A. & Lash, S. (1994) *Reflexive Modernisation*. Cambridge: Polity Press.

Becker, H., Greer, B., Hughes, E. & Strauss, A. (1961) *Boys in White: student culture in a medical school*. Chicago: University of Chicago Press.

Billett, S. (1996) Situated learning: bridging sociocultural and cognitive theorising, *Learning and Instruction*, 6: 267–279.

Billett, S. (1997) Constructing vocational knowledge: histories, communities and ontology, *Journal of Vocational Education and Training*, 48: 141–154.

Blauner, R. (1964) *Alienation and Freedom*. Chicago: University of Chicago Press.

Braverman, H. (1974) *Labour and Monopoly*. New York: Capital Monthly Review.

Bridges, D. (1993) The skill of transfer, *Studies in Higher Education*, 18: 43–51.

Britton, J. (1987) Vygotsky's contribution to pedagogic theory, *English in Education*, 21(3): 22–26.

Brookefield, S. (1987) *Developing Critical Thinkers*. Buckingham: Open University Press.

Brown, A. (1993) Expertise in the classroom, in G. Saloman (ed.) *Distributed Cognition*. Cambridge: Cambridge University Press.

Brown, A., Evans, K., Blackman, S. & Germon, S. (1994) *Key Workers Technical Training and Mastery in the Workplace*. Bournemouth: Hyde Publications.

Brown, J., Collins, S. & Duguid, P. (1989) Situated cognition and culture of learning, *Educational Researcher*, 18: 32–42.

Casey, C. (1995) *Work Self and Society*. London: Routledge.

Chaiklen, S. & Lave, J. (eds) (1993) *Understanding Practice*. Cambridge: Cambridge University Press.

Cole, M. (1985) The zone of proximinal development: where culture and cognition create each other, in J. Wertsch (ed.) *Culture Communication and Cognition: Vygotskian perspectives*. New York: Cambridge University Press.

Cole, M. & Engestrom, Y. (1993) A socio-historical approach to distributed cognition, in G. Saloman (ed.) *Distributed Cognition*. Cambridge: Cambridge University Press.

Collins, A., Brown, S. J. & Newman, S. E. (1989) Cognitive apprenticeship, in L. B. Resnick (ed.) *Knowledge, Learning and Interaction: essays in honour of Robert Glaser*. New Jersey: Erlbaum, New Jersey Press.

Coy, M. (1989) *Anthropological Perspectives on Apprenticeship*. New York: SUNY Press.

Davydov, V. V. & Radzikhovski, L. A. (1985) Vygotsky's theory and the activity orientated approach to psychology, in J. Wertsch (ed.) *Culture Communication and Cognition: Vygotskian perspectives*. New York: Cambridge University Press.

Dreyfuss, H. L. & Dreyfuss, S. E. (1986) *Mind Over Machine*. Oxford: Blackwell.

Engestrom, Y. (1991) Towards overcoming the encapsulation of school learning, *Learning and Instruction*, 1: 243–261.

Engestrom, Y. (1995) *Training for Change*. London: International Labour Office.

Engestrom, Y. & Middleton, D. (eds) (1996) *Cognition and Communication at Work*. Cambridge: Cambridge University Press.

Engestrom, Y., Engestrom, R. & Karkkainen, M. (1995) Polycontextuality and boundary crossing, *Expert Cognition Learning and Instruction*, 5: 319–337.

Engestrom, Y., Viorkkunen, J., Helle, M., Pihlaja, J. & Poiketa, R. (1996) The change laboratory as a tool for transforming work, *Lifelong Learning in Europe*, 2: 10–17.

Fennell, E. (1994) Insight Comment, *Insight*, 31. Sheffield: Employment Department Information Branch.

Fuller, A. (1996) Modern apprenticeships process and learning: some emerging issues, *Journal of Vocational Education and Training*, 48: 229–249.

Garrison, D. R. (1992) Critical thinking and self directed learning in adult education, *Adult Education Quarterly*, 42(3): 136–149.

Geer, B. (ed.) (1972) *Learning to Work*. London: Sage.

Ghererdi, S., Nicolini, D. & Odella, F. (forthcoming) Towards a social understanding of how people learn in organizations: the notion of a situated curriculum.

Gott, S. (1995) Rediscovering learning: acquiring expertise in real-world problem solving tasks, *Australian and New Zealand Journal of Vocational Education Research*, 3(1).

Griffen, P. & Cole, M. (1985) Current activity for the future, In B. Rogoff & J. Wertsch (eds) *Children's Learning in the Zone of Proximal Development*. San Francisco: Jossey Bass.

Guile, D. & Young, M. (forthcoming) The question of learning and learning organisations, in M. Kelleher & C. Mulrooney (eds) *Learning Around Organisations*. Maidenhead: McGraw Hill.

Hughes, E. (1958) *Men and their Work*. Chicago: Chicago Free Press.

Hughes, E. (1971) *The Sociological Eye: papers on work, self and the study of society*. Chicago: Aldine.

Keep, E. & Mayhew, K. (1995) Training policy for competitiveness: time for a new perspective, in H. Metcalf (ed.) *Future Skill Demand and Supply*. London: PSI Publishing.

Kolb, D. (1984) *Experiential Learning: experience as the source of learning and development*. New York: Prentice Hall.

Knowles, M. S. (1980) *The Modern Practice of Adult Education: from pedagogy to andragogy*. Chicago: Follet Publishing.

Lave, J. (1993) The practice of learning, in S. Chaiklen & J. Lave (eds) *Understanding Practice*. Cambridge: Cambridge University Press.

Lave, J. (1996) Teaching as learning in practice, *Mind Culture and Society*, 3(3): 9–71.

Lave, J. & Wenger, E. (1991) *Situated Learning*. Cambridge: Cambridge Press.

Layton, D. (1991) Science education as praxis: the relationship of school science to practical action studies, *Science Education*, 19: 42–79.

Leontiev, A. N. (1978) *Activity, Consciousness and Personality*. New York: Englewood Cliff.

Leymann, H. & Kornbluh, H. (eds) (1989) *Socialisation and Learning at Work*. Aldershot: Avebury Press.

Marswick, V. J. (1987) *Learning Within Workplaces*. London: Croom Helm.

Marx, K. (1844) Economic and philosophical manuscripts, in R. Tucker (ed.) (1978) *The Marx–Engels Reader*. New York: Norton.

Mezirow, J. (1990) *Developing Critical Self Reflection*. San Francisco: Jossey Bass.

Noble, D. (1991) Social choice, in H. Mackay, M. Young & J. Benyon (eds) *Machine Design: the case of automatically controlled tools in understanding technology on education*. London: Falmer Press.

Orr, J. (1991) Narrative at work, in D. Middleton & Y. Engestrom (eds) *Collective Remembering*. London: Sage.

Pea, D. (1993) Distributed intelligence, in G. Saloman (ed.) *Distributed Cognition*. Cambridge: Cambridge University Press.

Pipan, R. (1989) Towards a curriculum perspective of workplaces, in H. Leymann & H. Kornbluh (eds) *Socialisation and Learning at Work*. Aldershot: Avebury Press.

Pratt, D. (1992) Concepts of teaching, *Adult Education Quarterly*, 42(4): 207–220.

Prospect Centre (1991) *Growing and Innovative Workforce*. London: Prospect Centre.

Raizen, S. (1991) Learning and work: the research base, paper presented at the United States Department for Education and The Overseas Education Centre for Development Conference, Phoenix: Linkages in Vocational Technical Education and Training.

Rogoff, B. (1990) *Apprenticeship in Thinking: cognitive development in social contexts*. New York: Oxford University Press.

Schön, D. (1986) *The Reflective Practitioner*. New York: Basic Books.

Schribner, S. & Cole, M. (1973) Cognitive consequences of formal and informal learning, *Science*, 82: 553–559.

Smith, A. (1974) *The Wealth of Nations*. Harmondsworth: Penguin.

Starr, S. L. (1996) Working together: symbolic interactionism, activity theory and information systems, in D. Middleton & Y. Engestrom (eds) *Cognition and Communication at Work*. Cambridge: Cambridge University Press.

Streek, W. (1989) Skills and the limits of neo-liberalism, *Work, Employment and Society*, 3: 89–105.

Streek, W. (1994) *The Social Institutions of Economic Performance*. London: Sage.

Tikhomirov, O. V. (1981) The psychology of computers, in J. V. Wertsch (ed.) *The Concept of Activity in Soviet Psychology*. Armonk: M.E. Sharpe.

Vygotsky, L. S. (1978) *Mind in Society*. Cambridge: Cambridge University Press.

Warner, M., Wobbe, W. & Brodner, P. (eds) (1990) *New Technology and Manufacturing Management: strategic choices for flexible production systems*. Chichester: Wiley.

Wertsch, J. V. (1981) *The Concept of Activity in Soviet Psychology*. Armonk: M.E. Sharpe.

Wertsch, J. (ed.) (1985) *Culture Communication and Cognition: Vygotskian perspectives*. New York: Cambridge University Press.

Womack, J. P., Jones, D. T. & Roos, D. (1991) *The Machine that Changes the World*. New York: Harper.

Wood, S. (ed.) (1982) *The Degradation of Work? Skill, De-skilling and the Labour Process*. London: Hutchinson.

Wood, S. (ed.) (1989) *The Transformation of Work Skill Flexibility and the Labour Process*. London: Unwin Hyman.

Young, M. (1995) Post-compulsory education and training for a learning society, *Australian and New Zealand Journal of Vocational Educational Reserch*, 3(1).

Zuboff, S. (1988) *In the Age of the Smart Machine*. London: Heinemann.

6

Questioning the Concept of the Learning Organization

Tara Fenwick

Hit the ground running or you won't keep up!, shouts Nuala Beck (1995), a Toronto economist and popular speaker-consultant in Canadian human resource circles. Beck warns that only workers who learn and change continuously to accommodate the demands of the market-place will survive in the new economy. Educators and human resource developers have adopted this rhetoric of urgency, declaring that 'learning is the necessary response to change' (Dixon, 1993: 18). The concept of the 'learning organization' is gaining momentum in both private and public sectors as the new panacea for coping with the most perplexing and frightening changes swirling about the labour market. An ideology of values, structure and prescriptive strategies, the learning organization concept offers a cuddly vision, of 'community' and collegiality, a workplace where trust, sharing, reflective practice and empowerment flourish. Common principles reiterated among learning organization theorists direct organizations to reinvent themselves so that they might: (1) create continuous learning opportunities, (2) promote inquiry and dialogue, (3) encourage collaboration and team learning, (4) establish systems to capture and share learning, (5) empower people toward collective vision, and (6) connect organizations to their environments (Watkins and Marsick, 1993).

Certainly such principles hold promise for creating a more humanitarian, egalitarian, growth-oriented workplace. But amid the enthusiasm attending flurried efforts to implement these principles, important questions remain unasked in the dominant literature on the subject, questions about what is meant by a learning organization, what it values, its assumptions about learning and the nature of knowledge and how its discourse structures the relations and practices of the workplace. As organizations come to recognize their position in the continual flux of an unpredictable global economy, the place of the worker in a learning organization has become relegated to one of eternal, slippery deficiency: workers must learn continuously and embrace instability as the normal order of things. That the workplace appoints itself as the individual's educator, personal development counsellor and even spiritual mentor is rarely questioned.

This chapter critically examines the ideology and discourse of the learning organization in two sections. The historical context, principles and people involved in developing the learning organization concept will be outlined briefly in the following section. The second section challenges assumptions embedded in learning organization ideology.

Historical Contexts and Principles of the Learning Organization

The 'learning organization' arose from the convergence of three important currents: (1) the tradition of organizational development (OD) and particularly concepts of organizational learning; (2) economic shifts to globalization, deregulation and information-based industry; and (3) Total Quality Management (TQM).

Organizational learning is not a new concept. Finger and Woolis (1994) argue that five schools of thought about organizational learning led to the appearance of Senge's (1991) learning organization concept. The earliest notions of organizational learning centred on organizational continuity and assumed the essential stability and coherence of the organization. Learning was viewed conservatively as a process to 'encode, store and retrieve the lessons of history despite the turnover of personnel and the passage of time' (Levitt & March, 1988: 319) or to continually improve existing procedures for adaptation. Later approaches viewed organizational learning as a transformative process.

Organizational development — a process that actively implements planned change to help organizations examine and change their routines and cultural norms – was well established in the work of Argyris and Schon (1978). The OD goal was to develop the organization's ability to maintain a pattern of homeostasis despite fluctuations in the external environment through an *action science* approach. Because the organization was encouraged to incorporate critical thinking into a continuous evaluation of its routines and norms – what Argyris called 'double loop learning' – the change process was dynamic and even subversive, although fundamentally conservative.

Finger and Woolis (1994) argue that a third group writing in the 1980s took a more sophisticated view of learning (i.e., Fiol & Lyles, 1985), clarifying important distinctions between organizational change on the one hand and learning on the other. They described different levels of learning and different learning systems and acknowledged the complex dynamics of the organization interacting with the various communities and forces comprising its environment. Thus, the concept of learning organization was incubated during growing interest in the nature of collective learning and the notion of an organization as a continuously adaptive and proactive agent.

The economic shifts of the 1980s was the second trajectory associated with the emergence of the learning organization concept. These shifts raised considerable alarm: business viewed itself in constant jeopardy in a new competitive climate that moved at fibre-optic speed, embraced global dimensions of cultural and market influences and communicated through constantly changing technologies. Businesses envisioned themselves as caught in a 'paradigm shift' and looked for new organizational structures and leadership approaches. Continuous learning offered a survival strategy.

During this period, the third contributing influence to learning organization notions, the movement toward Total Quality Management (TQM), tranformed business and government. Under TQM dictates, organizations were restructured to become flatter and more fluid, action-oriented, accountable for outcomes focusing on quality, mission and culture. People wer grouped in multi-skilled teams that ideally defined and regulated their own work. These changes prepared the ground for the germination of the learning organization ideology.

Senge (1991), whose book *The Fifth Discipline: The Art and Practice of the Learning Organization* is often credited with popularizing the concept, defines learning organization as 'a place where people continually expand their capacity to create the results they truly desire, where new and expansive patterns of thinking are nurtured, where collective aspiration is set free, and where people are continually learning how to act together' (p. 3). The learning organization concept presumes continuous change to drive the centre of the organization's activity and stresses continuous innovation as the key to productivity in an environment of constant change (Watkins & Marsick, 1993). For Senge and his associates (1994), there are five interwoven forces or 'disciplines' to cultivate when 'building' a learning organization: (1) personal mastery, or making personal capacities and dreams explicit; (2) mental models, or examining and overturning deep personal beliefs; (3) team learning, or collaborating to develop and share knowledge effectively in small groups; (4) shared vision, or building a collective dream to guide future action; and (5) systems thinking, or coming to view one's own actions and agendas from a big-picture perspective that accepts one's fundamental inter-connectivity with everyone else. Central to these disciplines is the assumption that employees need to engage in critical reflection and open dialogue, exposing their own belief systems and critically challenging others' belief systems, to break free of thinking patterns which perpetuate dysfunction and prevent innovation. A flexible, self-reflexive, but vividly clear vision is supposedly essential to carry the organization through the rapids of tumultuous change.

The Fifth Discipline was treated like a manifesto, cited so often in boardrooms and journals of the early 1990s (e.g., see Gavin, 1993; Shaw & Perkins, 1991; Wick, 1993; Ulrich, Jick & von Glinow, 1994; Redding & Catalenello, 1994) that it began exercising wide influence on organizational reform and restructuring efforts. Canadian federal task force reports and policy background papers in 1992–94 (e.g., CCMD, 1994) demanded that public instititions restructure to integrate continuous learning principles. Large corporations such as Canadian banks (Flood, 1993), and NOVA (Sass, 1996) announced commmitment to transform themselves into learning organizations. A consortium for organizational learning launched in early 1995 by the Center for Public Management invited private and public organizations to collaborate as they worked through issues in becoming a learning organization (Prospectus, 1994).

So why question this enthusiastic Canadian plunge into intentions of continuous learning and innovation, trusting communities and caring, collaborative teams? Critics from the left dismiss the human capital orientation embedded in learning organization literature, which regards people as 'resources' that serve the organization's pursuit of profit [. . .]. The power structures of the market-place and the selected knowledge it values remain unexamined, argue Finger and Woollis (1994), and learning is distorted into a tool for competitive advantage. Learning theorists might argue that the learning organization concept largely ignores current knowledge about adult learning and development. The ideals associated with learning organizations of interrelations, unity, co-operation and wholeness have been criticized by Edwards and Usher (1996) as rampant moralism subordinated to overarching order, the system's totality. Meanwhile the moralism-by-consensus that constructs the shared vision supposedly guiding the organization is relativist, 'emotive and inherently subjective', argues Campbell (1995: 94); such a vision lacks a deep conceptual grounding in objective principles of right and wrong, and the possibilities for variant values are infinite.

Problems with the Learning Organization Concept

What follows is a critical examination of six premises of the learning organization that focus on: (1) the organization of a site and frame for learning, (2) the dominant role of managers and educators, (3) the subordinate role accorded to employees as undifferentiated learners-in-deficit, (4) the emphasis on problem solving and instrumental knowledge, (5) the organization's appropriation of critical reflection, and (6) the reliance on 'open' dialogue for group learning in the workplace.

The organization as a site and framework for learning

Learning in the workplace is spatially and temporally bounded by the organization's contours. The individual's learning becomes understood as a 9:00 to 5:00 phenomenon that is motivated by the job, developed through the job and measurable only through observable behaviours linked to competencies that benefit the job. Learning is recognized only in knowledge that the organization can access, knowledge which can be spoken, deconstructed and shared (for example, through dialogue), rather than knowledge which might be tacit and embedded in practice, communicative relations, visions, choices and intuition.

One problem here is the conflation of individual and organizational learning. There is a leap from individual learning processes of action and reflection, constructing and transforming meaning perspectives, to applying these concepts somewhat cavalierly to an organization. The organization is thus construed as a unitary, definable, intelligent entity. It is not, nor is it stable and bounded. Consider the multiple sub-groups comprising an organization, each characterized by distinct cultures, each changing according to its dynamic interplay with other groups and shifting shape with the nomadic movement of individual workers. How can this fluctuating combination of sub-groups be totalized as a single, monolithic organism that somehow 'learns' and has memory?

From the individual's lifeworld perspective, a single workplace organization is only one part of the individual's purposes, growth curve, dilemmas and preoccupations. People often work part time, hold jobs in different organizations or work at home while loaning themselves to many different organizations to conduct business. People flow among various overlapping organizational communities. When learning is defined in terms of what perspectives and skills one particular organization most values, such as its own shared vision and need for multi-skills, each person's multiple identities (and knowledges) are obscured in the organization's perceptual field, which coheres around itself. The meanings, dilemmas, insights and changes comprising people's daily experience are neither acknowledged nor valued because these various kinds of knowledge do not fit the organization's perception of itself as a unitary, rational container of subjects. Marsick and Watkins (1990) go so far as to describe as 'dysfunctional' a person's ongoing 'incidental' learning that does not advance the organization's purposes. Too rigid and narrow a formulation of what counts as knowledge in the organization's gaze potentially alienates the individual from his or her own meanings and fails to allow these meanings to flourish and contribute to the community.

The dominant role of managers and educators

Literature about the learning organization tends to be written by and for those most concerned with the overall health and existence of the organization, those whose own identity is most closely aligned to the organization's goals and success. These are the managers of the organization and the educators who serve them. Two issues attending this circumstance deserve attention. First, despite the emphasis placed on dialogue among 'multiple perspectives', the production and consumption of the learning organization discourse omits many important perspectives. Among the excluded are workers' agendas and visions, small businesses struggling to compete in the accelerated markets of constant innovation, growing multitudes of independent contractors serving corporations through part-time temporary service, labourers in semi-skilled or de-skilled activities whose work is not knowledge reliant, and those who lack the learning capabilities required for critical reflection, visioning and team learning.

Second, the literature typically approaches the learning project as something that 'empowers' others, or 'helps' others to learn. The voice of the learning organization sculptors is not self-reflexive. The agenda and vision of the leader or educational agent is bracketed out, obscuring the partiality and positionality of the voices calling for continuous learning and learning organizations. This situation is reminiscent of the emancipatory pedagogue who presumes the privilege to enlighten and speak for the 'oppressed'. Who is controlling the vision, the goals, the definitions of learning – and for what purposes? The pragmatic issue attending such myopia is the inevitable incongruence between the workers' perspectives and those of the manager or educator.

Employees as undifferentiated learners-in-deficit

If managers and educators are the architects of the learning organization, employees are colonized as its subjects. Constituted as always learning and exhorted to remain balanced on the precipice of risk, these subjects are particularly vulnerable. In a climate of 'continuous' innovation the individual theoretically can never be grounded in a sense of expertise or stability. Nor does the individual have control over pronouncing what counts as knowledge, including personally constructed knowledge. From the continuous learning perspective, the individual is supposed to learn more, learn better and learn faster, and is therefore always in deficit. An ideology of 'constant improvement' tends to create a competitive track where the racing dogs never reach the mechanical rabbit. The anxiety-inducing press to avoid 'being left behind' is common in workplace learning literature. Meanwhile the organization's knowledge – considered the key to success – is linked directly to the employee's demonstrable ability and willingness to learn. The worker becomes responsible for the organization's health without the authority to determine alternative frameworks to 'learning' through which this health might be considered and measured.

The focus of the learning organization is on employees whose work is knowledge reliant. Thus the only individuals who are explicitly included in continuous learning initiatives are those whose learning power and stock of learnings are valuable to their employing organization as commodities that can help accelerate the productivity, improve the competitive performance of the business and generate profit. Workers who do not generate knowledge, who, according the Paquette (1995), are increasingly the kinds of employees most hired and required to fill Canada's job openings, are excluded from or outside the borders of the maps being constructed of today's market-place by the continuous learning promotors. Many writers are currently drawing attention to technology's dehumanizing impact in workplaces, diminishing the need for workers who think, create, change and proactively generate new knowledge (Zuboff, 1988). Agendas for continuous learning and growth evidently are oriented most towards the continuing privilege of the technocratic-professional-managerial elite, who are already the likeliest to be most educated and to have most access to learning opportunities.

Learning organization literature makes little attempt to distinguish meaningfully among the unique learning processes of individual worker-learners. Learning is understood to be essentially problem solving; 'deeper' learning supposedly transpires through processes of critical reflection (especially through verbal disclosure and deconstruction of belief systems), and a self-directed approach to learning becomes an ideal toward which employees should be encouraged to strive. These assumptions ignore literature showing that self-directed learning is *not* a generalizable approach among adults (see [. . .] Pratt, 1988; Collins, 1991) and that activity and tools more than dialogue affect what and how people learn (Lave & Wenger, 1991). Gender, race and class dimensions, all ignored in the learning organization discourse, create important distinctions among individuals in what holds meaning for them and how they construct these meanings. For example, studies in women's workplace learning (MacKeracher & McFarland, 1994) report complexities in relational learning and the centrality of self that contradict many learning organization assumptions. Individuals' workplace learning has been shown to vary dramatically according to their intentions, the disjunctures they apprehend, their positionality and relations in the workplace community, their values of knowledge and views of themselves as knowers (Fenwick, 1996). The target group for continuous learning in the workplace neglects large groups of people who are implicitly 'other' but whose individual work-learning struggles continue to produce knowledge, whether or not these kinds of knowledge are recognized by the learning organization. Meanwhile, learners with special needs, disabilities, low literacy skills or other characteristics which don't fit the learning organization's preferred approaches (self-directed learning, critical reflection, risk and innovation and dialogue) are in danger of being discarded altogether.

Emphasis on problem solving and instrumental knowledge

The learning organization literature emphasizes two kinds of knowledge: innovative problem solving and 'detecting error' (Argyris, 1993). The problem-solving orientation frames learning as continually seeking freedom from difficulty, which is a negative orientation to understanding cognitive construction of meaning (Prawat, 1993). When the understanding of learning becomes driven by a metaphor of problem solving and innovation, learning is limited to instrumentality. Productivity is thus used as the ultimate criterion to evaluate efforts towards personal growth, building relationships in teams and building cultures and close communities. The usefulness of what is being produced is removed from the question. Worse, the unpredictable, fluid, emergent process of learning is linked to the production of goods, which depends on certainty, bounded time periods and concrete products. Strange fruit is produced from the union of learning and production, evident in business literature that discusses 'intellectual capital' (Stewart, 1994) as though the ephemerality of meaning making could be packaged, measured, bought and sold.

The purpose of 'continuous learning', indeed the very term, promotes an expansionary view of development. The question 'Learn what?' is rarely addressed. Employees might discern that the organization will premise future staffing decisions on particular skills or work experiences. The question 'Learn how?' is the programmatic focus of most learning organization literature, which provides lots of advice about learning process derived from romanticized humanistic principles of holistic learning and building family-like communities that care and share and notions modelled from action research. Because there is no explicit curriculum (naturally in the ideology of constant change, the learning architects can defer commitment to particular content: content emerges unpredictably), decisions about the 'what' of learning presumably are never made. Innovation to 'keep up' with constant change is the focus. This not only ties employee learning to the bumper of the overall company direction controlled by management, but also privileges breakthrough thinking and 'new' (profitable) knowledge over other kinds of knowledge, such as relational, cultural, procedural and personal. From such a perspective, alternative views of learning are invisible. For example, learning might include deepening inward rather than expanding outward; enriching existing meaning structures, confirming and extending them, rather than adding to them or transforming them; might be recursive, circling back to concepts and internalizing them into behaviours and beliefs, rather than generating new concepts.

Hart (1992; 1993) offers an elegant critique of the current imperatives driving the workplace and its learning orientation. She raises questions about what is truly important and productive work, and to what extent the expansionary, innovation-oriented perspective fits how individuals view their learning in the workplace. Hart's vision of 'sustenance' work, predicated upon communicative dimensions rather than the hyperactive productivity driving the industrial machine, is only one example illustrating the possible alternatives driven to the margins by the domination of continuous learning initiatives for organizational competitive advantage.

The organization's use of critical reflection

Watkins and Marsick (1993), like Senge *et al.* (1994) and Argyris (1993), emphasize reflection, especially critical reflection through small-group talk, as a key activity in a learning organization. They assume that learning occurs when understandings become shaped through rational thought and language. This cognitive bias is evident in Bohm's (cited in Senge, 1991) description of the importance of talk to clarify an individual's ambiguous, disordered, contradictory or 'inaccurate' meanings. Thus knowledge that is generated and embodied through sensual, kinesthetic, intuitive, relational, spiritual and emotional meaning systems would not count as 'learning' until it is made explicit and conscious to the rational mind. Strands of research exploring workplace intuition (Mott, 1994) and the 'feeling-sense' developed by professionals through non-rational learnings (Boreham, 1992) refute this dominance of cognitive reflection in learning organization precepts.

Critical reflection in learning organization literature presumes that if people could just detect their dysfunctional and paralysing taken-for-granted assumptions and deep-seated beliefs, they would be free to find new and more creative ways to frame the problems of practice and thus improve their performance in the workplace. In demanding explicit confessional critical reflection of its employees, the organization appropriates for its own purposes the most private aspects of individuals' worlds – their beliefs and values – and conscripts them for the organization's purposes. Good examples of this practice are the personal development exercises described in popular learning organization handbooks (e.g., see Senge *et al.*, 1994), leading individuals through intensely private scrutiny.

Assuming that all people can engage in dialectical, critical reflection – a dubious premise in light of cognitive and psycho-social adult development theory (Benack & Basseches, 1989; Belenky *et al.*, 1986; Perry, 1970) – serious questions need to be raised about the goals of critical reflection in the learning organization ideal. The assumption is that individuals' current beliefs and moral structures, which make up their identity and whatever stability they can manage to create in a whirling workworld, are not good enough. Whatever perspectives exist in a person probably need to be critically challenged and changed, but it is incumbent only on the individual employees to critically reflect upon and change their mental models. Thus the Canadian Imperial Bank of Commerce (CIBC) chairman declares, 'Learning is now everybody's business', and the organization's job is to 'encourage' people to 'adopt different mental models that better reflect competitive and workplace realities' (Flood, 1993). The objects for critical focus are carefully delineated to exclude the fundamental structures of capitalism, the CIBC's and other corporate interests, and assumptions like 'life serves economic imperatives', and 'learning will save business'. Employees are supposed to reflect critically on the operational procedures of the corporation, but only its surface. From a radical left perspective (i.e., see Noble, 1990; Cunningham, 1993), employees' minds are expected to remain colonized and loyal to the imperial presence of their employing organization. Critical scrutiny is deflected from the power structures and the learning organization ideology itself and focused on the individual.

The organizational perspective is oriented to the status quo and is self-serving: it cannot conceive of its own death or life after its death. Workers' learning is to be innovative and critically reflective so long as the outcomes ensure the survival, indeed the prosperity, productivity and competitive advantage, of the employing organization. Learning that threatens the existence of the organization, such as liberated workers finding ecological and communicatively nurturing ways to achieve their purposes that begin with dismantling the organization, are not possible from the organization's perspective. Meanwhile the focus is on changing individuals to become the kinds of workers corporations demand. From the organization's perspective the continuously learning individual is in perpetual deficit, harnessed to Beck's (1995) vision of the 'powerful engines' of the economy and struggling to 'keep up'.

The reliance on 'open' dialogue for learning in the workplace

The most promoted vehicle for reflection in learning organization literature is team dialogue. Extensive strategies are offered to promote a balance between 'inquiry' and 'advocacy', to create open, trusting climates where honesty is not punishable and personal disclosure is permissible, where communication is clear and authentic, where people are exposed to multiple perspectives and where challenges to one another's assumptions are encouraged. This literature accepts the possibility of an 'ideal speech situation, where, according to Habermas (1984), participants communicate accurate but often incomplete information, are free from coercion or deception, are able to weigh evidence and assess arguments objectively, arc open to alternative perspectives and are able to reflect critically on their own assumptions. Dixon (1993) recommends the 'ideal speech condition' as the best way an organization may help staff turn all experience into learning: presumably they will listen to each others' experiences, find causal relationships and overall consequences, talk about failures and analyse each others' mistakes. Emphasis is on achieving 'transparency' through talk.

Thus words are privileged over other means of expression between people, such as kinesthetic, sensual, oral non-verbal, artistic and intuitive. All complexities of meaning are supposedly reducible to the linear stream of language structures. This is an orientation of management and control that raises questions about agenda and about the links among all languages and learning. Is the most valuable workplace learning produced in the dynamic of interchange? Is giving voice to experience necessarily a useful process or a necessary part of learning? Usher and Edwards (1995) argue that a related problem with dialogue is its disciplinary function. To disclose one's opinions, and particularly to disclose for the purpose of critical scrutiny one's belief systems and values, is to surrender the last private space of personal meaning to the public space of workplace control. The demand for such disclosure could be construed as an exercise of surveillance and disciplinary regulation constituting gross violation of an individual's rights.

Simplistic understandings of workplace dialogue also ignore power asymmetries as these configure the communication process, especially in the workplace when conversations and relationships are structured according to politics of gender, class, age, job status and other factors. Critics have shown the difficulties of achieving truly democratic 'ideal' speech situations when little or no attention is given to the multiple social positions, conscious and unconscious pleasures, tensions, desires and contradictions present in all subjects in all historical contexts (Ellsworth, 1992; Orner, 1992). The reality in the workplace is that all people cannot possibly have equal opportunity to participate, reflect and refute one another in a 'team dialogue'. Brooks (1995) reports contradictory meanings, conflicting interests and subversion in her studies of workplace teams. Shaw and Perkins (1991) report many barriers that preclude reflective talk in many workplaces: pressure, 'competency traps', bias towards activity, people's sense of powerlessness, a focus on measurable performance and strong inter-group boundaries.

The notion of dialogue is grounded in Senge's 'fifth discipline' of teaching employees in an organization to view themselves as connected in a webwork of groups that function interdependently and benevolently to achieve a common purpose. Systems thinking essentially equates a social and cultural entity structured by power and composed of complex, constantly shifting human relations with physical phenomena. Thus the organization is conceptualized as a biological stystem. A short jump allows ideologues to envision a learning system where all system components are equitably and functionally interlinked. Systems thinking is a-structural, a-contextual, a-historical and apolitical. Knowledge is considered to be freely available to all; conflict is viewed as resolvable differences between equally competing individuals; and culture is treated as a set of environmental conditions which can be manipulated through thoughtful leadership. Such assumptions cannot reasonably be validated against organizational reality.

Paradoxes in the Learning Organization

The fundamental problem with the concept of the learning organization is that the popular notion of 'empowerment', while prevalent in learning organization literature, is not critically examined. Questions as to whose empowerment and to what ends are not asked. West (1994) concludes in his critical review of this literature that the learning organization meets the learner's needs only if these are not in conflict with the orgnaization's needs. He shows that despite rhetoric representing itself as a worker-centred philosophy, the learning organization concept emphasizes productivity, efficiency and competitive advantage at the expense of the worker. And as Shaw and Perkins (1991) point out, these goals orient the company culture to values and activities which actually inhibit learning.

Another paradox is that learning organization literature is often prescriptive, performing a normalizing and regulatory function while claiming to emancipate workers. Thus the very hierarchies of power and technical knowledge that are supposedly democratized in the learning organization are in fact wielded by the organization to control and subvert worker resistance to corporate downsizing and restructuring. A third paradox is created by context: the warm rhetoric in the literature of connectedness, trust and opportunity is unfurled in a climate darkened by an ethos of anxiety, a darkness that is not acknowledged in the rosy visions of the learning organization. Employees, told to trust in the corporation's benevolent human-growth-centred agenda, are invited to confess and transform their innermost desires and beliefs, to stick out their necks and keep learning and forget that they are in constant danger of being summarily ejected.

In the implementation of concepts of a learning organization there is perhaps another paradox: assumptions of continuous learning, based on a theory of knowledge produced thorough exploratory experimentation and innovation, collide with organizational norms of productivity, accountablity and results-based measurement using predictable outcomes. Rough (1994) shows how traditional assessment measures of organizational performance and training are still prevalent and distort the holistic and dynamic notions of learning in the new paradigm. Moreover, the learning organization concept, based on adminstrative control of staff dialogue, paradoxically precludes the assumptions of the open, provisional, relational knowledge the technologies of learning organizations are supposed to produce. Multiple perspectives are urged by the learning organization ideology, but the ideology itself is a universal coherent set of simplistic ideals. What perspectives and differing abilities truly would be tolerated?

These paradoxes and the problematic implications of the six focuses of the learning organization become internalized in the workers, creating a problem in the constitution of worker identity and knowledge. Workers struggle to find and/or create an identity, meaning and purpose within their work (Fenwick, 1996). The learning organization discourse presents itself as a romantic ideal encouraging workers' personal growth and imaginative engagement – yet this discourse continues the workplace tradition of dictating which kind of growth counts most, what imaginative endeavours are most valued, what kinds of talk, relationships and identities are allowed and which are out of bounds or even meaningless. Perhaps the situation is rendered even worse by the learning organization's ubiquitous adjuration to workers to be 'open and honest' and name the 'undiscussables' (Argyris, 1993). The reality of workers' multi-situated and continually shifting identity, as well as the complexities of their workplace learning (Fenwick, 1996), are neither valued nor even acknowledged. The practical outcome may be the precise opposite of what the learning organization ideal hopes to achieve: rather than co-operation, commitment, and community, what may be produced is workers' withdrawal or cynicism, confusion and alienation.

Conclusion

Questions about these issues are posed not to destroy the promise held by learning organization approaches to workplace learning but to clarify its discourse. Until its premises become clear, efforts to implement the learning organization ideal will continually be challenged by real human beings and their needs, which weave together to create an organization. Meanwhile, educators need not discard precepts of continuous learning but should continue to work with others to explore their potential. Educators can provide fresh perspectives towards truly empowering work-learning activities.

References

Argyris, C. (1993) *Organizational learning*. Cambridge, MA: Blackwell.

Argyris, C. & Schon, D. (1978) *Organizational learning: A theory of action perspective*. Reading, Mass: Addison-Wesley.

Beck, N. (1995) *Shifting gears: Thriving in the new economy*. Toronto, ON: Nuala Beck and Associates.

Belenky, M. F., Clinchy, B. M., Goldberger, N. B. & Tarule, J. M. (1986). *Women's ways of knowing: The development of self, voice, and mind*. New York: Basic Books.

Benack, S. & Basseches, M. A. (1989). Dialectical thinking and relativistic epistemology: Their relation in adult development. In M. L. Commons, J. D. Sinnitt, F. A. Richards & C. Armon (eds), *Adult development*. New York: Praeger.

Boreham, N. C. (1992). Harnessing implicit knowing to improve medical practice. *New Directions for Adult and Continuing Education*, 55: 71–78.

Brooks, A. K. (1995) The myth of self-directed work teams and the ineffectiveness of team effectiveness training: An argument with special reference to teams that produce knowledge. *Proceedings of the 26th Annual Adult Education Research Conference* (pp. 41–48). Edmonton, AB: University of Alberta.

Campbell, E. (1995) Raising the moral dimension of school leadership. *Curriculum Inquiry*, 25(1): 87–99.

CCMD Report No. 1. (May 1994) *Continuous learning: A CCMD Report*. Canadian Centre for Management Development. Minister of Supply and Services Canada.

Collins, M. (1991) *Adult education as vocation: A critical role for the adult educator*. New York and London: Routledge.

Cunningham, P. (1993) The politics of workers' education: Preparing workers to sleep with the enemy. *Adult Learning*, 5(1): 13–17.

Dixon, N. (1993) *Report to the Conference Board of Canada on organizational learning*. Report prepared for the Conference Board of Canada, Ottawa.

Edwards, R. & Usher, R. (1996). What stories do I tell now? New times and new narratives for the adult educator. *International Journal of Lifelong Education*, 15(3): 216–229.

Ellsworth, E. (1992). Why doesn't this feel empowering? Working through the repressive myths of critical pedagogy. In C. Luke and J. Gore (eds), *Feminism and critical pedagogy* (pp. 90–119). New York: Routledge.

Fenwick, T. J. (1996). Women as continuous learners in the workplace. Unpublished doctoral dissertation, University of Alberta, Edmonton, Alberta.

Finger, M. & Woolis, D. (1994) Organizational learning, the learning organization, and adult education. *Proceedings of the Adult Education Research Conference* (pp. 151–156). Knoxville, TN: University of Tennessee.

Fiol, M. C. & Lyles, M. A. (1985) Organizational learning. *Academy of Management Review*.

Flood, C. (1993) The learning organization. *The Worklife Report*, 9(2): 1–4.

Gavin, D. (1993) The five practices of a learning organization. *Harvard Business Review*, July–August, 271–282.

Habermas, J. (1984) *The theory of communicative action*. Vol. 1: *Reason and the rationalization of society*. (McCarthy, T., trans.). Boston: Beacon.

Hart, M. (1993) Educative or miseducative work: A critique of the current debate on work and education. *Canadian Journal for the Study of Adult Education*, 7(1): 19–36.

Hart, M. U. (1992). *Working and educating for life: Feminist and international perspectives on adult education*. London: Routledge.

Lave, J. & Wenger, E. (1991) *Situated learning: Legitimate peripheral participation*. New York: Cambridge University Press.

Levitt, B. & March, J. G. (1988) Organizational learning. *Annual Review of Sociology*, 14: 319–340.

MacKeracher, D. & McFarland, J. (1993/94) Learning working knowledge: Implications for training. *Women's Education Des Femmes*, 10(3/4): Winter, 54–58.

Marsick, V. & Watkins, K. (1990) *Informal and incidental learning in the workplace*. London: Routledge.

Mott, V. W. (1994) The role of intuition in the reflective practice of adult educators. *Proceedings of the 34th Adult Education Reserch Council Conference*. University of Tennessee, Knoxville, TN.

Noble, D. D. (1990) High-tech skills: The latest corporate assault on workers. In S. London, E. Tarr & J. Wilson (eds), *The re-education of the American working class*. Westport, CT: Greenwood Publishing Group.

Orner, M. (1992) Interrupting the calls for student voice in 'liberatory education': A feminist poststructuralist perspective. In C. Luke & J. Gore (eds), *Feminisms and critical pedagogy* (pp. 74–89). New York: Routledge.

Paquette, J. (1995) Universal education: Meanings, challenges, and options into the third millennium. *Curriculum Inquiry*, 25(1): 23–56.

Perry, W. (1970) *Forms of intellectual and ethical development in the college years*. New York: Holt, Rinehart, and Winston.

Pratt, D. D. (1988) Andragogy as a relational construct. *Adult Education Quarterly*, 38(3): 160–181.

Prawat, R. S. (1993, August–September). The value of ideas: Problems versus possibilities in learning. *Educational Researcher*, 5–16.

Prospectus. (1994, November 21) Consortium for Organizational Learning: An invitation to join. Centre for Public Management.

Redding, J. C. & Catalanello, R. F. (1994) *Strategic readiness: The making of the learning organization*. San Francisco: Jossey-Bass.

Rough, J. (1994) Measuring training from a new science perspective. *Journal for Quality and Participation*, October/November: 12–16.

Sass, B. (1996) NOVA looks up learning. *Edmonton Journal*, February 20, DI.

Senge, P., Ross, R., Smith, B., Roberts, C. & Kleiner, A. (1994) *The fifth discipline fieldbook: Strategies and tools for building a learning organization*. New York: Doubleday.

Senge, P. (1991) *The fifth discipline: The art and practice of the learning organization*. New York: Doubleday.

Shaw, R. B. & Perkins, D. N. T. (1991) The learning organization: Teaching organizations to learn. *Organization Development Journal*, 9(4): 1–12.

Stewart, T. A. (1994) Your company's most valuable asset: Intellectual capital. *Fortune*. October 3: 68–74.

Ulrich, D., Jick, T. & von Glinow, M. (1994) High-impact learning: Buildings and diffusing learning capability. *Organizational Dynamics*.

Usher, R. & Edwards, R. (1995) Confessing all? A 'postmodern guide' to the guidance and counselling of adult learners. *Studies in the Education of Adults*, 27(1), 9–23.

Watkins, K. & Marsick, V. J. (1993) *Sculpting the learning organization*. San Francisco: Jossey-Bass.

West, G. W. (1994) Learning organizations: A critical review. *Proceedings of the Annual Midwest Research-to-Practice Conference in Adult, Continuing, and Community Education* (pp. 210–217). University of Wisconsin-Milwaukee, Milwaukee, Wisconsin.

Wick, C. (1993) *The learning edge: How smart managers and smart companies stay ahead*. New York: McGraw-Hill.

Zuboff, S. (1988) *In the age of the smart machine: The future of work and power*. New York: Basic Books.

7

What is Skill and How is it Acquired?

John Sloboda

There are two rooms in my house that have recently been repainted, one by a professional decorator, the other by me. The decorator was skilled at his job. I was not. By what marks might one detect the difference? Well, the end product certainly tells something. If you look closely at the walls that I painted you will find unevenness of texture; too much paint here, barely enough to cover there. You will find faint vertical streaks where the paint has run, and you will find small overshoots and undershoots at the edges. The walls painted by the professional are even in texture, and the edges are beautifully straight.

Notwithstanding these differences, I actually managed to cover my tracks quite well. Unless you gave my walls a very close examination you would not find any obvious faults. The most dramatic diferences between myself and the professional would have been apparent had you actually stood and watched us at work.

To begin with, the professional finished the job in about half the time it took me. Not only were his individual strokes faster, but he stopped less often, I was stopping very regularly, not through laziness, but because I continually needed to assess what I had done, and decide what needed doing next. Other delays occurred too. For instance, I ran out of paint with only three-quarters of the job done, and had to go to the shop for more.

Second, the professional made his job appear easy. The paint just seemed to flow onto the wall in a relaxed and co-ordinated sequence of movements. My own movement sequence was jerky and effortful. For instance, one brushful would have too much paint on it, the next too little; once I would start with an upstroke, next with a down; I would constantly be attending to minor 'bugs', such as spillages and drips.

Finally, the professional's sequencing was impeccable. He arranged things so that he was not constantly having to move apparatus around. He always ended up in the right place at the right time (for example, returning to put on the second coat just at the time when the first coat was dry enough), and was completely systematic in the way each wall was tackled. I worked haphazardly, treating each wall in a different way, leaving odd patches unpainted when, for example, a ladder was not conveniently placed. I was constantly having to stop painting in order to get something I needed or to move obstacles out of the way.

The Characteristics of Skill

For a long time, psychologists have wanted to specify exactly what the characteristics of skilled activities are. My painting example informally includes many of the major characteristics, but I would like to deal with them in a more systematic way under five principal headings: fluency, rapidity, automaticity, simultaneity, and knowledge. The first-letter mnemonic FRASK may be helpful in keeping these in mind.

Fluency

An activity is fluent if the components of it run together in an integrated and uninterrupted sequence. The term 'fluency' is usually applied to the microstructure of a task (elements occurring over a span of a few seconds) rather than to its long-term structure. Thus we speak of a fluent translator as one who can provide an appropriate translation with a minimum of pauses or hesitations. A fluent typist is one who can maintain a relatively even and continuous output of key presses.

It seems likely that fluency is brought about by two things. One is the overlapping in time of a sequence of movements. That is to say, preparatory movements for action B are begun whilst action A is still being completed. The other is the building of a set of actions into a single 'chunk', which can be controlled and run off as a single unit of behaviour.

The existence of chunking in skilled typists has been elegantly demonstrated by Shaffer (1976). In this study, typists saw a computer console on which was displayed a single line of text. The console was linked to a keyboard in such a way that every time a key was pressed the text moved one space to the left. This meant that the leftmost character (or space) 'fell off' the screen and a new character appeared on the right.

Shaffer was able to vary both the window size (that is, length of line displayed) and also the amount of preview (that is, how far from the right a letter had moved before the subject was required to type it). With no preview, a subject had to type a character as soon as it appeared on the right of the screen. With preview, the subject typed a character as it arrived at a preordained position towards the middle of the screen. Typists were given three different varieties of text to work on:

1 normal English prose;
2 jumbled prose in which English words were printed in random order;
3 jumbled words, where letter order was randomized.

These three conditions are illustrated in Figure 7.1.

Shaffer found that typists required about eight characters of preview to obtain their fastest speeds. Increasing preview beyond eight characters did not result in further improvements in speed and accuracy. Fastest consistent speeds were about 10 characters per second (100 words per minute) in

The vertical line indicates the position of the letter to be typed under 8-character preview

(a) in Ayrshire. I told John about the meeting, |and also

(b) meeting told. About, John also in the Ayrs|hire I and

(c) metegni idto. Atoub, nJoh slao ni eht sirAe|yha I dna

Figure 7.1   *Types of text used in Shaffer's typing study*

conditions (a) and (b), but were only two characters per second in condition (c). It seems that skilled typists can deal with familiar English words much better than with strings of nonsense letters. We can get a better insight into *why* words are typed faster when we look at what happened when Shaffer reduced preview below eight characters. In condition (c), reducing preview to zero had no effect whatsoever on speed, which remained at two characters per second. However, such reduction had a dramatic effect in the other two conditions which dropped right down to two characters per second as well.

It seems that fluent typing depends on the typist being able to see the whole of an average English word (six characters) before beginning to type it. Only then can the full set of finger movements required to type the word be assembled into a single performance unit. Such a unit can be 'rattled off' at speed. When there is no preview, or when the letters do not make up familiar words, such chunking is not possible, and the job must be done letter by letter.

The lack of difference between conditions (a) and (b) is also of interest. It shows that these typists were not forming chunks bigger than individual words. If they had been then we would have expected condition (a) to be even faster than condition (b). It looks as though in general any given pair of adjacent words occurs too infrequently to be chunked in the way that individual words are. It is, however, likely that word sequences such as 'Dear Sir' or 'Yours sincerely' could attain the status of chunks for some secretaries.

There are, of course, two levels of chunking occurring in fluent typing. There is what one might call *input* chunking – the perceptual act of grouping letters into units such as words; and there is also *output* chunking – the assembling of co-ordinated movement sequences. Perhaps the best way of appreciating the nature of output fluency is to experience the loss of it. One effective way of disrupting fluency is to upset the sensory feedback we normally receive from motor behaviour. This interferes with the ability to dovetail separate movements with one another. For instance, suppose you were wearing a set of headphones and speaking into a microphone which fed into the headphones. Under these conditions it is possible to introduce a delay, so that instead of hearing your own voice as you speak you hear it a little while later. Delaying the auditory feedback from one's own voice by about 0.2 second usually causes severe speech disruption. It induces stuttering, repetition of sounds, and excessive pausing between words and syllables. Fluent behaviour is crucially dependent upon normal feedback arriving at the normal time. More commonly, loss of fluency is experienced when we are nervous. We trip over our feet and stumble on our words. Fluency is usually the last feature of skill to be acquired and its loss the first sign of disruption due to disease, intoxication, or fear.

Rapidity

Most skills involve the ability to make an appropriate response quickly. The skilled tennis player must not only get to the right place on the court and choose an appropriate stroke, he or she must do these things in an incredibly short time. It is the ability to make the right response almost immediately that is so characteristic of all skills.

One of the most widely quoted and influential studies which demonstrates the speed of skilled performance is a study of chess players carried out by Chase and Simon (1973). They took subjects at differing levels of expertise from novice up to grandmaster and showed them chessboards on which were placed some pieces copied from the middle of an actual game between experts. Subjects were allowed to view the board for five seconds. It was then removed and they were asked to reconstruct the positions of the pieces on a blank board. A novice was able, on average, to replace about four out of 20 pieces correctly. A master, in contrast, replaced about 18 out of 20 correctly.

Since the subjects viewed the board for the same period of time, these results show that a master is able to deal with the same amount of information much more rapidly than a novice. A second part of the study shed substantial light on the mechanisms involved. In this, the boards shown to subjects contained pieces placed on them at random, in a way that could not have occurred in any rational game. Faced with such boards, a novice performed exactly the same as in the first experiment, getting about four out of 20 pieces correct. The master, however, showed a dramatic drop in performance, from 18 down to four out of 20. On these random boards the master was no better than the novice.

This shows us that the master's skill does not rest simply on superior perception or memory, it is linked to the detection of familiar and game-relevant patterns in the stimulus. The master immediately 'understands' what is seen in meaningful terms so that, for instance, one group of four pieces becomes a 'castled king', another a 'knight fork' and so on. This view is confirmed by the way in which the master carries out the reconstruction, tending to put down linked groups of pieces together, with longer pauses between groups. The ability of the knowledgeable player to perceive meaningful patterns on the board is analogous to the ability of a knowledgeable football spectator to recognize carefully rehearsed moves amidst the frantic activity on the pitch.

Automaticity

One of the most universal characteristics of skill is the way in which it becomes 'easy' to its practitioners. We no longer experience any effort when carrying out some well-learned skill such as walking. It 'just happens' without us having to think about it. If this were not the case, our ability to act upon the world would be drastically limited. Our whole time would be spent attending to the simplest things.

The sight-reading of piano music is a complex skill. In a study of professional sight-readers, Wolf (1976) interviewed several practitioners and asked them what were the principal problems in sight-reading. One pianist answered: 'for me, personally, there are none'. This is not arrogance, but an honest answer about a highly automated skill. It is the kind of answer that most of us would have to give if asked about the problems we had in walking. Yet that is a skill of comparable complexity to piano sight-reading, and one that takes infants a long time to learn.

One of the ways of testing whether a skill is automatic is to see whether the practitioner can deal appropriately with a situation, even when not concentrating or expecting it. So, for instance, a skilled driver is able to brake rapidly at a potential hazard, even if the mind were on something else in the immediately preceding moments. [. . .]

Another characteristic of automatic skills seems to be that they are, in some sense, mandatory. That is to say, a stimulus triggers its automatic response regardless of whether we wish it to or not. When we look at a familiar printed word we usually cannot help experiencing its meaning. We find it almost impossible to experience it just as a set of letters. Similarly, we find it almost impossible not to recognize a familiar face as a person we know and to see it instead as a set of individual features.

The tendency of automatic skills to be called into play 'despite ourselves' can sometimes lead to embarrassing and amusing occurrences which have been studied in the context of 'absent-mindedness' (for example, Reason and Mycielska, 1982). The mother of a large family tells of the time when she was at a dinner party and found herself cutting into small pieces the dinner of her surprised neighbour while holding a conversation with someone else. If we laugh then we should laugh with rather than at the unfortunate mother since diary studies have shown that most people are able to record large numbers of slips of this kind in their everyday lives. The outcomes need not always be as embarrassing but the principle is the same. Slips of this nature seem to be an inevitable consequence of the automatization of skilled behaviour.

Simultaneity

I still remember with horror my first driving lesson. My instructor was trying to teach me how to change gear. This involved a complicated sequence of movements involving clutch, accelerator, and gear lever simultaneously. If this was not enough, my instructor kept shouting 'keep your eyes on the road, keep steering'. The multiple demands on my attention seemed impossible to fulfil. Now, some 20 years later, it all seems so trivially easy. Changing gear is a fluent and co-ordinated movement sequence which I can do without losing any of my attention on the road. I can do all these things whilst maintaining an intellectually demanding argument with my passenger on some unrelated topic.

Simultaneity is a characteristic of skill in two senses. First, the components of a skilled activity can be executed simultaneously (as in conjoint movements of hands and feet for gear changing). Second, because of the high degree of automaticity, it is often possible to carry out an unrelated activity at the same time as performing a skilled activity. One way that psychologists test how automatic a skill has become is to measure the effect on performance of adding a second, simultaneous task for the subject to perform.

One of the most strikingly counterintuitive demonstrations of simultaneity was provided by Allport *et al.* (1972), in an experiment where they examined performance on two skills: sight-reading of piano music and prose 'shadowing'. Subjects were experienced sight-readers. They were first asked to perform each task alone. For the sight-reading test, an unfamiliar piano piece was placed in front of the subject who was required to perform it on the piano without rehearsal. In the shadowing test the subject heard a prose passage through headphones and was required to speak it out as it was being heard. The two tasks were then combined. A subject was asked to continue as best she could with both tasks together.

After a very small amount of practice, subjects were able to perform the two tasks together. They did not break down in either of them. Even more surprising was the fact that the two tasks did not seriously affect one another. Each task was performed in the dual condition almost as well as each task was performed alone.

There has been a lengthy debate in psychology about whether or not it is possible to attend to two things at once. Some theorists have proposed that attention is like an individual beam which can only be pointed at one thing at a time. Dual task performance must then be explained in terms of rapid switching of attention between the two tasks (Broadbent, 1982). Others have seen it more as a *quantity* of resource which can be devoted entirely to one task or split up between several. Proponents of both views broadly agree that automatic tasks require little or no attention to be allocated to them. Therefore, when at least one of a pair of simultaneous activities is automatic, then there is enough attentional capacity to maintain both tasks. In the above experiment it seems likely that sight-reading had attained a high degree of automaticity.

Knowledge

When I get into a dispute about some topic close to my heart, I don't always win. As I nurse my wounds afterwards I often come up with the perfect response that I *should* have made to my opponent's apparently devastating blow. In the heat of the debate, however, I was just unable to gain access to the appropriate piece of knowledge, the argument I wanted to bring out. In a similar manner, examination candidates often realize what they *should* have written minutes after walking out of the examination room.

I use these examples to make the point that skill is not simply a matter of having knowledge. It involves this knowledge being readily available at the appropriate time, in response to the situation that demands its use. For instance, what is important for driving is that I should immediately slow down when I see green traffic lights turning to amber. It is no use having the conceptual knowledge that amber means 'stop' unless I can apply it in the driving situation. Recently, cognitive psychologists have paid increasing attention to the possible role in skilled behaviour of what are called *associate pattern-action pairs*. Such associations are like rules which an organism can apply to particular situations. They have the form: *'If Condition X Applies then Carry out Action Y'*. They look rather like the stimulus-response bonds which have had a venerable history in behaviourist explanations of animal learning. However, in these so called 'production rules', X need not be a simple external stimulus, and Y need not be an overt behaviour. We can include such things as internal mental states and goals as well. So the rule, 'If you see a police patrol car in your rear-view mirror, then feel panic' is a production rule, though one we would perhaps like to be without.

A set of production rules sufficient for carrying out some coherent task can be incorporated in a *production system*. One of the major reasons why psychologists have begun to think about skills in terms of production systems is the fact that such systems can be very easily simulated on a computer. [. . .]

Production system theory provides a useful way of understanding how knowledge may be organized in the service of skill at several different levels. First is the level of individual actions. Particular environmental patterns can trigger immediate knowledge about the right thing to do in that circumstance. In driving, for instance, a green light turning to amber triggers an immediate application of the brakes. Two significant facts about such knowledge stand out. One is that the knowledge may be completely inaccessible (or 'out of mind') until the circumstances which demand its use occur. Do you know without trying, for instance, which muscle you would use first when standing up from a seated position? The second fact is that our capacity to acquire new pattern-action pairs seems limitless.

The point about accessibility is made nicely by a study on taxi-drivers (Chase, 1983). Experienced Pittsburgh taxi-drivers were called into the laboratory and asked to describe the best routes between pairs of points in the city. This they were able to do. It turned out, however, that their routes were not always the best routes or the routes that the drivers would actually take. This was shown by repeating the study in real life; actually asking drivers to *drive* from A to B. When this happened the drivers would often remember better short cuts than the ones they had produced in the lab. These short cuts seemed to be triggered by the experience of arriving at particular locations. A driver would realize 'of course, if I turn left here I can cut round such and such a bottleneck'. This is, of course, completely adaptive. Taxi-drivers need to find good routes when on the job, not when thinking about it.

A complex cognitive skill such as chess playing is also amenable to production system analysis. We may suppose that the chess master has many thousands of production rules which link each commonly occurring pattern or chunk to a good move associated with the pattern. In this way, masters experience good moves 'just springing off the board' at them. Poor players have to work through the consequences of many bad moves before stumbling on a good move.

The Structure of Skills

We can also use the notion of a production system to elucidate the nature of planning and structuring in skill, and the ability to keep track of where one is at. For this, in addition to production rules, we must postulate a working memory-system in which a goal stack may be held. A simple example of a common skill much quoted in this context is the ability to travel around an industrialized country. If I am in a rural location and need to get to a big city quite quickly then I could set the goal of, for instance, 'getting to London'. This goal can act as the X condition of a production rule which might be, '*If the Goal is to Get to London then Set the Goal of Getting to the Nearest Railway Station*'. So the goal of getting to London is 'pushed down' the stack and the second goal of 'get to the station' sits on top as the current goal. You can imagine a goal stack to be rather like the spring-loaded plate racks found in canteens. Now the operative goal is 'get to station'. This may well call up a further rule which says, '*If the Goal is to Get to the Station then Set the Goal to Call a Taxi*'. So now 'call a taxi' becomes the current goal, with two unachieved goals stacked beneath it. This may call up further goals such as 'look up telephone number'. At some point there will be a goal which calls into play a production rule involving behaviour which achieves the topmost goal. When this happens, this goal can be jettisoned from the stack and the previous goal becomes current. This can then be achieved, and so on through the stack until there are no further goals left. The goal stack gives structure and direction to the total behaviour.

Without the structuring of a goal stack behaviour would tend to be uncoordinated and entirely driven by the current situation. Indeed, when the retention of goals in the stack is inadequate a partial breakdown of behaviour occurs. We can observe this through a particular class of absent-minded error. This occurs to most of us. You walk into a shop, and then stand there foolishly, trying to remember why you came in. The goal of 'buying X' led to the new goal of 'go to the shop', but on your way you started to think of other things and this intervening mental activity led to the loss of the original goal from the stack.

In real life, most of us are not pursuing just one set of goals, such as described above, but many disparate goals. It is sometimes hard to keep them all in mind, and we can never be directly working on more than one or two of them. It follows that the ability to remember what one's multiple goals are, and where one has got to in achieving each of them, is an important skill in its own right. We all know people who always seem to be forgetting to do things, whilst others seem to be able efficiently to keep on top of a wide variety of different but complex commitments. The role of external memory aids seems very important here. These are such things as diaries, knots in handkerchiefs, lists of things to do, and notes to oneself. We can see the mobilization of these aids as an explicit recognition of the fact that external stimuli are the best and most reliable triggers for action. Skill in fulfilling multiple commitments seems to be skill in engineering one's own environment to provide the necessary reminders at the right place and time.

Acquiring Skill

[. . .] We now turn to a related question: what does one have to do to become skilled? The human animal is unique in the number of skills that are acquired through learning. We are also unique in the diversity of our skills. Some of us are skilled mathematicians, others are skilled musicians, yet others are skilled mechanics. How is it that people can be so different in their skill profile?

Many animals appear extremely skilful. Observe, for example, how a cat stalks a bird. It crouches low so as to be concealed by ground cover; takes care to move slowly and quietly towards its prey. Then, when it becomes difficult to remain unobserved, it springs forward with claws outstretched to give the prey minumum time to react. My cat's skill at this operation is evidenced by the number of dead birds and mice that are proudly deposited on my kitchen floor. I could learn quite a lot about hunting techniques from carefully observing my cat.

Where did the cat's skill come from? As far as we know, most animal skills are inherited rather than learned. Kittens reared in isolation still show an appropriate repertoire of stalking and hunting behaviours (Hinde, 1966). They appear to be instinctual. Moreover, all individuals of a given species appear to inherit roughly the same set of skills.

Is it possible that human skills are inherited? In the next section we shall examine the view of skill acquisition that attributes it to 'talent' or 'innate potential'. We will then go on to contrast it with the view that talent is less important than opportunity and practice. We will conclude by looking at a case study of an exceptional skill, which shows that we really need both views to understand properly the acquisition of skill.

Talent and skill acquisition

It is indisputable that gifted parents tend to have gifted children. Sometimes specific talents such as musical talent seem to run in families for several generations. Unfortunately, it has long been realized that this finding, in itself, tells us very little about how the skill was acquired. It could be that the son of a musician has inherited some special propensity for musical achievement. Equally, it could be the case that a musical parent provides more opportunity and encouragement for a child to learn musical skills than does a non-musician. In real life, the influences of heredity and environment are inextricably mixed together, and it is very hard to establish that a particular influence is decisive.

Much of the serious psychological research in this area has centred around the notion of intelligence, and has been the subject of great controversy. One controversy concerns the question of whether there is some unitary capacity or faculty that comprises the basis for intelligent action, or whether intelligence is simply the conjunction of several distinct and independent skills. Supporters of the first view point to the fact that people who are good at one type of thing tend to be good at a whole range of other things. This fact forms the basis of intelligence testing. It is precisely because many skills correlate with one another that we can obtain a useful picture of a person's ability by just sampling a few skills. But the correlation is not perfect, and we find in almost every person areas of skill that are either much better or much worse than one might predict on the basis of intelligence measures. A good example of this is the dyslexic, who reads less well than his other intellectual achievements would predict. Gardner (1983) provides an accessible overview of the issues surrounding this general controversy.

A second controversy concerns the degree to which we can find reliable ways of measuring the separate effects of environment and heredity. This topic is fraught with methodological and theoretical difficulties. It is also a political and ideological minefield, since it is frequently linked to the issue of putative racial differences (Eysenck versus Kamin, 1981). Very few people come to the issue with an open mind. None the less, I will stick my neck out and say that there are probably three ways in which inherited characteristics might have a significant effect on skill acquisition:

1 There are some genetically transmitted conditions that cause largely irreversible mental retardation, presumably as a result of abnormal development of the brain or nervous system (for example, Down's

Syndrome). These conditions may destroy capacities that are essential for some skills. All such conditions, unfortunately, tend to handicap their possessors. There are no known conditions of this sort that confer significant advantage.

2 Inherited physical characteristics are undoubtedly a factor in determining achievement in some skills. It will depend largely on the shape of your vocal cavities as to whether you have a chance of becoming an opera singer. It will depend largely on your size and the shape of your skeleton as to whether you could become a ballerina, and so on. Inherited physical characteristics of the nervous system are also likely to be of importance.

3 There are a whole set of what one might call dispositional or motivational factors that could have an indirect effect on skill acquisition. From very early in life, infants seem to differ from one another in their degree of activity, the amount of sleep they require, their primary mood, and so on. Research on adult personality shows significant individual differences in such factors as ability to concentrate on boring tasks for long periods of time. There is also evidence for stable preferences for certain domains of activity. Some people seem to be biased toward visual activities, others towards verbal. These preferences may be linked to very early infancy, where significant differences in developmental profile may be observed (Kagan *et al.*, 1978). Some children develop early language skill but lag behind in physical development. Others show the reverse trend. All of these factors could have a strong influence on both the type and level of skill acquired. We can imagine the physically precocious extrovert as being more likely to acquire football skill, whilst the verbal introvert might be more likely to develop skill at poetry. This is not so much a question of *capacity*. Rather, it represents the amount of effort that a person is likely to want to devote to particular types of activity. Some activities seem to 'go against the grain', others seem intrinsically rewarding.

Practice and skill acquisition

Paul Tortelier was one of the world's foremost professional cellists. He was born to poor working-class parents who had no particular background of musical accomplishment. Before he was born they decided that their child should achieve great things in the world, and that they were going to have him trained as a cellist. By hard work, saving, and self-sacrifice, they were able to buy instruments, lessons, and other forms of support; and their son achieved their intentions for him.

Such rags to riches stories strike a deep chord in many of us, and prompt the following question. Suppose the young Tortelier had been snatched from his cradle at birth and replaced by another baby, chosen at random from the population at large? Suppose further that his parents were unaware of the switch, and treated the substitute in exactly the same way. Would they have turned *anyone* into that world-class cellist?

To the extent that we are inclined to answer 'yes' to that question we are basing our answer on the assumption that skills are not acquired by virtue of what you *are* but by what you *do*. Anyone can acquire a skill if only he or she does the right things.

It is impossible in practice to run the hypothesized substitution experiment. What we can do, however, is look at people in the process of acquiring skills and ask whether there is anything that seems to be linked with successful acquisition for a wide variety of skills and for a wide range of people. It will not come as a great surprise to be told that the single most important factor that psychologists know about is practice. Just as practice is the ingredient most emphasized by sports coaches and piano teachers.

A great deal of research has looked at the effects of practice on simple perceptual-motor skills. A frequently used task is one in which the reaction time is measured for pressing a button in response to a light turning on. Sometimes there is only a single light and a single button, while in other experiments there may be several of each, with subjects having to respond perhaps to one light at a time or to various patterns of lights coming on together. A study of Siebel (1963) is representative. Subjects viewed ten lights arranged in a horizontal row. Below the lights were ten buttons, one for each light. The subjects rested their fingers on the keys and watched the lights. After a signal, a random subset of the lights would go on. Subjects were required to depress the keys corresponding to the illuminated lights (and no others). Individual subjects repeated this task for upwards of 40,000 trials.

Siebel measured mean reaction-time to depress the correct combination of keys. Rapidity of response is a crucial characteristic of skill, which is why many researchers have used reaction time as a primary measure of skill level. The faster you can respond, the more skilled you are (given, of course, that your response remains accurate). Siebel found that reaction time dropped from an initial level of about two seconds down to 0.4 seconds with this large amount of practice. One can hardly imagine that this task had any interest for the subjects, yet sheer, dogged repetition caused continued improvement right through the 40,000 trials.

More detailed information can be gained by plotting reaction time (RT) against trial number, and Figure 7.2 shows the typical result of doing this. It illustrates what is sometimes called the 'law of diminishing returns'. Early practice results in quite large gains in speed, but equivalent amounts of practice later on yield only small gains. Sometimes this flattening-out of the acquisition curve occurs because one is coming up against physiological limits – for example, the fixed speed at which your nerves will conduct impulses. More often, though, the flattening out begins to occur long before any such limits are being approached.

Why do we get diminishing returns with practice? One possibility could be that people concentrate less and less as they repeat a task, becoming

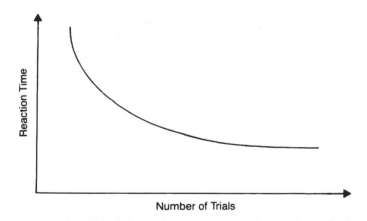

Figure 7.2 *A typical graph of reaction time plotted against number of trials*

unable to benefit from late trials to the extent of early ones. This might be a plausible explanation for decline in a single session. It would hardly account for a smooth decline over 40,000 trials spread over many days. If learning were entirely dependent on concentration, one should see many fluctuations up and down as concentration waxed and waned. [. . .]

Explaining the 'law of diminishing returns'

A line of explanation for diminishing returns has been suggested by Newell and Rosenbloom (1981) and is built directly on the notions of chunking and pattern-action production rules that we have already explored. They propose that, as a subject carries out some task such as Siebel's, continuous attempts are made to chunk the lights into patterns. Each such chunk will be associated with a particular finger pattern of response. To begin with, the display will be processed as ten separate lights, and a response must be made to each individually. As time passes, the subject will come to respond, say, to *pairs* of lights as single units, then to triplets, and so on, until some theoretical ceiling is reached when the complete ten-light array is seen as a single pattern. [. . .] If we assume, for simplicity's sake, that it takes a constant time to perceive and respond to a single chunk, then we can see that the larger the chunks are, the less time it will take to respond to the whole display.

It is quite easy to see intuitively that the more chunks a person learns the quicker will be the response to any particular set of lights, because there is more possibility of detecting a familiar pattern in it. Thus, practice will increase task speed. What is less easy to see is why this notion also predicts the law of diminishing returns, but in fact it does do so. This is because a given small chunk will occur in the array more frequently than a large one, and so can be learned and put to use more quickly.

To see why this should be important, consider first the effects of chunking the display into five pairs of two adjacent lights. Each pair can take on one of four configurations (off-off, off-on, on-off, and on-on). There are five pairs, so in all there are five times four configurations, which is 20. All of these need to be learned, together with their 20 associated response patterns. If on any trial of the experiment a random half of the lights come on, then any given configuration of a pair is likely to appear once in every four trials on average. So since each of the 20 chunks appears frequently, there is a lot of opportunity to notice and learn to respond to each one. Given our assumption that it takes a constant time to respond to any chunk, then a person who has learned these 20 pair-patterns will be able to halve the response time, always seeing the display as five chunks rather than as ten individual lights. This is the reason that the early stages of practice can result in large performance gains.

Now consider what would be involved in learning to respond to the display as two chunks each containing five items. There are 32 different configurations of on and off that a set of five lights can take up. There are two chunks in the display of ten, so there are 64 configurations in all that need to be learned (32 times two). If on any trial a random half of the lights come on then each configuration of a chunk will only appear once in every 32 trials. There are more patterns to learn, and much less frequent opportunities to observe any given pattern. Thus it will take a subject a great deal longer to move from processing the display as five chunks to processing it as two chunks than it will have done to move from ten to five. The first move reduces reaction time by a half, say from two seconds to one second. The second move reduces reaction time by three-fifths, from one second to 0.4 of a second. Not only will it have taken longer to bring about the second move, but this will also have yielded a smaller absolute increase in speed. This explains the phenomenon of diminishing returns, and its approximation to a logarithmic function.

Studies such as Siebel's, and the theorizing built round them, offer opportunities for mathematically precise thinking about skill. They show in a particularly elegant way why it takes so long to become really good at something. And yet such studies are lacking in several respects. First, the skills studied are very simple. They involve a single response to a stimulus rather than a co-ordinated sequence. Second, the stimuli themselves lack natural pattern and structure. It is very rarely in the real world that the material we deal with is so unpredictable. There are similarities between new situations and old ones that we already know about. We can make informed guesses and plans. Some patterns crop up much more often than one would expect by chance, and so on. Third, we normally have the opportunity to decide *how* we will practise a skill. In Siebel's task, subjects had to respond to all ten lights on every trial. It might be that a better strategy would be to learn the responses for each hand separately.

This leads to the fourth criticism. In such experiments as Siebel's, the subjects usually work entirely on their own, the skill is wholly without a social context. This is not true of real-life skills. These are usually learnt with the aid of some form of coaching. The coaching may be from an older practitioner, it may come from a book, it may amount to no more than trying to copy what you once saw someone else do. Nevertheless, there is normally available some source of comment and suggestion. For all these reasons, the rate of improvement on a task such as Siebel's probably represents a pessimistic estimate of our ability to acquire real-life skills.

Enhancing the Effects of Practice

In this section, we will look briefly at some things which have been shown to help many types of practice become more effective. These are features of practice around which any coaching programme must be constructed. The first and most important of them is *feedback*.

Feedback

Feedback is, quite simply, knowledge of what your actions have achieved. It can come in two forms, intrinsic and extrinsic. Intrinsic feedback is that provided as a direct consequence of bodily movement and sensation. If you move your arm, you can both feel the result through *kinaesthesis*, and you can see where the arm is through vision. Extrinsic feedback is that provided by some external source or agent, frequently a coach or teacher. Being told whether an answer you supply is right or wrong is a type of extrinsic feedback. Feedback of one sort or another is essential to all skill acquisition. One cannot improve unless one has ways of judging how good present performance is, and in what direction change must occur.

There are several ways in which one may harness feedback to achieve more successful skill acquisition. The first is actually to pay attention to existing feedback. This can be something as simple as checking over what one has written when writing a letter or an essay. Many students and others omit to do this, and suffer as a result. The second is to make sure that the feedback is immediate. Comments on an essay returned after several weeks are of little use because the author has probably forgotten the precise steps taken in preparing the essay. It is no longer possible to link feedback to specific aspects of behaviour. In an ideal world the tutor would supervise every step of the essay-writing process, offering suitable comments at each stage. This means that the two persons would have to be in close and prolonged contact, with the likelihood of an intense relationship developing. And intense relationships are familiar in contexts where there is a master and an apprentice, a trainer and an athlete, or a drama coach and a student. An example from literature is the relationship between Svengali and the young singer, Trilby, in Du Maurier's novel of that name.

More exotic than ordinary feedback are ways of helping people to become aware of internal sensations of which they are are not normally

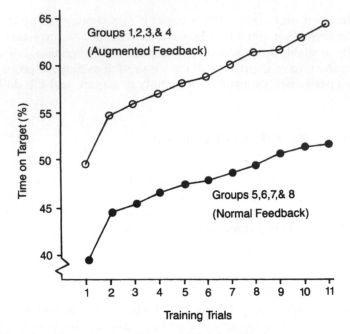

Figure 7.3   *The effects of giving different kinds of feedback*

conscious. By making use of a visual display which monitors some aspect of body state (such as heartbeat or galvanic skin response) one can learn to identify the bodily sensations which accompany changes in these states, and some people are able to control these states even when the augmented feedback (often known as *biofeedback*) is removed,

Sometimes feedback seems to have primarily a motivating effect. It provides information which is not strictly essential but which seems to increase involvement in the task. For instance, Smode (1958) asked subjects to practise what is known as a 'tracking task', in which a randomly moving needle could be kept on a central mark by rotating a dial in compensatory movement. After each trial all subjects were given 'normal' feedback in the form of the length of time that they had managed to keep the needle centred during that trial. In addition, one group of subjects were given 'augmented' feedback in the form of a counter on which their total score over trials was accumulated. This augmented feedback had a dramatic effect on performance, as Figure 7.3 shows. The advantage also persisted after the augmented feedback had been removed. In a second day of learning where all subjects just received normal feedback, those subjects who had received augmented feedback on day 1 continued to do better.

Spacing

If you are able to devote six hours to practising a given skill should you do six solid hours of work, or six separate hours on different days? In general, it seems that it is better to *space* practice over several sessions than to *mass* it all together (Welford, 1968). There are several reasons why this might be so. One is that fatigue and lowering of attention tend to occur as a repetitive task is continued. As a result bad habits may be formed, with further practice strengthening this undesirable behaviour. Frequent rests can allow the fatigue and the bad habits to dissipate. On the other hand, when motivation is high, it is quite possible to become totally immersed in a task for many hours without any noticeable loss of attention, so the prescription to space one's practice is by no means a universally beneficial one.

Attitude

A third issue relates to the question of what mental attitude or activity should accompany practice. Should you repeat a task fairly mechanically with an essentially passive mind, intending, as it were, to stamp the skill in by sheer repetition; or should you be actively structuring the task, looking for patterns and similarities, guessing what might come next? This is a somewhat vexed question, and psychologists have not been able to supply any definite answers. It is very clear that sheer dogged repetition does have beneficial effects (see the Siebel study described earlier). There is also a lot of talk in such areas as the psychology of sport about the importance of stopping being too cerebral and letting one's body 'take over'. There is certainly plenty of evidence that we do things better if we can get them to the level of automatic control, sitting back and letting the system 'get on with it'; and it is possible that where physical movements are concerned part of such a process may be the retrieving of early, partly instinctive movement patterns which have become overlaid by maladaptive attempts to control them (Tinbergen, 1974).

Even at a more complex cognitive level, a lot of skill learning seems to be largely incidental and unintended. It sometimes seems that if you are interested enough in an activity, your involvement will, in itself, result in the acquisition of some degree of skill. It is when you attempt to acquire a skill that relates to an activity which does not intrinsically interest you that a substitute for interest must be manufactured. Educational researchers have clarified the nature of effective study strategies and skills, and the teaching strategies needed to support them. It can be helpful to see these strategies as ways of getting the unmotivated learner to do what, with motivation, would come naturally. If you think that this seems like a poor substitute for letting people study what actually interests them, and some kind of indictment of our educational system, then you would not be alone (Illich, 1973). But this view is incomplete on its own. For even when we are interested to master a particular skill, we can still benefit from advice and feedback. In the acquisition of skills, it is the function of a coach to provide these.

An Exceptional Talent – a Case Study

I would like to conclude this chapter by describing a quite extraordinary skill, which I have recently been involved in studying (Sloboda *et al.*, 1985). The subject of this study, who will be referred to as NP, is an autistic man in his early twenties. Like many autistic people, he is severely mentally retarded. He has almost no spontaneous language, shows social withdrawal and other bizarre behaviour patterns, and he requires the total care of a specialist residential institution. What makes him different from the majority of autistic people is the fact that in one small area of his life he is anything but retarded. He has an amazing capacity to memorize piano music.

In tests that we carried out, NP was able to memorize a classical piano piece (Grieg Opus 47, no. 3) lasting over two minutes, almost note-perfectly in 12 minutes. He did this simply by listening to sections of a tape-recording of a piece and copying what he heard on the piano. A day later, with no intervening opportunity for rehearsal, he was still able to reproduce the piece almost perfectly. At no stage did he observe the printed music, see anyone else demonstrating the fingering, or receive any other extrinsic feedback. He was not told what key the piece was in, but was instantly able to choose the right notes and play them with the right combinations of fingers, even though he had probably never heard the piece before, and certainly had never attempted to learn it.

This level of memory skill is very rare, even among musicians of above-average intelligence. It is probably equalled only by the legendary accomplishments of a handful of prodigies, such as Mozart or Erwin Nyerghihazi (Revesz, 1925). NP provides an ideal test case for some of the questions about skill acquisition that we have raised in this chapter.

First, we can ask whether the skill fits the notions of inherited talent that we discussed at the beginning of the chapter. There is certainly little evidence of musical accomplishment in NP's immediate family background, which is one of quite severe social deprivation. He did, however, show early precocity in music, without a great deal in the way of family encouragement. Recordings which survive from the age of six show a level of skill much above that of a normal six-year-old. It is reported that although he had no piano at home, he made a coherent performance on his very first public exposure to the instrument. Given what is known about his circumstances, the possibility of secret coaching can almost certainly be ruled out. Even today, there is a real sense in which NP cannot actually be taught. His 'lessons' consist of his teacher playing him new pieces to memorize. No one has taught him how to memorize as he does. No one *knows* how he does it, and he is not able to explain himself. Opportunities have been put in his way, but NP must be one of the purest examples of a self-taught expert that exists.

On the face of it, NP looks like providing very strong evidence for the existence of an inherited gift for music. His lack of achievement in any other area of skill makes it look like a quite *specific* gift for music. But appearances can be deceptive, and we would do well to examine this 'gift' a little more closely. The first thing to notice is that the measure of the gift is equalled by the measure of what one can only call NP's obsession with music. Whenever he has a free choice of activity, he almost always chooses either to listen to music (on radio, record, etc.) or to play it. It also seems that when not doing either of these things, he is turning music over in his mind. It would not be unreasonable to suppose that his mind is engaged with music, in an intensely concentrated way, for five or six hours each day. Like Mozart, music is his life and his love. It is hard to know where this obsessive fascination with music came from. It could be a genuinely inherited disposition, or it could come from some crucial early experience. One general aspect of the autistic personality seems to be obsessiveness, and there are in existence people who have similar exceptional skills in other areas, such as mental calculation. Maybe the autistic mind is primed to latch onto an obsession, but the particular obsession may be determined entirely by circumstance.

A second argument against treating NP's skill as a specifically *musical* gift comes from a closer analysis of the way he memorizes music. As well as playing him some classical pieces such as the Grieg, we tried him on a piece which broke many of the rules of 'normal' music. This was an atonal piece by Bartok. Although this Bartok piece (Mikrokosmos, Whole Tone Scales from Book 5) had many fewer notes than the piece composed by Grieg, NP found it almost impossible to memorize. We interpret this as showing that NP's memory skill is based on the ability to chunk conventional musical input into higher-order patterns. When, as in the Bartok, these patterns are absent, performance is severely disrupted. This is just like the chess studies reported earlier, where the master player's memory for the positions of pieces was superior only when the board was taken from an actual game, not randomly constructed. This is confirmed by an analysis of the few errors NP made on the Grieg piece. They were nearly all structurally plausible errors, in which one musically appropriate chunk was replaced by something similar and equally appropriate (much as one might misremember a sentence by substituting synonymous expressions).

All the evidence we have is that extensive practice is the only and inevitable route to the formation of chunks which can make such impressive skills possible. But, as Siebel's random light data show, this chunking process operates on any material whatsoever, and seems not to be essentially different for music or any other specialized material. NP provides strong corroboration for the general equation that *Motivation + Practice = Skill*. The roots of specific motivations are almost entirely mysterious, but could easily have an inherited component. Practice can be accomplished, however, without any particularly strong motivation, and it seems that our cognitive system will respond by chunking both the inputs and outputs of any task that we practise enough. None the less, amounts of practice of the sort required to attain expertise are almost always unsustainable without strong motivation. Given the most supportive and enhanced environment in the world, most of us would fail to acquire many skills, not because we are, in some ultimate sense, incapable of doing so, but rather because, to us, they just don't seem to matter that much.

Note

This is an edited version of two chapters in A. Gellatly (ed.), *The Skilful Mind*, Milton Keynes, Open University Press, 1986.

References

Allport, D. A., Antonis, B. and Reynolds, P. (1972) 'On the division of attention: a disproof of the single channel hypothesis', *Quarterly Journal of Experimental Psychology*, 24, 225–35.

Broadbent, D. E. (1982) 'Task combination and selective intake of information', *Acta Psychologica*, 50, 253–90.

Chase, W. G. (1983) 'Spatial representations of taxi-drivers', in D. R. Rogers and J. A. Sloboda (eds), *Acquisition of Symbolic Skills*, New York: Plenum.

—— and Simon, H. A. (1973) 'The mind's eye in chess', in W. G. Chase (ed.), *Visual Information Processing*, New York: Academic Press.

Eysenck, H. J. versus Kamin, L. (1981) *Intelligence Controversy*, New York: John Wiley.

Gardner, H. (1983) *Frames of Mind*, London: Heinemann.

Hinde, R. A. (1966) *Animal Behaviour*, New York: McGraw-Hill.

Illich, I. D. (1973) *Deschooling Society*, London: Penguin.

Kagan, J., Lapidus, D. R. and Moore, N. (1978) 'Infant antecedents of cognitive functioning: a longitudinal study', *Child Development*, 49, 1005–23.

Newell, A. and Rosenbloom, P. S. (1981) 'Mechanisms of skill acquisition and the law of practice', in J. R. Anderson (ed.), *Cognitive Skills and their Acquisition*, Hillsdale, N.J.: Erlbaum.

Reason, J. and Mycielska, K. (1982) *Absent Minded? The Psychology of Mental Lapses and Everyday Errors*, New York: Prentice-Hall.

Revesz, G. (1925) *The Psychology of a Musical Prodigy*, London: Kegan Paul, Trench & Trubner.

Shaffer, L. H. (1976) 'Invention and performance', *Psychological Review*, 83, 375–93.

Siebel, R. (1963) 'Discrimination reaction time for a 1023 alternative task', *Journal of Experimental Psychology*, 66, 1005–23.

Sloboda, J. A., Hermelin, B. and O'Connor, N. (1985) 'An exceptional musical memory', *Music Perception*, 3, 155–69. University of California Press Berkeley, California.

Smode, A. (1958) 'Learning and performance in a tracking task under two levels of achievement information feedback', *Journal of Experimental Psychology*, 56, 297–304.

Tinbergen, N. (1974) 'Ethology and stress disease', *Science*, 185, 20–7.

Welford, A. T. (1968) *Fundamentals of Skill*, London: Methuen.

Wolf, T. (1976) 'A cognitive model of musical sight-reading', *Journal of Psycholinguistic Research*, 5, 143–71.

8

Theories of Professional Expertise

Michael Eraut

This chapter reviews [some] theories of expertise to be found in the literature and discusses their scope and validity. In particular, it notes how different theories of expertise emphasize different professional processes and asks whether some theories presented as conflicting may not better be treated as complementary. It begins with the Dreyfus model of progression from novice to expert [. . .], then moves on to consider theories of clinical decision-making by physicians. These are more strongly linked to research evidence, yet encompass both intuitive models based on memory and analytic models based on probabilities and reasoning. The full range, including mixed models, is mapped out by Hammond's Cognitive Continuum Theory which links the mode of cognition induced to the characteristics of the process of task. [. . .]

The Dreyfus Model of Skill Acquisition

The Dreyfus brothers' model of skill acquisition has attracted considerable interest in professional education. Hubert is a philosopher and Stuart an industrial engineer working in computing and operational research. The title of their book *Mind Over Machine, the Power of Human Intuition and Expertise in the Era of the Computer* (1986) reveals that their theory first developed as an attack on the claims made by experts in artificial intelligence, before becoming a more broadly based theory of expertise. Moreover, they see their model as defending the contemporary experiential approach to philosophy against the rationalist tradition of analytic reasoning and the formulation of rules, and as supporting 'Merleau-Ponty's claim that, perception and understanding are based in our capacity for picking up not rules, but flexible styles of behaviour' (p. 5). Their use of the term 'picking up' stands in marked contrast to the behaviourists' emphasis on direct instruction, behavioural modelling and coaching [. . .]. So also does their endorsement of the existentialist view that:

> Human understanding was a skill akin to knowing how to find one's way about in the world, rather than knowing a lot of facts and rules for relating them. Our basic understanding was thus a *knowing how* rather than a *knowing that*.
>
> (Dreyfus and Dreyfus, 1986: 4)

Although the Dreyfuses describe their model as depicting five stages of skill acquisition (see Table 8.1), the emphasis is on perception and decision-making rather than routinized action. Thus they define skill as an integrative overarching approach to professional action, which incorporates both routines and the decisions to use them, while still maintaining that the term 'skilled behaviour' connotes semi-automatic rather than deliberative processes. They cite two groups of examples: those taken from the application of rational methods such as decision analysis, mathematical modelling and 'intelligent' computer systems which are used to demonstrate the inadequacy of those methods; and those judged as authentic representations of expertise which are taken from the areas of chess, car-driving, plane-flying, senior management and daily life. However, the most comprehensive account of the applications of the Dreyfus model to professional work is provided by Benner (1984) who used it to analyse evidence collected from critical incident interviews with a sample of ninety-three nurses. Significantly she did not choose examples only to explain and justify the model, but also to describe the nature of nursing expertise as a whole. Thus she applied the model to each of thirty-one competencies, classified into the following seven domains:

- the helping role;
- the teaching-coaching function;
- the diagnostic and patient-monitoring function;
- effective management of rapidly changing situations;
- administering and monitoring therapeutic interventions and regimens;
- monitoring and ensuring the quality of health care practices; and
- organizations and work-role competencies.

The main features of the Dreyfus model are depicted in Table 8.1. As befits its philosophical underpinning, the emphasis is almost entirely on learning from experience with only occasional references to theoretical learning or the development of fluency on standard tasks. The pathway to competence is characterized mainly by the ability to recognize features of practical situations and to discriminate between them, to carry out routine procedures under pressure and to plan ahead. Competence is the climax of rule-guided learning and discovering how to cope in crowded, pressurised contexts. Whereas proficiency marks the onset of quite a different approach to the job: normal behaviour is not just routinized but semi-automatic; situations are apprehended more deeply and the abnormal is quickly spotted and given attention. Thus progress beyond competence depends on a more holistic approach to situational understanding.

Table 8.1   *Summary of Dreyfus model of skill acquisition*

Level 1   Novice
  • Rigid adherence to taught rules or plans
  • Little situational perception
  • No discretionary judgment

Level 2   Advanced Beginner
  • Guidelines for action based on attributes or aspects (aspects are global characteristics of situations recognizable only after some prior experience)
  • Situational perception still limited
  • All attributes and aspects are treated separately and given equal importance.

Level 3   Competent
  • Coping with crowdedness
  • Now sees actions at least partially in terms of longer-term goals
  • Conscious deliberate planning
  • Standardized and routinized procedures

Level 4   Proficient
  • Sees situations holistically rather than in terms of aspects
  • Sees what is most important in a situation
  • Perceives deviations from the normal pattern
  • Decision-making less laboured
  • Uses maxims for guidance, whose meaning varies according to the situation

Level 5   Expert
  • No longer relies on rules, guidelines or maxims
  • Intuitive grasp of situations based on deep tacit understanding
  • Analytic approaches used only in novel situation or when problems occur
  • Vision of what is possible

Usually the proficient performer will be deeply involved in his task and will be experiencing it from some specific perspective because of recent events. Because of the performer's perspective, certain features of the situation will stand out as salient and others will recede into the background and be ignored. As events modify the salient features, plans, expectations, and even the relative salience of features will gradually change. No detached choice or deliberation occurs. It just happens, apparently because the proficient performer has experienced similar situations in the past and memories of them trigger plans similar to those that worked in the past and anticipations of events similar to those that occurred.

(Dreyfus and Dreyfus, 1986: 28)

Progression from proficiency to expertise finally happens when the decision-making as well as the situational understanding becomes intuitive rather than analytic; and thus requires significantly more experience. The Dreyfuses describe the distinction as follows:

The proficient performer, while intuitively organising and understanding his task, will still find himself thinking analytically about what to do. Elements that present themselves as important, thanks to the performer's experience, will be assessed and combined by rule to produce decisions about how best to manipulate the environment. The spell of involvement in the world of the skill will thus be temporarily broken.

(Ibid: 29)

> An expert generally knows what to do based on mature and practiced under-
> standing . . . An expert's skill has become so much a part of him that he need be
> no more aware of it than he is of his own body . . . the expert business manager,
> surgeon, nurse, lawyer, or teacher is totally engaged in skillful performance.
> *When things are proceeding normally, experts don't solve problems and don't*
> *make decisions; they do what normally works*
>
> (Ibid: 30–1)

Thus most expert performance is ongoing and non-reflective. The Dreyfuses do acknowledge that experts will deliberate before acting on some
occasions, either because the outcomes are particularly critical or because
they feel uneasy with their first choice of action. But this deliberation is
described as being not so much problem-solving as critical reflection on
their own intuition.

Before proceeding to critique this model, we should note that the
Dreyfus definition of competence is based on how people approach their
work, not on whether they should be judged as qualified to do it. Indeed
Benner suggests that competence is typically acquired by a nurse who has
been on the job in a same or similar situation for two or three years, so that
regular procedures have become standardized and routinized.

> The competent nurse lacks the speed and flexibility of the proficient nurse but
> does have a feeling of mastery and the ability to cope with and manage the many
> contingencies of clinical nursing. The conscious, deliberate planning that is char-
> acteristic of this skill level helps achieve efficiency and organisation.
>
> (Benner, 1984: 27)

One could describe the situation as one where the nurse has become proficient at the level of the individual task but is not yet proficient in the
integrated performance of the whole role. That integration, Benner estimates, is likely to take another three to five years in the same kind of
situation. We shall return to the question of situational specificity in a later
section.

The strength of the Dreyfus model lies in the case it makes for tacit
knowledge and intuition as critical features of professional expertise in
'unstructured problem areas'. The Dreyfuses also provide a devastating
critique of what they call 'calculative rationality', the world of mathematical modelling, decision analysis and computerized simulation. However,
they tend to regard their own model as the only alternative, devoting much
of their argumentation to the attack on calculative rationality with very
little attention to other options. This is clearly demonstrated by their ambiguous treatment of deliberative processes:

> This Hamlet model of decision-making – the detached, deliberative, and some-
> times agonising selection among alternatives – is the only one recognised in much
> of the academic literature on the psychology of choice. While that type of care-
> fully thought-out behaviour certainly sometimes occurs, frequently for learners
> of new skills and occasionally for even the most skillful, an unbiased examination
> of our everyday behaviour shows it to be the exception rather than the rule.
>
> (Dreyfus and Dreyfus, 1986: 28)

Not only does this ignore the work of the *gestalt* psychologists and other empirical studies of professional judgment but it makes questionable assumptions about everyday behaviour. Deliberation may not be a daily occurrence but it is certainly not rare, nor is it based on mathematical models. Moreover, many professionals are continually complaining about the lack of thinking time.

This ambivalence is continued in a later section about deliberation in management:

> Experienced intuitive managers do not attempt to understand familiar problems and opportunities in purely analytic terms using calculative rationality, but realise that detached deliberation *about the validity of intuitions* will improve decision-making. Common as it is, little has been written about that conscious deliberative buttressing of nonconscious intuitive understanding, probably because detached deliberation is often incorrectly seen as an *alternative* to intuition.
>
> (Ibid: 163–4)

Here, their obsession with attacking mathematical models is revealed in the use of the term 'calculative rationality' and the weakness of their arguement disguised by including the word 'purely'. Analysis is being associated with quantitative methods and the logic of computer programming while the analytic skills of a historian, which might be much more relevant, are conveniently disregarded. Their statement about using deliberative methods to check the validity of intuitions is important, but represents just one way in which to combine intuition with deliberation. Another is when prior experience, apprehended intuitively, suggest which lines of deliberative inquiry are most worth pursuing. Yet a third is when after a period of analysis and discussion, the problem is mulled over until one particular option seems to provide the best fit: here it is intuition which follows deliberation and analysis, rather than the other way round. There are also many situations in which several people need to be consulted and their differing intuitions fed into group deliberations.

My other concern with the model is its neglect of the metaprocesses involved in controlling one's own behaviour, especially the self-evaluation dimension of professional work. The only image we are given of the process of learning from experience is that of the gradual accumulation of memories of cases. The problem of how this huge volume of information is selected, organized and retrieved is not addressed. Important aspects of a case may not have been retained, theories are likely to have been developed of dubious validity which then become self-confirming. In short the process of learning from experience has been idealized and psychological research in the fallibility of human judgment ignored.

In conclusion, therefore, we can note that the Dreyfus model provides an analysis of skilled behaviour under conditions of rapid interpretation and decision-making, in which the logically distinct processes of acquiring information, following routines and making decisions are fully integrated. It depicts not so much the simple skill of riding a bicycle but the more complex process of riding a bicycle through heavy traffic. It accounts for the greater complexity of professional work and the long time needed to develop proficiency and expertise. Its description of the role of tacit knowledge is consistent with professionals' self-accounts and with other research we review later in the chapter. But it leaves two important questions unanswered: How serious is its neglect of the problem of expert fallibility? – and – What proportion of professional work does it cover? My own view is that it constantly underestimates the former and overestimates the latter.

Theories of Clinical Decision-Making

Medicine is probably the most thoroughly researched of the professions, with clinical expertise being most strongly linked to the process of diagnosing an illness and deciding how to treat and manage it. Whether this process is more appropriately described as skilful behaviour or deliberative action is a matter of some contention. The Dreyfuses regard it as skilful behaviour because their model emphasizes intuition rather than reasoning as the major characteristic of expertise. But they offer no explanation of how learning from experience, the central feature of their model, occurs in practice. Cognitive scientists working in the field of medical education have attempted to address this important question empirically as well as conceptually; and have reached conclusions that are not so far removed from the Dreyfus model, a somewhat ironic outcome since it was the criticism of cognitive science which originally stimulated the Dreyfuses to develop their model.

The traditional assumption has been that diagnosis is based on two distinctive kinds of knowledge: propositional knowledge about diseases and their symptoms and a generalizable skill of clinical reasoning. In this context it should not perhaps be forgotten that the first attempt to legislate the requirements for qualified physicians, the decree of Frederick II in c.1241, specified a first degree in logic before embarking on the study of medicine. However, research into the differences between novice and expert physicians has revealed little significant differences between them on tests of deductive reasoning: there is even a slight decline when people become recognized experts. The conclusion to be drawn is not that doctors do not reason, but that they are already sufficiently competent at it at the time of qualification. Tests of propositional knowledge then showed that propositional knowledge about diseases, symptoms and treatments reaches a plateau at the time of acquiring a specialist qualification (knowledge, that is, which comes within the domain covered by the qualification). Recently qualified specialists have as good an information base as most experts. This led to the hypothesis that it was not propositional knowledge in itself which characterized expertise, but having it better organized and more readily available for use. Certainly there was plenty of evidence that experts made decisions more rapidly. But just how do experts organize their accumulated clinical knowledge, and in what form does it become available for use?

The traditional textbook approach to the organization of clinical know-ledge involves developing classification systems rather like those used by botanists and zoologists. But this raises questions about which principles of classification are appropriate. Most diseases have multiple symptoms and many symptoms can come from several diseases. The patient may have more than one disease at the same time. More fundamental distinctions based on pathophysiological causes of disease depend on these causes having already been established beyond reasonable doubt. The greatest problem, however, is that while any cause-based classification system that is well indexed can retrieve information relevant to the confirmation of a diagnosis or the treatment of a disease, it cannot logically assist with recog-nizing that disease in the first phase.

During the mid-1970s cognitive scientists began to put forward alterna-tive ideas for the representation of knowledge in memory, using what Boreham (1988) calls a 'template model'. Instead of diseases being stored in memory like a filing system, indexed according to their critical attributes, it was suggested that they are stored in the form of schemata or stereotypes against which data patterns for new patients could be compared until a suitable match was found. Although this accounts in a more satisfactory way for evidence that expertise is built up from many years of relevant experience, it does not in itself explain how the template represents know-ledge of a disease, nor how matching data against a large store of disease templates can be achieved so quickly. A librarian, for example, would still opt for a category system, in spite of its many disadvantages.

Minsky's 'frame-system' theory (1977) was an early and extremely influ-ential revision of this template model. Minsky characterized a 'frame' as 'a data-structure for representing a stereotyped situation', to which several kinds of information could be attached, both a pattern which could be recognized and matched to new data sets and a connection box with links to other frames or appropriate behavioural responses:

> A *frame* is a data-structure for representing a stereotyped situation like being in a certain kind of living room or going to a child's birthday party. Attached to each frame are several kinds of information. Some of this information is about how to use the frame. Some is about what one can expect to happen next. Some is about what to do if these expectations are not confirmed.

> We can think of a frame as a network of nodes and relations. The 'top levels' of a frame are fixed, and represent things that are always true about the supposed situation. The lower levels have many *terminals* – 'slots' that must be filled by specific instances or data. Each terminal can specify conditions its assignments must meet. (The assignments themselves are usually smaller 'subframes'.) Simple conditions are specified by *markers* that might require a terminal assignment to be a person, an object of sufficient value, or a pointer to a subframe of a certain type. More complex conditions can specify relations among the things assigned to several terminals.

> (Minsky, 1977: 355)

Boreham (1988) describes how Swanson (1978) applied Minsky's theory to cardiologists, using the term 'disease frame' to represent the diagnostic expectations of an expert in a form which could be built into a computer programme to provide other less experienced cardiologists with assistance in diagnosis. This theory of expertise depends on two assumptions: that a disease frame can provide a sufficient representation of relevant information to be useful and reliable in diagnostic process; and that through professional practice the diagnostician is able to build up a larger and more differentiated store of frames.

> over the years, the expert sees cases not quite fitting the expectations of existing frames, and creates new ones which encode the differences, refining his initial knowledge in the light of experience.
>
> (Swanson, cited in Boreham, 1988: 99)

This quotation raises a question, however, about the relationship between levels of representation, suggesting that these might be a set of several linked frames for representing a disease rather than a single disease frame. The underlying problem is that assessing a frame will be easier if there are less matches to be made, at least initially; and this would form a single disease frame. But representing a disease will be more accurate if there is scope for handling a range of situational variations; and this would favour a set of linked disease frames. These criteria can be reconciled by recourse to images of frames and subframes, or Minsky's notion of higher levels for pattern recognition and lower levels for connecting to further information. But such speculation has little empirical support, apart from well documented evidence that expert physicians do in practice succeed in interpreting these two different requirements.

A more fundamental criticism, perhaps, is Boreham's argument that frame-system theory ignores the effect on the diagnostic process of the personal character of the physician. [It is important to recognize] the very personal nature of conceptual frameworks developed through experience. Not only does the personality and prior experience of physicians affect the way in which they acquire and interpret information but each encounters a unique series of cases during the process of constructing and further developing their frame systems. This perspective is still compatible with the notion of representation by frames, but not with the concept of a standard frame which can represent a body of expertise rather than that of a single expert. Minsky had to assume that standard frames were possible in order to develop computerized models, but we are under no such compunction.

Two further questions which need to be addressed by this and other models concern the nature of both the diagnostic process and the learning process. Frame-system theory allows the possibility of a staged process in which the matching of data to a frame or subframe triggers the next diagnostic stage, but when and why does such staging occur? It may be enforced by the situation if diagnostic tests take time or symptoms require time to mature. But is it ever necessary to reduce the cognitive overload? Then secondly, there is the problem of how the frame system is developed and refined by experience. To what extent is this a process of conscious reflection or can it be accomplished, as the Dreyfuses suggest by intuitive adjustment alone?

A more sophisticated approach which both encompasses and broadens frame theory is the four-stage model of developing clinical expertise put forward by Schmidt, Norman and Boshuizen (1990). They argue that 'memory is the overriding source of differences in diagnostic performance between medical students and physicians having different amounts of experience'; and that the functioning of memory is dependent on the knowledge structures used to represent the information being stored. The gradual progress from novice to expert can be depicted by four developmental stages, each characterized by the emergence of a distinct type of knowledge structure. However:

> these representations do not decay or become inert in the course of developing expertise but rather remain available for future use when the situation requires their activation.
>
> (Ibid: 613)

The first two stages of the model are reached during training. Stage 1 involves the development of richly elaborated causal networks which medical students can use to explain the causes or consequences of diseases in terms of underlying pathophysiological processes. This knowledge is largely derived from lectures and books, and accounts of cases are very lengthy. Stage 2 then involves the transformation of these elaborated networks into abridged networks using high-level causal models, with information about signs and symptoms being 'subsumed under diagnostic labels' rather than spelt out in detail. This is exemplified by two contrasting protocols for the same case: that from a fourth-year student contained over 250 words and forty separate propositions, while a sixth-year student summarizes it more accurately with only thirty-four words and six propositions. The latter had developed the capacity both to select only the most critical information and to use higher-level concepts to handle clusters of interrelated detail. Although this change is attributed to the student being exposed to real patients, there are other possible explanations. This particular change involves a transition from an academic environment which stresses the elaborate presentation of knowledge to a clinical environment which stresses rapid decision-making and action [. . .]. It may also be compared to the increase in conceptual sophistication expected of graduate students as they begin to understand the central theories and paradigms of their disciplines.

Stage 3 is more obviously dependent on accumulated experience of working with patients, but takes much longer to reach. Its principal feature is the emergence of a particular kind of template called an 'illness script' (Feltovitch and Barrows, 1984). Constructing such scripts involves organizing one's knowledge about an illness to conform to the pattern depicted in Figure 8.1, which uses temporal more than causal relations to order information in a format that resembles a story rather than an argument:

An important feature of an illness script is its serial structure: items that make up the script appear in a specific order. This order closely matches the way in which physicians inform other physicians about their patients' conditions; as such, one could say that illness scripts obey certain conventions regarding an optimal story structure in medicine.

(Feltovitch and Barrows, 1984: 615)

Illness script

Enabling conditions →	Predisposing factors, boundary conditions, hereditary factors etc.
Predisposing factors →	Compromised host factors, travel, drugs, etc.
Boundary conditions →	Age, sex, etc.
Fault →	Invasion of tissue by pathogenic organism, inadequate nutrient supply, inability of tissue to survive, etc.
Consequences →	Complaints, signs, symptoms
Complaints →	Etc.
Signs →	Etc.
Symptoms →	Etc.

Figure 8.1   *A generic illness script*

Schmitd *et al.*, summarize evidence in favour of the gradual development by physicians of this script mode of representation. Less experienced physicians can recall information more effectively when it is presented in the order of a script, but more experienced physicians do this for themselves and gain no special benefit from having it done for them in advance. Their notion of script derives from Schank and Abelson (1977) who saw scripts as 'a specialisation of the frame idea', but there is also a wider research literature on the use of narrative structures to convey knowledge. Another significant finding was that expert physicians made greater use of information in the 'enabling conditions' category than less experienced colleagues, suggesting that the construction and use of this type of knowledge requires greater experience.

Confirming Boreham's critique of frame theory [. . .], Schmidt, *et al.*, describe the illness scripts developed by physicians as highly idiosyncratic, depending both on the character of the physician and the particular examples of the disease that he or she encounters:

based on his or her unique experience with a certain disease, each physician develops rich, idiosyncratic scripts for that disease, which may or may not resemble the scripts of other physicians or the textbook. This may explain why some doctors have difficulty diagnosing some diseases where others immediately recognise the essential patterns. It may also explain why extensive exposure to many different cases may be the crucial factor in developing expertise.

(Schmidt *et al.*, 1990: 617)

The fourth stage of development involves yet another type of knowledge structure, the use by experienced physicians of memories or previous patients. Significantly, and one could argue in perfect counterbalance with illness scripts, these case memories are retained as individual entities rather than merged into the prototypical form expoused by Cantor *et al.* (1980) and Bordage and Zachs (1984). Again Schmidt *et al.*, cite evidence that such memories play a significant part in diagnosis by experts; but they do not offer any explanation as to why this particular mode of knowledge representation should develop at a later stage than illness scripts. However the following passage does suggest that the organizational conventions established by illness scripts may be needed before recollections of prior patients can become a reliable and accessible form of knowledge.

> The different representations we have described coexist in the mind of the physician. In other words, the ways in which a disease expresses itself in human beings are represented both as 'generalised experience' in the form of illness scripts for the disease, pathophysiologic descriptions, and so forth, and as an elaborate set of lively recollections of specific patients who suffered from that disease. These representational formats have a synergistic effect. The recollections of prior patients, indexed by the relevant illness scripts, are stored in episodic memory, which makes them very easily accessible.
>
> (Ibid: 617)

Although the earlier modes of representation get used much less as later modes become available, Schmidt *et al.*, emphasize the essential complementarity of all four modes. Moreover they hasten to add that:

> we are not implying that experts work at some 'deeper' level of processing but rather that expertise is associated with the availability of knowledge representations in various forms, derived from both experience and formal education.
>
> (Ibid: 618)

Like other researchers thay note the relative absence of basic science information in clinicians' protocols, thus ruling out the frequently proposed theory that such knowledge forms the basis of expertise. However, they do not examine the extent to which scientific knowledge is embedded into practice in ways that disguise its underpinning contribution. There is clearly a danger in assuming that, because experts do not appear to possess or use scientific knowledge more than those who are recently qualified, such knowledge is unimportant. Different kinds of research would be needed to investigate that question.

The Schmidt theory successfully explains the frequently confirmed research finding that expertise in medicine is domain-specific. A physician with acknowledged expertise in one speciality will perform at no better than average level in another. But it goes beyond this now accepted conclusion in suggesting that the expertise of different scientists in the same domain will differ according to their accumulated store of illness scripts and individual cases. Earlier Elstein *et al.* (1978) had shown that in most cases the intuitive phase of diagnosis leads to hypotheses which still have to be confirmed or modified, in others it helps to narrow the range of possibilities so that subsequent diagnosis becomes a more achievable problem-solving task. Hence Schmidt *et al.*, were able to conclude that:

(1) there are at least two separable levels or stages – a rapid, non-analytical dimension, which is used in the majority of problems, and a slower, analytic approach, applied to a minority of problems that present difficulties; (2) neither is to be preferred, since both may lead to a solution; (3) it is not now possible to predict which kinds of problems will cause difficulty for an individual, since difficulties arise from individual experience.

(Ibid: 619–20)

Although Schmidt *et al.*, describe their theory as 'a stage theory of clinical reasoning' it focuses entirely on the process of diagnosis. Rather different models of reasoning appear when the treatment or management of illness are under review. Boreham (1989) analyses the expertise needed for making decisions about the optimum dose of the drug *phenytoin sodium* in the management of epilepsy. Too small a dosage fails to prevent seizures but too large a dosage is toxic. The problem for the physician is first to achieve, and then to maintain, the optimum concentration of drug in blood serum for each individual patient. The situation is accurately represented by a mathematical equation, but this contains two constants the value of which depends of the individual patient. So the equation can only be used after two measurements of serum concentration have been made, separated by a significant time interval. The physician's response to a new patient has to involve either (1) an initial 'loading' dose to significantly increase the concentration followed by 'maintenance' doses with a level adjustment as more information becomes available, or (2) withdrawing the drug until toxic effects have dissipated and it is safe to restart with (1). By interviewing an expert about three different cases, Boreham was able to establish that his dosage decisions were based on a set of fifteen If-Then rules which covered all possible circumstances. The most difficult group of decisions concerned the first dose to prescribe for patients currently having seizures, for which he measured the current concentration of serum then applied the following 'rule of thumb':

if serum concentration is less than 7 mg/l, an increase of 100 mg a day is safe. Between 7 and 10 mg/l, an increase of 50 mg a day is safe. Over 10 mg/l, one would want to edge up in 25 mg increments.

(Boreham, 1989: 192)

which Boreham represented as three If-Then statements as follows (p. 172):

If   (10 mg/l < serum concentration)
Then   (add 25 mg to present daily dose *and* reassess after several weeks)

If   (7 mg/l < serum concentration < 10 mg/l)
Then   (add 50 mg to present daily dose *and* reassess after several weeks)

If   (serum concentration < 7 mg/l)
Then   (add 100 mg to present daily dose *and* reassess after several weeks)

This decision system was evolved from professional experience over several years. It was consistent with, but could not be derived from, the equation; and it was completely successful in predicting current doses for a series of simulated cases. However, the expert did not claim to follow these rules rigidly; and a second expert, while generally regarding the decisions for the simulated cases as correct, suggested that they were occasionally suboptimal. One suggested modification was intended to improve the safety margin in a case where (1) previous evidence of toxicity at a certain level provided enough information to use the equation to calculate the optimum dose instead of having to rely on rules of thumb, and (2) the low body weight of the patient also suggested a more cautious approach. This is an example of a 'normal' decision being modified both by recourse to theory and by making good use of additional contextual information. The other adjustment recommended by the second expert also required an appreciation of the underlying mathematical model: the first new dose in a toxicity case was administered a little earlier to take into account the lapse of time before it would come into effect and the time which had already lapsed since the 'current' concentration had actually been measured.

Boreham's study also covered an aspect of clinical decision-making neglected by Dreyfus and only briefly discussed by Schmidt, the interactive and progressive nature of decision-making. The process of collecting information about a case is rarely instant and may be extremely protracted. Apart from the need, as in Boreham's study, to wait and see what happens next and to monitor the effects of any treatment, diagnosis can involve decisions about what information to collect and in what order, which require judgments balancing the time and expense of getting some particular kind of information against its anticipated contribution to the diagnosis. Such decisions lend themselves to evolving personal rule systems, which experts can then modify for cases they perceive as abnormal. But changes in scientific knowledge or investigative technology can make rules out of date, as well as generating a significant period of uncertainty while people find out how best to take advantage of them. The quality of judgments about collecting information and the capacity to change established patterns in the light of advances in science and technology could both be considered as aspects of process expertise in diagnosis. So also might the process of interacting with one's patients, an issue to which we shall shortly return.

Medicine is a field where decisions have to be made under conditions of considerable uncertainty. So physicians have to deal with probabilities whether or not they choose to express them in figures. At least three kinds of probability are highly relevent:

- the probability that a test for a particular condition will give the right result, a false positive or a false negative;
- the probability that a given treatment will lead to a particular outcome; and
- the probabilities associated with risks of complications, infections, mortality.

Where only one of these probabilities is relevant and there is a single, simple decision, the decision situation is easy to conceptualize. But when there is a chain of decisions and several sets of probabilities to consider, the problem is difficult to conceptualize and intuitive decison-making unlikely to be a good option. The technique of decison analysis was developed to bring some clarity of thinking to such situations and to work with multiple probabilities in a disciplined manner. Like most professions, there are those who are perceived as enthusiasts for quantitative methods and those who avoid them whenever possible. Given the very qualitative flavour of the discussion so far it is time to examine these more quantitative aspects of expertise.

Let us begin with a case quoted by Lilford (1992) of a woman with an early cancer of the reproductive tract. A small tumour was removed by an excisional biopsy which enabled the pathologist to estimate a 2 per cent probability of residual tumour. This risk could be halved by further surgery which has a mortality rate of 0.5 per cent. The technique involves exploring all possible outcomes than calculating their respective probabilities. This suggests that further surgery will improve her chances of survival, but the analysis is only there to provide a guide. Three other factors have to be considered: the reliability of the probability estimates used in the calculation; the likelihood of further contextual information about the woman suggesting an adjustment in one or more of the probability figures; and her preferences for the possible outcomes. In this case a woman who wishes to continue to have children might wish to take a slightly higher risk of mortality in order to retain her fertility.

Lilford gives considerable emphasis to the role of decision analysis in facilitating consultations with clients; and argues more generally that the technique exposes assumptions for discussion which should not be allowed to remain hidden. For example, he points out that it is quite common to suggest that amniocentesis should be recommended to pregnant women when the risk of their child having Down's Syndrome is greater than the risk of miscarriage caused by the procedure. But, although this advice sounds plausible, it implicitly assumes that the women places equal value on both a Down's birth and foetal loss, which could be true for only a small percentage of women. There are a range of treatments and outcomes to be considered when making a decision. The physician's role is to explain the choice to his or her patient using the best available estimates of outcome possibilities. The relative desirability of the possible outcomes is a matter for the patient, who may need assistance in recognizing the implications for his or her future quality of life. This model suggests three distinctive areas of expertise

1. The physician has to be able to draw up a decision analysis using up-to-date information about possible treatments and outcomes, their respective probabilities and the reliability of the figures. This latter requires a critical reading of research.
2. Research may also provide some information about how probabilities may vary according to context and patient. This together with the physician's ability to collect and interpret relevant information about context and patient will enable him or her to make appropriate adjustments to the probabilities.

3. The physician has to be able to interact with patients in order to best prepare and advise them, without unduly influencing their choice. Even in this situation, however, there may be some empirical evidence that is relevant.

Decision analysis uses the term 'utility' to indicate the weight to be attached to an outcome which reflects a client's preference and in some cases researchers have attempted the difficult task of establishing the range of values commonly associated to certain outcomes. Where the evidence is accompanied by information about people's arguments and feelings, it provides a useful background to discussions with individuals (and often counteracts physicians' first intuitive assumptions about utilities).

The danger inherent in analytic approaches is overestimating the significance of the typical case which conforms with published estimates of probabilities and utilities, and underestimating the variation between patients. It can also be more time-intensive than many medical institutions are prepared to allow. However, there are other reasons why many physicians shy away from it. They may not feel competent in the mathematical handling of multiple probabilities; or they may feel their autonomy threatened by any suggestion that their unaided diagnosis of individual patients might need external guidance, especially when that guidance 'appears' to devalue the significance of individual cases. Intuitive approaches, on the other hand, tend to get reported in a manner that assumes that they always result in the right decision. The expert-oriented theories of the Dreyfuses and Schmidt *et al.*, start from the assumption that how clinical decisions *are made* by experts is also how clinical decisions *ought to be made*.

The limitations of a purely intuitive approach have been reviewed by Elstein and Bordage (1979), using Elstein *et al.*'s earlier (1978) research as a starting point.

> physicians engaged in diagnostic clinical reasoning commonly employ the strategy of generating and testing hypothetical solutions to the problem. A small set of hypotheses is generated very early in the clinical encounter, based on a very limited amount of data compared to what will eventually be collected. Often the chief complaint or the data obtained in the first few minutes of interaction with the patient are sufficient to establish this small set of working hypotheses. The clinician can then ask: 'What findings would be observed if a particular hypotheses were true?' and the collection of data can be tailored to answer this question.
>
> This reasoning process transforms the ill-defined, open-ended problem 'What is wrong with the patient?' into a series of better-defined problems: 'Could the abdominal pain be caused by acute appendicitis? or a twisted ovarian cyst? or pelvic inflammatory disease? or ectopic pregnancy?' This set of alternatives makes matters more manageable. By constructing a set of hypothesised end points, it becomes possible for the clinician to work backwards from the diagnostic criteria of each hypothesis to the work-up to be conducted. The search for data is simplified because only certain points will be addressed.
>
> (Elstein and Bordage, 1979)

The empirical evidence strongly confirms the intuitive nature of 'hypothesis generation', but does not suggest that it is error free. The heavy dependence on memory suggests that it is the most salient hypotheses which are most likely to be identified [. . .] and not necessarily the most probable. The research suggests that the most prevalent cause of incorrect diagnosis was a 'failure to generate and consider the relevant diagnostic hypothesis'. Experienced clinicians try to counteract this problem by deliberately constructing alternatives to those immediately suggested by the problem, a process which also draws on experience but clearly differs from the pattern recognition method of the template model.

The process of moving from a small set of hypotheses to a diagnosis involves both acquiring new data and interpreting the data already collected, often a major information processing task. Elstein and Bordage note that experienced physicians simplify this task by interpreting cues on a three-point scale: 'as tending to *confirm* or *disconfirm* a hypothesis or as *non-contributory*'. Then finally all this data has somehow to be interpreted and integrated in the clinician's head. Nor surprisingly, a number of problems arise at this stage. The most common error is to treat non-contributory evidence as confirming a hypothesis; and there is also a strong tendency to re-emphasize negative findings. Other problems can arise from the tendency to give equal weighting to all the confirming or disconfirming issues, when some may be much more reliable and significant than others. This is less likely during later work-up when routines are likely to have been established that start with the most reliable ones, unless of course those particular tests involve time delays or are highly expensive. In general, the interpretation of data tends to be biased against the adoption of the totally intuitive approach described by Dreyfus, though not against the use of intuition *per se*. [. . .].

Hammond's Cognitive Continuum Theory

Our review of clinical decision-making has yielded models of expertise that are relevant outside the field of medicine, and drawn attention to empirical evidence that is rarely available for other professions. In particular, it has highlighted the role necessarily played by intuitive thinking, together with its advantages and limitations. The need for long periods of practical experience in order to develop and refine professional expertise has been explained in terms of theories about the role of memory in supporting intuitive thinking. The important role of more analytic approaches such as decision analysis and logical argument has also been discussed, raising important questions about the appropriate balance between intuitive and analytical approaches and the best ways in which they can be combined. Hamm (1988) points out that this last problem involves two important factors: the nature of the task, and the nature of the practitioner's expertise. Hence the initial questions to be answered are:

1. What kinds of thinking, analytic or intuitive (or a mixture) should be used in various types of situation?
2. How does the practitioner discover or decide which mode of cognition to use?

3. How can the appropriate kind of thinking be performed as well as possible?

(Hamm, 1988: 80–1)

These questions are addressed by Hammond's Cognitive Continuum Theory (1980) which defines analytic and intuitive thinking as poles of a continuum, arguing that most thinking is neither purely intuitive nor purely analytical. A variety of 'quasi-rational' modes of cognition lies somewhere in between. At the fast and ill-structured end of the continuum these quasi-rational modes include peer-aided judgment and system-aided judgment (decision analysis) while at the slow and well-structured end of the continuum are modes of inquiry involving surveys or quasi-experiments. It is interesting to note that on the time-scale in which clinicians work, decision analysis is perceived as the most analytic mode whereas for an engineer or a manager it would be perceived as closer to the intuitive end of the spectrum. However, even for them it would require information from previous analytically conceived research to supply the necessary evidence of probabilities.

Elstein's work, discussed earlier, drew attention to the 'mixed mode' of inquiry in which intuitive and analytical approaches are combined in a problem-solving approach to diagnosis. Similar results were obtained by Boreham (1987) from a study of expert management consultants. His account is worth quoting at some length as it epitomizes what many now regard as one of the most fruitful approaches to problem-solving.

> The subjects' expertise was quite obviously strongly dependent on their intuitive abilities to operate on mental models of what they implicitly recognised in the problem givens. Their initial problem spaces included constraints (not part of the problem givens, but recalled from the subjects' memory of similar situations) which drastically reduced the amount of the problem domain which needed to be searched for the causal factor. This was unmistakably the result of a pattern recognition process similar to those postulated in the knowledge-based theory outlined earlier.
>
> However, the problem was not actually solved just by activating these templates. Despite the substantial prior experience of these consultants, and the fact that the problem was one which they had 'seen a lot of' in industry, the solution was not actually contained in the schemata which were activated. The intuitive processes were used only to generate a problem space which isolated the crucial aspects of the problem and guided subsequent search.
>
> In order to model the consultants' problem-solving behaviour accurately, it was necessary to represent the process of diagnosis as an alteration between knowledge-driven operations on a mental model of the situation, and sensory-driven operations on the problems givens. Insights gained in the former type of episode narrowed down to the cause of the problem remarkably quickly, but the management consultants still felt the need for local search to verify that what they suspected was actually the case, and to delineate the nature of the problem exactly.
>
> (Boreham, 1987: 94)

Boreham's evidence also showed very clearly that the local-search stage involved the use of inferential procedures which conformed to models of logical deduction rather than pattern recognition. The subjects' reasoning followed the classical laws governing inferences from categorical propositions. He also found that performance by post-experience students of management science was improved by practice in the formal operations involved in hypothesis-testing.

The second part of Hammond's theory is a 'task continuum' to differentiate those features of a task which should determine the most appropriate mode of cognition to use. Thus:

> In Cognitive Continuum Theory, tasks are considered to occupy a position on a task continuum, ranging from analysis-inducing to intuition-inducing, indicated by task features that influence the model of cognition that the thinker will adopt. These features include the complexity of the task, the ambiguity of the content of the task, and the form of task presentation.
>
> (Hammond, 1980)

For example, the greater the number of pertinent cues and the higher the extent of their overlap or redundancy, the more likely there will be an intuitive response. The availability of a complex organizing principle is likely to encourage analysis. Pictorial forms of presenting information induce intuition and quantitative forms induce analysis. Decomposition into subtasks will also aid analysis, but lack of time causes people to adopt a faster, more intuitive approach.

Hammond's central argument is that people's reasoning is more effective when the mode of thinking they adopt corresponds to these critical features of the task. But to many professionals this advice must seem a little idealistic. The time factor alone forces people into a more rapid, intuitive mode of cognition; and as routines get developed, many would rather keep it that way. While some professionals are disposed to take time over their decisions and tasks, others clearly prefer not to linger. The current emphasis on professional productivity severely limits the choice.

[. . .]

To conclude this chapter, perhaps we should note the revolution in thinking about professional expertise. Thirty years ago, professional expertise tended to be identified with propositional knowledge and a high theoretical content, regardless of whether such knowledge ever got used in practice. Whereas most of the theories of expertise discussed in this chapter appear to have assumed that expertise is based mainly on experience with further development of theoretical knowledge having almost ceased soon after qualification. Why has the pendulum swung so far in the other direction? Several explanations come to mind. One is the strong anti-intellectualization of the 1980s exacerbated by the exaggerated claims of the immediate post-war era. Another is the failure to properly recognize theory in use, a point strongly emphasized by Argyris and Schön (1974). A third, I could argue is the failure to recognize how theory gets used in practice, that it rarely gets just taken off the shelf and applied without undergoing some transformation. The process of interpreting and personalizing theory and integrating it into conceptual frameworks that are themselves partly inconsistent and partly tacit is as yet only minimally understood. [. . .]

[A further discussion of issues in professional education and learning in the workplace is provided in Eraut (2000).]

Note

This is an edited version of a chapter in Eraut, M. (1994) *Developing Professional Knowledge and Competence*, London, Falmer Press.

References

Argyris, C. and Schön, D. A. (1974) *Theory in Practice: Increasing Professional Effectiveness*, San Francisco, Jossey-Bass.

Benner, P. (1984) *From Novice to Expert: Excellence and Power in Clinical Nursing Practice*, Menlo Park, Calif., Addison-Wesley.

Bordage, G. and Zacks, R. (1984) 'The structure of medical knowledge in the memories of medical students and general practitioners: Categories and prototypes', *Medical Education*, 18: 406–16.

Boreham, N. C. (1987) 'Learning from experience in diagnostic problem solving', in Richardson, J. *et al.* (eds) *Student Learning: Research in Education and Cognitive Psychology*, Guildford, SRHE, pp. 89–97.

Boreham, N. C. (1988) 'Models of diagnosis and their implications for adult professional education', *Studies in the Education of Adults*, 20: 95–108.

Boreham, N. C. (1989) 'Modelling medical decision-making under uncertainty', *British Journal of Educational Psychology*, 59: 187–99.

Cantor, N. *et al.* (1980) 'Psychiatric diagnosis as prototype categorisation', *Journal of Abnormal Psychology*, 89: 181.

Dreyfus, H. L. and Dreyfus, S. E. (1986) *Mind over Machine: The Power of Human Intuition and Expertise in the Era of the Computer*, Oxford, Basil Blackwell.

Elstein, A. S. and Bordage, G. (1979) 'Psychology of clinical reasoning', in Stone, G. *et al. Health Psychology – A Handbook*, San Francisco, Jossey-Bass.

Elstein, A. S., Shulman, L. S. and Sprafka, S. A. (1978) *Medical Problem Solving: An Analysis of Clinical Reasoning*, Harvard, Mass., Harvard University Press.

Eraut, M. (2000) 'Non-formal learning and tacit knowledge in professional work', *British Journal of Educational Psychology*, 70: 113–36.

Feltovich, P. J. and Barrows, H. S. (1984) 'Issues of generality in medical problem solving', in Schmidt, H. G. and De Volder, M. L. (eds) *Tutorials in Problem-Based Learning*, Assen, The Netherlands, Van Gorcum, pp. 128–42.

Hamm, R. M. (1988) 'Clinical intuition and clinical analysis: Expertise and the cognitive continuum', in Dowie, J. and Elstein, A. (eds) *Professional Judgement: A reader in clinical decision making*, Cambridge, Cambridge University Press, pp. 78–105.

Hammond, K. R. *et al.* (1980) *Human Judgement and Decision Making*, New York, Hemisphere.

Lilford, R. J. (1992) 'Decision logic in medical practice', *Journal of the Royal College of Physicians*, 26(4): 400–12.

Minsky, M. (1977) 'Frame-system theory', in Johnson-Laird, P. N. and Wason, P. C. (eds) *Thinking: Readings in Cognitive Science*, Cambridge, Cambridge University Press, pp. 355–76.

Schank, R. and Abelson, R. P. (1977) 'Scripts, plans and knowledge', in Johnson-Laird, P. N. and Wason, P. C. (eds) *Thinking: Readings in Cognitive Science*, Cambridge, Cambridge University Press, pp. 421–32.

Schmidt, H. G., Norman, G. R. and Boshuizen, H. (1990) 'A cognitive perspective on medical expertise: Theory and implications', *Academic Medicine*, 65(10): 611-21.

Swanson, D. B. (1978) *Computer Simulation of Expert Problem Solving in Medical Diagnosis*, Ph.D dissertation. University of Minnesota, cited in Boreham (1988).

9

Teaching Self-teaching

Pip Eastop

In this chapter I will discuss my approach to the teaching of horn students within the context of music conservatoires which prepare students for the musical profession. After describing the conservatoire learning context I will explain some of the specific training needs of performing musicians and outline aspects of my approach to teaching them.

Music conservatoires differ from other establishments of higher education in that they exist as places of practical, rather than academic, learning for performing musicians. Although their courses have some academic elements, which form compulsory parts of the students' degrees, the main emphasis is on the students developing their performance skills to the highest possible professional level. For this reason, in the conservatoire context, instrumental teaching is done on a one-to-one basis by established performing musicians of the highest calibre.

Entrance to the music conservatoires is by audition and the standard is extremely high. Only a very small number of school leavers who play musical instruments are proficient enough to consider auditioning for a conservatoire place and, out of those who make the attempt, only very few actually gain entrance. Once accepted, their training focuses on improving their technical and musical performance abilities to such a standard that they are professionally employable when they leave. The reality is, however, that in proportion to the numbers of hopeful college leavers there are relatively few vacant jobs for performing musicians so, again, a filtering takes place and only the best of them make it into the profession.

I teach undergraduate level horn[1] students at two of London's music conservatoires. Their courses last four years and towards the end of each academic year they have examinations in which students are expected to demonstrate their performing achievements. At the end of their course they have to perform a 'final recital', to a high degree of technical and musical excellence as a major part of their B.Mus degree qualification.

On leaving college the newly graduated professional must have the resources to continue improving their playing because due to fierce competition the acceptable standard is not only high but keeps on rising, a fact which poses a continual challenge to all musicians, even established ones, who wish to have long careers.

Typically, after the conservatoire years, a horn player will want to make a living in the employment of an orchestra. Unfortunately, although the standard of playing reached by this stage is often very high it is quite rare for newly graduated horn players to find such work immediately upon leaving. Some, in anticipation of the difficulties ahead, opt for a postgraduate year or two to develop their playing expertise while still under the shelter of the college. Some realize that they will not make the grade and switch to alternative careers. Most, however, will try to set themselves up as freelance players and begin developing networks of employment contacts in the hope of gradually building up their work to the extent that they can earn a living by their playing. Many fall by the wayside by failing to keep up a high enough standard.

During the years of a horn player's career many aspects of their working materials and environment can change. In particular the teeth can move, leading to a need for subtle changes in lip technique. Also, the instrument and mouthpiece may be altered, or perhaps the kind of repertoire played, the place of practice, the amount of practice time available and its regularity. Thus, what works today might not be so effective in several years' time. Indeed it is often the case that horn players who have played beautifully for decades begin to feel their ability to play coming slowly unravelled. This can be a dangerous time for a horn player, particularly if they have no investigative resources and are thus unable to overhaul and rebuild their technique.

Although the study of a musical instrument is never complete, when a student leaves the conservatoire, ideally, they should not need the help of a teacher again. Thus, an essential element in a student's preparation for a professional working life is their acquisition of flexible, self-analytical tools for problem finding, problem-solving and sustaining continuous personal development of their own technique and musicianship. The skills needed for this 'self-teaching' are among the most valuable a performing musician can have but also the most difficult to acquire. It is because of this difficulty that I believe 'self-teaching', as a discipline in itself, should be instilled in the student as deeply as possible during their conservatoire training.

Horn playing is very technique-intensive, by which I mean that a lot of technical work must be done before its output will be recognized as musical sound rather than grotesque noise. Once painstakingly acquired, the collection of discrete skills which in combination make up a full working technique must all be maintained in as stable and reliable a way as possible to minimize future breakdowns in ability, disasters in performance and to keep the playing generally on top form. In contrast to, for example, the piano, where production of its individual notes is taken care of by the keyboard and hammer mechanism, the horn demands that each note must be formed using the lips and the breath in a way which does not come naturally at all to most people. In fact, the instrument itself is of little help to the player. Anyone who can coax music from a horn can generally get a similar result from a few metres of garden hosepipe or even a teapot. The horn, being topologically equivalent to a length of drainpipe, acts only as resonator with the *potential* to assist the player in making exceedingly beautiful tones. The same is true for all of the brass 'family' of wind instruments.

It has become a traditionally held belief that the horn is one of the most difficult instruments to play. Indeed, there is some truth in this as it usually takes years before the beginner can play even one note proficiently, let alone sequence them into an effective musical phrase. The horn player's lips must be trained to vibrate like the vocal cords of a singer, which is problematic enough but there is yet a further difficulty: whereas a singer's mouth will resonate and thus amplify any frequency at which the vocal cords vibrate, the horn will only do the same for the lips at a few precise frequencies, which are known as harmonics. It is only possible to make the horn ring out beautifully if the pitch at which the lips choose to 'sing' exactly matches that of one of the harmonics the horn allows. The particular array of these harmonics is entirely dependent on the length of the instrument, from its mouthpiece to the its final bell flare, which can be varied in the modern horn by the use of its four valves. These are simple devices, operated by the left hand, which in various combinations enable the length of the instrument to be changed instantly. The tension of the lips, and several other physical variables of breath and mouth which are too complex to describe here, must be set exactly right to blow any particular harmonic or there will be a disagreement between the intention of the player and what the horn 'wants' to do. The player must know exactly where, in 'pitch space', the required harmonics lie in order to have any chance of finding them quickly. The dreadful sound resulting from inaccuracy in this respect is commonly known as a 'split note' and a player who does this regularly will not last long in any of the better orchestras. Pitching horn notes accurately, then, is somewhat analogous to archery – any single good note being the equivalent of hitting a bulls-eye from several fields away in thick fog and high winds. The livelihood of the modern horn player depends on a very high degree of accuracy.

Apart from being notoriously difficult, horn technique is also a very hidden discipline. It is impossible to see what is going on from the outside. The mouthpiece[2] completely obscures that part of the mouth which a horn teacher would like to observe in order to 'see' evidence of poor technique. There are a variety of subtle ways in which the lips can be doing things badly but, generally speaking, these can only be spotted if the teacher has had some past experience of working through the same, or similar, problem and thus can somehow sense from a range of clues, intuition and guesswork what is going wrong. Once such a problem has been discovered it is often quite easy to find a fix for it, the diagnosis being the most difficult part.

When investigating such subtle problems I try to involve the student as much as possible in the processes of analysis and subsequent experimentation to find solutions. My first step is to get them to see, hear and feel the problem – a process which can be surprisingly difficult. Fixed habits of seeing, hearing and feeling can be very strong; often to the point of self-delusion. Who has not been surprised, or appalled, at the sound of their own recorded voice? What we self-observe as we actually carry out a complex task such as walking, speaking or playing an instrument is usually very different to what we see if we observe the same thing retrospectively.[3] An obvious solution, then, would seem to lie in the students using recordings or videos of themselves playing. However, while this can be helpful occasionally, it is not something that ought often to be relied upon because not only does it slow down valuable practice time but, more significantly, it discourages development of one of the most important skills in horn playing, namely, accurate self-observation in real time. It is of course much better to learn to hear the truth precisely, as it is happening, with one's own finely tuned perception. Acquisition of this skill can be a painful process because the truth sometimes hurts.

In order for the student to gain an accurate impression of how they are playing they need to have as much accurate feedback as possible, both aural and visual. The visual aspect here is quite important because, as is the case with musical performers of all descriptions, poor habits of posture if left unnoticed can exert a deleterious influence on the final musical result. To this end I may, for example, set up a mirror so that the student can see, at least superficially, what some of their visible playing musculature is doing, or indeed how some of what *ought* to be their non-playing musculature may be interfering. I might then give them a very simple exercise to work on, perhaps in the form of one single note, so they can hear without too much complication, and encourage them to listen with an intense focus of awareness.

If this kind of feedback is not developed a horn player's imagination tends to fill in any obvious gaps in understanding by creating mental pictures of what they *think* they do when they play. Such fantasies can be quite inaccurate and when used as a basis for further exercise, or even in the teaching of others, can be quite disastrous. An example of this is the commonly held belief among many brass players that the action of the tongue in contact with the roof of the mouth for the purpose of making notes start firmly is comparable to the action of a hammer striking a percussion instrument, whereas, in actual fact, the tongue in this context functions more like a valve which opens to let the breath flow or closes to stop it. It is easy to see that designing exercises to develop tongue co-ordination based on such misunderstandings of underlying physical functions will not be the most efficient way to train. Given better feedback, it is possible to avoid this and other forms of self-deception.

Deceptions of fantasy and imagination are not confined only to the realm of how a player perceives the mechanical 'doing' of their technique, but extend also to how they perceive the results of their playing – how they listen. There seem to be two forms of this – the first concerning the musical building blocks, *individual notes*, while the second concerns *musical phrases*. These compare well to the *pronunciation* of individual words and the *meaning* of sentences in spoken languages. The quality of individual notes, as heard in the practice room, should be, but is often not, studied through a cultivated awareness of comparisons between the carefully monitored input to the instrument and the exact resulting sound output. Having good acoustics in the practice room is very helpful here, but the specific requirement is quite the reverse of the rich resonant reverberation so desirable in a concert hall. I deliberately make my teaching room acoustically 'dry' because in such a room it is possible to hear details of sound analytically. This is the kind of acoustic most horn players would describe as 'unflattering', because a dry acoustic reveals even the tiniest of imperfections whereas a reverberant one tends to hide them. The abundant sound reflections found in reverberant rooms, although very satisfying for the player because of the complexity and richness they add to the sound, divert the ear from a true picture of what is emerging from the instrument. Without clear aural feedback it is very difficult to develop the production of really fine individual notes.

With musical phrases, there is a tendency to hear one's musical intention rather than the actuality. This is not surprising; if a beginner were able only to hear an objective version of their music, un-enhanced by their imagination, they would probably give up before long (this might have something to do with why it is that instruments seem easier to learn when young – while one's imagination is still believable!) To break free from dependence on teachers, in this respect, the student must work on refining their objectivity of listening.

Instrumental teachers preparing those at school level for entrance to a conservatoire are often excellent in many respects. They may inspire a love of music and enthusiasm for the instrument while nurturing the growth of good basic playing abilities. However, not generally being performers of an exceptionally high playing ability, they will most likely not have passed on an understanding of the intense level of self-awareness which is needed to refine horn technique up to a modern professional standard. Later, when the horn student begins study at the conservatoire the deepening of introspective self-awareness needed to take horn technique up to a higher level can come as something of a surprise.

While it is obviously the case that horn players need skilled tuition to accomplish the basic technical and musical skills which comprise horn playing at beginner or intermediate levels, there comes a time when in order to progress the horn player must go it alone to a large extent. One of the reasons it is so important for a conservatoire-level horn student to develop self-teaching, particularly of refined technical details at a high level, is because of the near-impossibility of such refinements being taught to them by anyone else. Indeed, many of the established horn players with whom I have discussed this issue feel themselves to have been largely self-taught, particularly at the higher level, despite having spent many years studying at a conservatoire. No teacher, apart from oneself, has the sensory feedback available to make really clear and accurate judgements about precisely what is happening during the process of playing the instrument. Thus, any teaching of the finer points of breath and lip control, apart from self-teaching, can be based on little more than intuitive guesswork.

Interestingly, most of the subtle skills of *listening* needed for effective horn teaching are exactly the same as those learned directly from the experience of monitoring oneself in learning to play. Indeed, I would argue that a teacher without the experience of successful self-teaching would find it virtually impossible to pass on anything of real technical value to high level students.

I have talked mainly about technique in this chapter and have said that horn playing is very technique intensive. While this is true, I must now redress the balance by saying that from the point of view of the listening audience, whose primary requirement is for a musical experience, the intricacies of horn technique are *of no interest whatever*. Naturally, there is a need for excellent technique in performance, but one of the dangers in emphasizing the importance of technique is the possibility of ignoring the development of a 'feel' for music, so-called 'musicality', or of neglecting aspects of style and phrasing. Music is a language which, like any other, can only be learned by immersing oneself in it and by nurturing a love of it.

It should be borne in mind by those who study technically demanding instruments that the musical notations we are trained to read and to translate into delightfully complex vibrations of the air are merely bare sketches – the bone structures of composed music. Composers have always written for musicians knowing that they will flesh out this basic notated structure and add musical meaning to it, add life to it, *interpret it*, in the same way a reciter of poetry will not simply say the words in a dull, mechanical monotone but animate and phrase them into a meaningfully expressive vocal line. Sadly, it is not as uncommon among horn players as one might expect to hear performances devoid of any communicative musical qualities. It can seem as though the performer is too busy 'doing' the playing to take much notice of the results, leaving the audience with nothing more to listen to than the technique of the player. This is a very bad situation because if the technique is perfect, and thus invisible, there will be nothing of interest to listen to, whereas if the technique is gritty with imperfections the attention of the audience will fall hungrily upon it and tear it apart.

For students of music, then, instrumental technique, however awesomely difficult, is only the beginning. Technique should never be an end in itself but a means to an end, the ultimate 'end' being a communicative performance of music charged with magic to move the listener.

Notes

1.   The 'horn' in this chapter is the modern French Horn. It is simply a long tube, looped several times, with a narrow end through which it is blown and a flared end from which a variety of sounds emerge. It commonly has four valves which are used to vary its length so that it is capable of playing every note within a range of at least four octaves.

2.   This is a little metal funnel which is placed over the central part of the lips and channels the outflowing breath into the narrow entrance of the instrument. Where the mouthpiece covers the lips it obscures a circle approximately one inch in diameter. A glass mouthpiece would seem a sensible solution to this problem were it not for the distorting refraction of the glass in addition to a tendency for it to steam up whenever blown rendering the lip aperture once again invisible.

3.   Along with many other musicians, I am indebted here to the work of F. M. Alexander, a pioneer, and teacher of, this form of self-observation. He became famous for developing his sophisticated 'Alexander Technique', a method which teaches the recognition, and subsequent re-training, of habitually inaccurate self-observation, neural motivation and physical execution of complex physical actions.

10

Computers and the Teacher's Role

Peter Scrimshaw

Introduction

Teaching is one of the most demanding social activities in our society, involving the presentation of a sophisticated cultural inheritance to a large group of learners while working within the constraints of a heavily bureaucratized National Curriculum. Compulsory computer use can easily be experienced as an extra burden rather than a potential aid. Nevertheless, while teachers have little choice over whether to use computers, they retain a great deal of control over how and when they use them.

However, the computer is not simply another curriculum innovation; it is also arguably the most important technical aid to teachers wishing to explore their own practice. This is because it is an immensely flexible (albeit often infuriating) device for generating and modifying curriculum innovations to enable learners and teachers to try out for themselves new approaches to teaching and learning. [. . .] The nature of the computer radically changes when the teacher replaces one piece of software with another; in choosing which software to use the teacher is making a first approximation at specifying what kinds of learning they are hoping to promote. Once chosen, most forms of software allow teachers and learners a great deal of freedom in how they make use of it. Thus the detailed formulation and implementation of computer-based classroom activities allows for a closer approximation to what kinds of learning can be achieved. But this requires teachers to see the computer not as an exotic extra, but as a responsive and integral element in a classroom curriculum that has been rethought to include a view of what computers might do. To ask how teachers need to use computers is in large part to ask how the computer might be used to support and explore the theoretical and practical implications of their own philosophy of education, with a view to its improvement.

The first part of this chapter offers a model of the curricular elements in the pre-computer classroom and then considers how different kinds of software relate to this framework. The later part of the chapter discusses the changes that the computer is bringing to the school and the world beyond, and considers some of the implications of all this for the professional development of teachers.

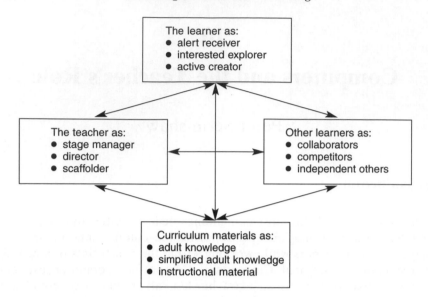

Figure 10.1   *Curricular elements of the pre-computer classroom*

The Structure of the Pre-Computer Classroom Curriculum

[. . .] There are various ways in which teachers can conceptualize classroom life. Behind [this] diversity of experiences lie a range of views that the contributors take of learners, curriculum materials, adult knowledge and the pattern of relationships between these and the teacher's role (see Figure 10.1).

How teachers regard each individual in a class varies greatly, but behind those variations it may be possible to distinguish a general disposition. One position is to consider that learners should be encouraged and enabled to become alert receivers and sensitive appreciators of externally generated knowledge; another that they are interested explorers of such knowledge; a third that they are active and imaginative creators of their own understanding. Many intermediate positions are possible here, but nevertheless many educational controversies are presented in terms of these underlying distinctions, such as debates about the relative importance of spelling, grammar, imagination and originality in writing.

There is again a choice to make when teachers consider how each individual should relate to other class members. A teacher may wish to promote a view of others as potential collaborators with whom the individual must learn to work, or as competitors to be related to in a pattern of healthy and good-natured conflict for fairly earned success. In contrast to both these perspectives stands the view that others in a class are irrelevant distractions and that ideally the individual should pursue his or her own activities independently. Here, too, intermediate possibilities are present, but simply to say that gets us little further forward unless some rationale can be offered for why a particular balance is favoured.

Our views on the characteristics of individual learners and their relationship to the group are in turn affected by how we think of classroom knowledge, and the connections between that and what we may call adult knowledge, i.e. the immense body of conflicting beliefs, values, skills and capabilities that form the human resources with which members of a society conduct their affairs and attempt to realize their individual and joint intentions.

One position here could be that classroom knowledge should be an unvarnished selection of the most important adult knowledge, to be confronted by learners with little or no mediation. Whether the learner, the teaching profession, the community, industry and business or the government should define what adult knowledge to present distinguishes several very significant variants within this general position. What they all share is a distrust of the education establishment and of what are seen as its self-interested attempts to interpose itself and its arcane and inefficient procedures between the learner and 'real' knowledge, as embodied in one or other notion of 'real life'. While this approach rightly emphasizes the value of schools in helping learners towards increasingly sophisticated conceptions of knowledge, it can allow the logical structure of adult knowledge to dominate unduly how it is best presented. [. . .]

Over against this position we can place the belief that it is essential that adult knowledge be carefully and professionally presented to school-age learners in ways that make it easier for them to grasp. One way in which this can be done is to introduce curriculum materials or activities that provide the learner with a series of simplifications of adult knowledge, each presentation progressively closer to the full picture. Some children's fiction, school assemblies, children's encyclopaedias, five-a-side football, Lego blocks and the infants' Wendy house exemplify this approach. Such constructions present unembellished simplifications of adult knowledge but do not of themselves generate learning. For this to emerge, the teacher (or perhaps another learner) must provide some framing, direction or instructional support.

However, a related category of curriculum materials builds in such directions from the start, thus partially filling a role that might otherwise be taken by the teacher. This category includes such things as textbooks, some educational television, worksheets and (as a marginal case) structured reading schemes. Here, too, teachers face choices: how far to rely upon curriculum material and experiences that have no instructional component, and how far to rely upon materials in while such instruction comes prepackaged.

If we turn now to the conception we might have of the teacher's function in all this, again there are a number of options. Different views on the relationships between learners and knowledge influence the extent to which we see teachers as dominant actors in the classroom directing activities or as stage managers of what are seen as largely self-generated learning activities emanating from learners as individuals or as a group. It is here that decisions on such matters as the ideal balance between instruction and support, between open and closed questions, between direction and enabling come into focus. We will return to the role of the teacher later, but first we need to consider how the use of computers might fit into this general framework.

The Computer as a More Effective Curriculum Resource

So how can we most usefully characterize the ways in which the computer can be used within the diversity of classroom cultures that we find in our schools? Clearly, what computers can do depends substantially upon what software they are running at any time; and there are many kinds of software. This suggests that we should ask instead what sorts of computer packages are best suited to supporting particular kinds of learning, and how far each kind of software is amenable to use within a different pedagogic framework from that for which it appears to have been designed. Here we could envisage a range of possibilities: at one end of the range the chosen software would completely determine the sort of activities needed to accompany its effective use; at the other end of the scale some kinds of software might be relatively neutral, being highly malleable and responsive to many different teaching approaches. Table 10.1 classifies (albeit in a simplified and debatable form) many commonly available kinds of software in these terms.

Some types of software (the 'open-ended' or 'tool' packages) assume that the learner is predominantly an active creator of knowledge. Productivity tools, such as presentation packages, word processors, outliners, ideas processors, spreadsheets, graphics packages, music composers and database packages, all allow users to collect and enter their own data and so are in this category because they all leave the initiative to the user. Programming languages and modelling packages, too, requires the user to take the lead in defining the purpose of the activity and in evaluating the results of his or her own choices as they are in effect devices for enabling users to externalize and evolve their own conceptualization of some process. [. . .] Various kinds of open-ended software are discussed in Scrimshaw (1993a), Straker (1989) and Underwood (1994).

While open-ended packages assume an active learner, as far as other dimensions of the classroom curriculum framework are concerned they are much more flexible. To start with, they all allow a variety of kinds of group relationships when they are being used; individual use, collaborative work by a group with a shared task or competitive working are all possible. They also have some capacity for what we might call self-adjustment to their users. As they are essentially empty shells into which users place and manipulate content of their own choosing (text, pictures, numbers,

Table 10.1 *Types of software and their educational characteristics*

Software type	Learner seen as	Group relationships encouraged	Knowledge embodied is
Word processors	Creator	Neutral	Adult/simplified
Desktop publishing packages	Creator	Neutral	Adult/simplifed
Presentation packages	Creator	Neutral	Adult/simplified
Spreadsheets	Creator	Neutral	Adult/simplified
Graphics packages	Creator	Neutral	Adult/simplified
Music composers	Creator	Neutral	Adult/simplified
Ideas processors	Creator	Neutral	Adult/simplified
Database packages	Creator	Neutral	Adult/simplified
Modelling packages	Creator	Neutral	Adult/simplified
Programming languages	Creator	Neutral	Adult/simplified
E-mail	Creator	Collaborative	Adult
Computer conferencing	Creator/receiver	Collaborative	Adult
Remote databases	Explorer	Neutral	Adult
Filled read-only tools	Explorer	Neutral	Adult/simplified
Text disclosure	Explorer	Neutral	Adult/simplified
Simulations	Explorer	Neutral	Simplified
Adventure games	Explorer	Neutral	Simplified
Instructional hypertexts	Explorer	Neutral	Instructionalized
Encyclopaedias	Explorer/ receiver	Neutral	Adult/simplified
Talking books	Explorer/ receiver	Neutral	Adult/simplified
Intelligent tutors	Explorer/ receiver	Independent	Instructionalized
Video games	Explorer/ receiver	Independent	Simplified
Data logging	Receiver	Neutral	Adult
Drill and practice programs	Receiver	Independent	Instructionalized

formulae or whatever), users can choose for themselves the level of complexity of that content, and the level of sophistication of the manipulation of it. This encourages learning, by reducing the risk of frustration and failure that more rigid packages are prone to ([Vaughan (1997)] offers a good illustration). However, in other contexts this openness can discourage learning for precisely the same reason; namely, that it does not make demands upon the user that they do not themselves choose to accept. [. . .] For example, Jon Jessel (1997) notes how children using word processors may not engage in discussion of their collaboratively written text without teacher intervention. This is presumably in part because the software does not require such activities of them or indicate the need for them. In addition open-ended packages, like any others, may create obstacles to learning simply through their lack of user friendliness in the sheer mechanics of operating them, rather than any intrinsic difficulty in the content they are used to order and modify.

However, not all types of open-ended packages are neutral as between different modes of use. Electronic mail and computer conferencing are (like the telephone and the postal service) impossible to use except in collaboration with others willing to act as recipients and initiators of messages too (see Davis, 1994, for a detailed consideration of this matter). Bernadette Robinson (1993) has also discussed this point at some length. As she notes, computer conferencing may be used not only for the transmission of factual information but also as a powerful tool for creative writing, a point supported and expanded elsewhere by Brent Robinson (1993). What we have in this sort of software, then, are learning media that are at least as flexible in most respects as other kinds of open-ended software, but which have a built-in requirement for shared use.

In the second main category of software types the emphasis swings from the learner as knowledge creator to the learner as interested explorer. Here either the software designer or the teacher provides a structured body of content that learners then explore. This category includes what we might call the 'filled' versions of the tool packages discussed above, i.e. those in which the database, spreadsheets or whatever is presented to the learners with some content already in place. Related types of software include text disclosure packages (Scrimshaw, 1993c), talking books for young children, video games, adventure games (Underwood and Underwood, 1990), simulations and the hypermedia simulations and encyclopaedias now appearing on CD-ROM. Finally, data logging devices are another rather different form of tool package. Here, however, the filling is provided through the ongoing collection of data from the environment itself. Thus these packages offer a distinctive mix of active data collection by the learner and close control over what kinds of data are collected by the program designer and by the nature of the environment in which the equipment is used.

These sorts of package are all neutral as between individual and collaborative use, but they differ not only in what knowledge they embody but also in the form that it takes. Many databases (for example most of those that can be accessed remotely) are designed for adult use, and to that extent can claim to be direct introductions to some aspects of the adult world. Conversely simulations, video games and adventure games (which can be seen as a rather exotic form of non-real-life 'simulation') are by definition simplifications, and thus potentially easier for younger learners to understand, although the underlying complexity of such popular simulations as *SimCity* and *Civilization* suggests that this point can be overstated. So, too, are many forms of control technology devices (see, for instance, Whalley, 1994), such as LOGO-based floor turtles. Between these two subgroups are packages that may take either adult or simplified forms, such as electronic encyclopaedias and all the filled tool packages, which may be presented with content that makes greater or lesser concessions to the relative lack of experience of younger users.

Another subgroup within these more exploratory kinds of software are instructional hypertexts, in which some teaching material is included to help the learner deal with the substantive content provided. Here, too, there can be wide variations in the level of complexity of the instruction provided. Related to these are the drill and practice programs in which learners reinforce and/or test their knowledge (for a discussion of one example, see Jones and Mercer, 1993). Such programs may have some form of branching (a simple hypertext structure) built in, through which the user is channelled from activity to activity according to the responses made. This kind of program has developed over the past fifteen years into intelligent tutor packages, which respond with a much greater degree of relevance and flexibility to the learner's inputs to the computer. These packages may have an explicit didactic element or may be designed in a more exploratory and occasionally collaborative mode. These programs assume an alert user who is willing to make choices, but one who reacts to the program's initiatives and definition of the task, rather than creating such a definition for him or herself, or exploring in a more or less open-minded way the information provided; they thus stand on the borderline between exploratory and receiver models of the learner.

CD-ROMs are becoming increasingly widespread in schools and homes. CD-ROM disks are simply another device for storing information, operating on the same general principles as audio CD disks. CD-ROM disks, however, store and play back a much wider variety of kinds of information; text, diagrams, photographs, animations and computer programs can all be included as well as sound.

The reason that CD-ROMs need separate discussion from an educational point of view is that they store far more material than floppies. This allows the designer to include around a quarter of a million pages of text on each disk, or to include items such as good-quality sound and animations (including short video clips) that take up so much space that only a CD-ROM can hold enough of them to make up an effective presentation. Consequently CD-ROM titles range from text-only designs, through multimedia encyclopaedias (where the text is leavened with many pictures and some sound and video clips) to CD-ROMs whose most obvious characteristic is a great deal of animation and sound. Thus far more complex software packages can be provided through this medium, such as general and special-interest encyclopaedias, annotated databases of pictures and a variety of 'talking books', in which learners follows an animated story with access to both a printed text and a spoken reading. Something of the potential of CD-ROMs in schools are beginning to be reported (Steadman *et al.*, 1992; Collins *et al.*, 1996) and first indications are positive.

What emerges from all this is that the distinctions drawn earlier between kinds of curriculum materials reappear in rather similar form when we look at computer packages. While there are also many differences in convenience and speed (not all favouring the computer), software packages can be grouped in the same ways as conventional materials as far as their potential roles in classroom teaching and learning are concerned.

The Computer as Catalyst for Radical Educational Change

The previous section assumes that the importance of computers lies in their capacity to help us pursue our current conceptions of education more efectively than we could do with traditional kinds of resource. It also assumes that the wider place of the school and teachers within society will remain the same. Can these assumptions be sustained? I think not, which means that the account so far, while plausible within its limits, seriously underestimates the impact that computers will have upon schools and therefore of the opportunities that they will offer for teachers.

If we look beyond the classroom and the school we see a world in which changes are continuous and diverse. Historically schools have been partly sheltered from these processes, because in their location, staffing and to some extent in the knowledge they were expected to transmit they were physically and organizationally separate from the society around them. But all these three screens between schools and society are, for good or ill, disintegrating, making schools far more open to external influences. This opens up another route by which computers will influence teaching and learning, because society itself is being powerfully and directly changed by the ways in which computers are being employed.

As we have seen earlier, electronic networking involves the connection of individuals to each other via the computer and to massive databases of stored information. This facility is already available to, and in some cases used by, schools but the fastest growth is in the electronic interconnection of companies, universities, government bodies and individual homes through computers. This is evolving into a vast network, precursor to an eventual 'Information Superhighway'. This is currently estimated to link over 20 million people worldwide. All of them have, in principle, access to each other and to the databases that each is prepared to make available to others, either free or for a small charge.

Schools can choose to link into this network, and to the extent that they do, they redefine both what constitutes learning groups for their pupils and the role of teachers. When the group includes other children and adults from all round the world, the teacher's contribution to the group's discussion is quite different from that which is possible and required when everyone involved is present face to face in the classroom.

This development also raises questions about how children themselves might use information available on the network. [. . .] How [. . .] will teachers help children deal with databases they encounter through the Internet, designed for adult specialists to use?

The Redefinition of Public Knowledge

So far I have discussed these issues as if the notion of adult knowledge itself was unproblematic; as if this was, if not a static entity, at least something that was evolving and changing slowly through time; but in fact adult knowledge and its mode of dissemination are both changing rapidly, and the computer is at the heart of this process, as the spread of computers through the wider world forces a reconceptualization of one human activity after another. In business management and commercial practice massive changes have already taken place and are already partially reflected in schools. But computers are also altering how, for instance, English, art and history are conducted and conceived of as academic and creative activities. In consequence the option of simply seeing computers as a better means of transmitting the traditional curriculum is already dissolving, especially for students now preparing for teaching.

First, in many areas the form and substance of what constitutes knowledge is being modified by the introduction of the computer, even in areas in which the motive for the change was simply to provide some improvement in ways of accessing or generating kinds of knowledge whose nature was assumed to be impervious to the effects of such changes. In many cases this was indeed so, but in others it was not. Novels written in hypertext format are not simply equivalents of the linear novels published on paper (see Scrimshaw, 1993b; and, for more detailed discussion, Bolter, 1991, and Landow, 1992). Art packages do not simply reproduce in a more convenient way the artwork produced with traditional media (although some of them to some extent can) and the same is true of computer-based musical composition and performance.

If we turn to more practical activities and the sorts of craft knowledge and skills that define them, the changes are, if anything, even greater. [. . .] Today computer-aided design is changing the ways in which all kinds of objects from dresses to aircraft are being created, while electronically generated simulated news studios now replace the images of real studios behind the (so far still real) news reader. Occupations such as accountancy, stockbroking, product development and marketing have been significantly altered in many firms by the introduction of spreadsheets and computer databases to identify, for instance, the quantitative aspects of possible future developments, and to locate patterns and problems in current practices.

More generally, electronic communications within companies are changing the balance between individual and group activity on a massive scale, with the development of such interesting devices as electronically shared personal diaries that allow members of a team to see at once when a suitable time for a group meeting is available, to set up that meeting and to have it recorded in everyone's diary automatically. In the same way shared files that several people can access and change, even if they are in offices in different countries, are transforming what can be meant by co-authoring.

Whether people are working at a checkout counter, stocktaking in a warehouse or producing a parish newsletter, computers are redefining what capabilities their tasks require, and in ways that cannot but feed back eventually into the school curriculum. These changes are not only in individual techniques and skills, but are also altering the whole balance in thought and action between the intuitive and the explicit, and between the rationally simplified and the qualitatively complex. These are changes that teachers not only should not, but in practice cannot, ignore.

The Teacher's Role

What are the consequences of such changes for the way in which teachers do their work? This is best approached by again looking separately at computers and software that can be seen as improving the effectiveness of current kinds of teaching and learning, and then turning to the more radical demands made by those new technologies that are beginning to require a wholesale rethinking of the teacher's role.

There is something to learn about any new piece of software of a straightforwardly technical kind, although perhaps less than might often be feared. I have argued earlier that teachers also need to see how different kinds of software relate to various views of learners, their relationship with each other, and the view of knowledge that the design of the software assumes. Below these more general considerations is the need to become familiar with the distinctive features of specific software packages, for as much of the educational potential of a program lies in the detailed structure as in its more general character.

How teachers use a particular program has to take account of all these aspects, but it is not completely determined by them, although both programs and more frequently the accompanying advice for teachers suggest that the designer favours a given approach. In practice teachers can employ software in ways that fit their own educational philosophies, rather than automatically taking up the particular educational stance that the designer may favour. In that sense virtually all software packages are, as far as the teacher's role is concerned, open to at least a fair degree of interpretation, as a variety of studies have shown (see, for instance, Olsen, 1988, and Cochran-Smith *et al.*, 1991). Open-ended packages can, as we have seen, be closed down by the teachers pre-specifying content for them that sets limits on the range of ways that children then use them. These limits can subsequently be selectively loosened or tightened as the activity progresses. On the other hand, the teacher may instead want to open up the ways in which a learner uses an open-ended package, because the learner has too restricted a conception of the possibilities it offers to use it to best effect. [. . .] Even where the package provides prestructured material that the teacher cannot change (as in adventure games, for example), the teacher can still use the package in various ways by presenting it to learners within a different framework of instructions and suggestions.

In practice, therefore, teachers are faced with very similar choices when using computer packages as they are when using any other kind of curriculum materials, namely how to adapt and interpret them to fit their own philosophy of education and the best interests of the learners they work for. But neither the full implications of what we each take our philosophy of education to be or what constitutes the best interests of learners are ever fully obvious to us, for our understanding of both evolves and changes continually in the light of experience. This is especially obvious when we face a new situation (such as that created by the introduction of a different kind of software package) which itself offers more possibilities and limitations than are immediately obvious. This implies the teacher's role, too, cannot be rigidly pre-specified and then applied in every situation. For instance, to ask if the teacher should be an unobtrusive stage manager or a hands-on director of classroom activities is to miss the point; sometimes one is appropriate and sometimes the other. The problem is to know which strategy to use when.

One approach to this problem has been to look to the notion of scaffolding. The terms refers to the actions that a helper (usually an adult) takes to reduce the demands of some task on a learner so that he or she can concentrate on gaining the particular skill or understanding that the task requires. This concept is clearly relevant to classroom learning (although it is by no means restricted to that arena). However, it needs a fuller definition if it is to be of practical use to teachers. Maybin *et al.* (1992: 188–9) offer the following provisional formulation:

> ['Scaffolding'] is help which will enable a learner to accomplish a task which they would not have been quite able to manage on their own, and it is help which is intended to bring the learner closer to a state of competence which will enable them eventually to complete such a task on their own . . . To know whether or not some help counts as 'scaffolding', we would need to have at the very least some evidence of a teacher wishing to enable a learner to develop a specific skill, grasp a particular concept or achieve a particular level of understanding. A more stringent criterion would be to require some evidence of a learner successfully accomplishing the task with the teacher's help. An even more stringent interpretation would be to require some evidence of a learner having achieved some

greater level of independent competence as a result of the scaffolding experience (that is, demonstrating their increased competence or improved level of understanding in dealing independently with some subsequent problem).

Scaffolding in this sense does indeed get us beyond thinking about what teachers do in terms of a single kind of approach, as the form that scaffolding might need to take would clearly differ from context to context. It also emphasizes the role both of the teacher's intentions and the learner's subsequent achievements in deciding whether scaffolding has been successfully accomplished. Finally, it makes very clear that such a view of the teacher's role requires a great deal of careful observation and reflection by the teacher, so that the links between what the teacher attempts and the subsequent learning can be identified with some confidence.

However, the concept of scaffolding is not by itself sufficient, for it makes no distinction in terms of the relative value of different kinds of learning; or, indeed, between ethical and unethical (as distinct from effective and ineffective) methods of scaffolding learning. It needs therefore to be set within a wider conception of education based upon a thought-through philosophy. This is even more clearly the case when we turn to those forms of software and delivery systems (such as CD-ROMs and electronic networking) which demand a radical rethinking of their role by teachers.

The first difference that these two technologies introduce is to increase greatly the range of knowledge available to learners. This alone changes the teacher's role. How, for instance, does the teacher respond to a situation where different pupils have based individual project work not upon the information contained in books in the classroom or school library, but upon data gathered from an encyclopaedia on CD-ROM or electronically from outside sources that, in total, are too many and diverse for the teacher to check directly for accuracy?

Electronic networking also widens the range of learners in a group far beyond the classroom walls, through computer conferences and e-mail. But when the group with which a learner interacts includes other learners and adults from all around the world, the teacher's contribution to the group's discussion is quite different from that which is possible and required when everyone involved is present face to face in the classroom.

Such networking also expands the range of 'teachers' available to children. These include not only those fellow learners elsewhere who can advise their peers on a particular topic, but adult experts. This raises the question of how, for instance, the teacher contributes to a discussion on science between pupils and a working scientist whom they have contacted for advice, or how two teachers in different countries jointly organize and support a shared project involving both their classes.

So how can schools and teachers respond to these new possibilities? One option is simply to view the wider resources as something to be closely controlled by the teacher by setting closed tasks that require only materials which the teacher already knows to be available on the CD-ROM or in the national database that the learner is to use. While such tightly focused activities have their place, they hardly make full use of the potential available and will not, if used exclusively, help learners develop their own capacity for independent study. Such closed tasks therefore need to be supplemented with activities and instruction that enables learners to benefit from both the wider range of knowledge available and from their interactions with learners and teachers outside their own school.

The implication of the first requirement is that teachers need to teach the processes of learning rather than its products. The conventional learning skills, such as locating, collating and summarizing information, and identifying connections and contradictions within a body of information, all need to be explicitly moved to the centre of the classroom curriculum. The development of such skills also needs to be done in ways that then enable learners to develop them further for themselves through using appropriate forms of software.

Another major contribution from the teacher is to assist learners to find out how to collaborate with and learn from others. This requires the explicit teaching and learning of ways of organizing co-operative activities involving computers, whether in face-to-face groups round a single machine or through co-operation at a distance via a conferencing or e-mail system.

In order to do this, teachers themselves need more opportunities and support in using the new technologies in collaborative contexts, so that they can both identify the problems and possibilities for themselves and find ways to model these activities in their own practice with learners. Finally, when introducing these newer technologies teachers too need time to reflect upon and research what is happening.

What all this suggests is that the ever-increasing influence of the computer in schools and in the wider community will demand a far deeper reappraisal of the teacher's role than is commonly recognized, requiring a fundamental and continual process of rethinking what is taught, how it is taught, and why. If this change is not to be externally imposed, teachers themselves will need to develop forms of reflective classroom practice that enable them to make the best use of the educational and professional opportunities as they open up.

References

Bolter, J. (1991) *Writing Space: The Computer, Hypertext and the History of Writing.* Hillsdale, N.J.: Lawrence Erlbaum Associates.

Cochran-Smith, M., Paris, C. L. and Kahan, J. L. (1991) *Learning to Write Differently: Beginning Writers and Word Processing.* Norwood, N.J.: Ablex.

Collins, J., Longman, J., Littleton, K., Mercer, N. Scrimshaw, P. and Wegerif, R. (1996) *CD-ROMs in Primary Schools: An Independent Evaluation.* Coventry: National Council for Education Technology.

Davis, N. (1994) 'Electronic communication', in J. Underwood, *Computer Based Learning: Potential into Practice*. London: David Fulton.

Jessel, J. (1997) 'Children writing words and building thoughts', in B. Somekh and N. Davis, *Using Information Technology Effectively in Teaching and Learning*. London: Routledge.

Jones, A. and Mercer, N. (1993) 'Theories of learning and information technology', in P. Scrimshaw, *Language, Classrooms and Computers*. London and New York: Routledge.

Landow, G. P (1992) *Hypertext: The Convergence of Contemporary Critical Theory and Technology*. Baltimore, MD: Johns Hopkins University Press.

Maybin, J., Mercer, N. and Stierer, B. (1992) 'Scaffolding learning', in K. Norman (ed.), *Thinking Voices: The Work of the National Oracy Project*. London: Hodder & Stoughton.

Monteith, M. (ed.) (1993) *Computers and Language*. Oxford: Intellect Books.

Olsen, J. (1988) *Schoolworlds/Microworlds: Computers and the Culture of the Classroom*. Oxford: Pergamon Press.

Robinson, B. (1993) 'Communicating through computers in the classroom', in P. Scrimshaw, *Language, Classrooms and Computers*. London and New York: Routledge.

Robinson, Brent (1993) 'Collaborative writing using distanced electronic communications', in M. Monteith, *Computers and Language*. Oxford: Intellect Books.

Scrimshaw, P. (ed.) (1993a) *Language, Classrooms and Computers*. London and New York: Routledge.

—— (1993b) 'Reading, writing and hypertext', in P. Scrimshaw, *Language, Classrooms and Computers*. London and New York: Routledge.

—— (1993c) 'Text completion programs', in P. Scrimshaw, *Language, Classrooms and Computers*. London and New York: Routledge.

Steadman, S., Nash, C. and Eraut, M. (1992) *CD-ROMs in Schools: Evaluation Report*. Coventry: National Council for Educational Technology.

Straker, A. (1989) *Children Using Computers*. Oxford: Blackwell.

Underwood, J. (ed.) (1994) *Computer Based Learning: Potential into Practice*. London: David Fulton.

Underwood, J. M. and Underwood, G. (1990) *Computers and Learning: Helping Children Acquire Thinking Skills*. Oxford: Blackwell.

Vaughan, G. (1997) 'Number education for very young children', in B. Somekh and N. Davis, *Using Information Technology Effectively in Teaching and Learning*. London: Routledge.

Whalley, P. (1994) 'Control technology', in J. Underwood, *Computer Based Learning: Potential into Practice*. London: David Fulton.

11

The Information Superhighway and Postmodernity: the Social Promise and the Social Price

Jane Kenway

Introduction

In developing an argument for systematic global analysis, Hennessy (1993: xvii) wrote

> it makes it possible to acknowledge the systematic operation of social totalities . . . across a range of interrelated material practices. These totalities traverse and define many areas of the social formation – divisions of labour, dimensions of state intervention and civil rights, the mobility of sites for production and consumption, the reimagination of colonial conquest, and the colonisation of the imagination.

Such a mode of analysis is sorely needed in education at the moment as studies of education have become increasingly fragmented and as the oversupply of micro-analyses hides from view a sense both of the big structuring forces at work and of their effects as they weave their way through everyday life. This is particularly the case in the educational research which focuses on new information and communications technologies – with some exceptions (for example, Cummins & Sayers, 1995). Here the emphasis is usually on such technologies as tools for learning or as a means of enhancement for more of the same. In such work there is usually a wilful blindness to the genuinely new and to the social and cultural contexts and implications of technology. However, technology is not just a resource for learning and we must also consider its significance as a context for learning (Bigum & Green, 1995). It is a context within and through which learning occurs and about which learning must occur. Given the implications of converging technologies for reshaping the lives of those in the so-called developed world and given their likely increasing importance for other parts of the globe, educators the world over have a responsibility to produce an agential citizenry which is well and critically informed about such technology's social and cultural implications. In particular, it is important to ask 'What are the quality of life and social justice issues which arise?' and 'What sort of polity will new technologies help bring into effect?' My intention in this chapter is to adopt the sort of analytic recommended by Hennessy (1993) in order to consider these questions in relation to the 'information superhighway'. These are difficult questions to answer given that the effects of technologies are notoriously difficult to predict and given the complexities of postmodernity. Nonetheless, it is important to try because, as I have argued elsewhere, they put new and profoundly difficult issues on the educational agenda (Kenway, 1995).

I will begin the chapter with a brief description of the information superhighway, followed by an equally brief discussion of its social and cultural context. I will then canvas the views of those who have developed informed speculations about the social and cultural implications of the information superhighway and, in the process, add some thoughts of my own. The argument I will mount is that despite its promise and promises we need to remain open-minded as well as sceptical and critical.

The information superhighway

The information superhighway metaphor refers to the unstoppable trend to replace current technologies for the delivery of information, communication and entertainment with new. It is about a move from narrow band to broad band which provides the capacity to deliver much more volume, more quickly. It is also about digital encoding which brings about the convergence of computing, telecommunications and broadcasting into a common digital format. This means that voice, text, graphics and video signals can be mixed and manipulated. It also means the increasing convergence of the computing, telecommunications and broadcasting industries. The Internet, which links computers and telephones, is the medium attracting most current interest.

The Internet is a network of computers which allows users access to databases worldwide. As we move from narrow to broad banding the quality and range of textual forms that the Internet provides access to will increase. However, there is more to the Internet than access to more and better information. It also offers a different economy of communication from other communications technologies. Until computer networks, these communication technologies fell into one or two categories: one to one (telegraph and telephone) and one to many (broadcasting – print, television, movies, and radio). Computer networks, on the other hand, offer many to many communications, multicasting in addition to one to one and one to many. The Internet, therefore, offers many different ways of communicating and, in short, it readily opens the way to membership of an array of new communities not grounded in local geography and makes it possible for people to become producers and distributors of their own cultural products. It is these changed relations of production and new opportunities for association that are seen to account for the Internet's tremendous popular appeal. [. . .]

At the same time as it is being constructed technologically, the information superhighway is being constructed discursively, with a range of very different values implied and interests at stake. Those who are constructing popular understandings tend to be advertisers and journalists and those vested interests whose perspectives they amplify. These mainly include representatives of the various industries involved, experts – usually from university research centres associated with science, technology and/or communications, enthusiasts and governments. The tendency amongst these groups is to celebrate and promote uncritically new communications media. The stress is on convenience, access, choice, enhancement and profit. Let us take some examples starting with the idea of the new networked home. Access from home is based upon new functions for a more extensively networked Internet and includes banking, paying bills, filling in forms and various sorts of home shopping. The latter include computerized catalogues with densely layered virtual shopping malls or with attractive video texts and payment from home possibilities. When the focus is entertainment the stress is on choice and interactivity. Multiple channel pay TV, video on demand and interactive TV are seen to open the opportunity for 'entertainment democracy'. For business and industry, the new media forms are promoted as providing new opportunities for profit. The digital gold rush is under way for large and small businesses alike. When the focus moves to education the emphasis is on access to more and better information unrestricted by geography, institutional location or teachers and on new opportunities for global communication between students and between students, teachers and 'experts'. Clearly, the information superhighway is a very successful and popular metaphor. However, those who regularly employ it say little about the direction and quality of its traffic, the difference activities in different lanes, who controls the lights or who gets to travel. Neither do they say much about the social and economic conditions which are helping to produce it or those which will result from it. Yet it would seem that new information and communications technologies are shaping up a new economic, social and cultural order and layering new inequalities over old.

Brand (1987: xiii) argued that 'Communications media are so fundamental to society that when their structure changes, everything is affected'. Most other analysts follow suit and the consensus amongst commentators is that these new media forms have the capacity to reshape our work, leisure, lifestyle, social relationships, national and cultural groupings and identities but in ways difficult but important to predict. For example, Poster (1994) claimed that as the new communications media which will arise as a result of convergence are so dramatically different from those preceding them, they represent a second media age and Drucker (1993) argued that the information or knowledge economy is the major economy of today and the future. Many on- and off-line cultural, social and educational analysts are currently exploring the implications of new communications media for various aspects of our lives. In order to get a sense of the complexity of what is afoot it is useful to canvass their ideas.

The information superhighway and postmodernity

Social and cultural theorists tend to place recent developments in information and communication technologies, such as the information superhighway, in the context of discussions of the massive changes associated with what is variously called postmodernity, the post-industrial age, post-Fordism, post-nationalism, new times, globalization, the information age, late capitalism, disorganized capitalism, casino capitalism and so on. Whatever their title, their stories are of dramatic irreversible, life altering, unpredictable change.

This range of titles suggests a number of things. Firstly, it suggests that we are going through a historical period which has certain features which distinguish it from previous times and that fundamental social conditions have radically changed. Secondly, the range of titles suggests differences of focus and emphasis, but it also points to some serious interpretive disagreement about the nature of the times we are going through. In turn, this implies that adequately coming to grips with these times is no easy analytical task. Much analysis is therefore a necessarily speculative and tentative exercise in seeking to understand this new context. However, all analysts, from whatever broad theoretical orientation, seem to agree that to understand these times it is necessary to adopt a global analytic and one which takes into account the relationship between capitalism and new technologies. Such an analytic recognizes that computer technology has 'intensified multinational capital's reach', provided it with a 'dense grid of information' and 'proliferated opportunities for investment and exploitation' (Hennessy, 1993: 15). To put it very simply, markets and information technology and the relationship between them are the primary forces driving economic, social and cultural change today. It is thus insufficient to talk either of the dominance and force of consumer culture or of technoculture. Our global, regional, national and local cultures and the identities they construct must be seen, in large part, although not exclusively, as the complex and shifting result of both as one. This point is eloquently demonstrated in the words of Rundle (1992):

> We live in the world of the office, the computer network, the outer suburb, satellite TV, the multi campus university. These are the outer signs of a global system which has been consolidated in recent decades by the fusion of science, the state and the market, by the development of the information society, by the growth of consumer capitalism and by the development of new systems of value and meaning. (p. 3)
>
> The contemporary period . . . is one in which the vastly speeded up and globalized system of information and production has produced a culture, a psychology and a system of values appropriate to it. Practically everyone . . . is, to a greater or lesser degree, caught up in this culture, from the young urban professional in the thick of the information lifestyle leisure culture, to the inhabitant of the outer suburb (who shops at a mall, gets 24 hour world TV, whose children are learning computers and Japanese) to the farmer watching satellite TV in the pub or contemplating the pros and cons of various genetically engineered species of wheat and all points in between.

Global markets and global technologies have significant implications for nation-states, for the power of policy to effect change justly and, indeed, for the inclination of policy makers to attempt such change. New technologies interact with economic matters to help facilitate transnational enterprises, the operations of which challenge the capacity of nation-states to control their own economies and cultural and natural environments. Indeed, new technologies of communication and the markets they support often bypass state boundaries altogether as electrons pass through national borders at will. The state thus attempts to steer but is also to some extent steered by the cultural and economic logic of these new media forms. Nowhere is this more evident than in relation to international money markets which are characterized by 'footloose capital' and shifting global economic landscapes (Wheelright, 1994: 26). As Wheelright (1994) noted, four principles prevail in the supranational corporate culture. These are 'think globally, act short-term, move money and buy and sell other corporations'.

These changes undermine the power of the nation-state to control its subjects and their form of life. The nation-state, therefore, seeks out new ways to survive in times which threaten its annihilation. These are often very destructive and exploitative (see Levidow, 1990). As states struggle to transform their national economies and as they direct their resources accordingly, what we see are a shedding of welfare responsibilities, rapid privatization, the rise of market forms in the remaining state-provided services and the development of new government and market technologies of ideological manipulation and control. As Dion, (1995) said of the USA case:

> The current task for the public relations workers at transnational corporations and their governmental allies had been how to recover the iconography of the American Dream as a positivity in a time of dislocation and disaccumulation. Specifically, they cultivate and circulate a claim that transborder informational and production practices do not represent the death of the American Dream. In the amended account, the American Dream is resurrected, phoenix-like, in the promised embodiment of a postindustrial, information-driven, 'next generation' form. In doing this, they refurbish the powerful and recurrent American ideology of techno-utopianism.

The Information Superhighway and Postmodernity: Social and Cultural Implications

It is not uncommon for governments to express concern about the implications of the information superhighway for social inequality and justice. The slogan for expressing this concern is 'information rich and information poor'. This slogan raises the questions 'Will converging technologies create new social divisions in terms of "information poor" and thus layer over current social inequalities another layer of inequality?' and 'How can this be prevented?' Seldom do such concerns translate into either an adequate understanding or enlightened social policy. This is no surprise, governments being what they are. But, to be fair, reaching an adequate understanding is no easy matter given the complex processes involved and the proliferation of both Utopian and dystopian narratives about communications technologies and their economic, social, cultural and political implications. Let me try to bring some clarity to the field by pointing to the main threads of both perspectives.

Utopian perspectives

Some usually astute observers, among them Internet Society President Vinton Cerf and Microsoft CEO Bill Gates, are predicting that the twenty million now on the Net is only the beginning. Cerf predicts 100 million by 1998 and Gates, in a recent interview, confided that his big mistake so far had been in underestimating the importance of the Internet. If they are right, if the hordes are going to start beating their drums in public, absolutely everything about the existing social order is about to be challenged. Not simply the mass media institutions, but all institutions. Everything is at stake.

(Weston, 1994)

Most Utopian arguments focus on the Internet and on developments associated with it. Basic to them all is the fact that the Internet has a fundamentally different economy of communication from other forms of communication technology. As I noted at the outset it allows multicasting or many to many communication. And, so the argument goes, the Internet offers people the opportunity of becoming producers and distributors of their own cultural products, rather than active or passive consumers of the products of others. As Weston (1994) pointed out, 'the mouse is more powerful than the remote control'. He argued 'It is impossible to understand much about the Internet's appeal by analysing its content. The Internet is mostly about people finding their voice, speaking for themselves in a public way' (Weston, 1994). In this view the Internet is less about content and information and more about new relationships to content and information. The mass media is seen as offering 'almost pure content' and a non-dialogical relationship that insulates the few content producers from their audiences. In Weston's (1994) view the Internet expands 'the locus of direct, self-mediated, daily political involvement'. Cultural producers of all sorts no longer have to kowtow before mass media agencies in order to gain a public voice. And, 'what was previously local, domestic, idiosyncratic amd private can, for the first time, become external and public. This is an abrupt reversal of the mass media's progressive appropriation of the idiosyncratic and private for their own institutional purposes.'

There are many implications here for those from subordinated groups who wish to rewrite their identities – always providing of course that such groups can get access to the new means of cultural production and have the skills necessary to use them. The Internet provides them with new opportunities to represent themselves in their own voices and own ways. This allows them to move beyond the constraining and often demeaning constructions of them produced by the mass media. It also allows them to move beyond the gendered, racialized and classed barriers often put in their way by those who control publication outlets and makes possible an outpouring of art, literature and music from subordinate groupings. In turn, this has implications for the notions of expert and novice, high and low culture – notions which have often positioned the socially subordinate on the down-side of the divide.

Some argue that this capacity provides a direct challenge to the mass media and the established institutional order which it supports – that the more public expression becomes distributed the more the institutions of modern society will be inconvenienced, destabilized and even threatened. Certainly digitized information has the capacity to subvert a market economy because it challenges fundamentally the nature of property and ownership. Challenges to the notion of property and ownership have important implications for the socially dispossessed who have often been viewed as property and are not to be the property holders.

Taking a somewhat different tack, some argue that the Internet not only provides people with a different relationship to cultural production but that it provokes a more democratic polity and offers new models of social and economic organization. Kapor (1993, reference not given) represented this point of view rather romantically perhaps, when he said

> The crucial political question is 'Who controls the switches?' . . . Users may have indirect or limited control over when, what, why and from whom they get information and to whom they send it. This is the broadcast model today and it seems to breed consumerism, passivity, crassness and mediocrity. Or, users may have decentralized, distributed, direct control over when, why and with whom they exchange information. That's the Internet model today and it seems to breed critical thinking, activism, democracy and quality.

Certainly, some of the metaphors of the Internet promise new ways and opportunities for relating and for the formation of identity. One metaphor is networking and the discourses within it include interactivity, interconnectedness, multidirectionality, flow and seamlessness. Fans of the Internet are particularly fond of the network metaphor (the WWW is one of the main systems on the Internet). To them it represents a new, non-hierarchical, democratic and reciprocal model of human relationships in which there are multiple and shifting centres, there is no obvious framework of constraint and in which the individual is the author of meaning. Indeed, as Burstein and Kline (1995: 104) pointed out the lexicon associated with the Internet includes such concepts as free, egalitarian, decentralized, *ad hoc*, open and peer to peer, experimental autonomous and anarchic. In contrast, the concepts associated with business and commerce are for profit, hierarchical, systematized, planned, proprietary, pragmatic, accountable and reliable.

As many argue, distributed public media require the renegotiation of the rights and freedom associated with public self-expression. They also require the renegotiation of issues associated with assembly and privacy. There is a well promoted view on the Internet that these issues will be worked out in community networks of various sorts and that community networks have particular implications for social justice. According to this view, the Internet provides opportunities not only for building new communities, but for renegotiating the rules of social life and for provoking a more democratic polity (Reingold, 1994). Agre (1995) went so far as to argue that as the collective life of the Internet community has unfolded, the politics of social life are being renegotiated:

> Concepts of identity, civility, and community were suddenly transformed beyond recognition – and not just in a theoretical way, but in a way that the system maintainers and the users themselves had to work with daily. System maintainers . . . have been, in many ways, rediscovering the basics of democracy as they negotiate the social contract that balances individual freedom and social harmony while confronting a whole range of social distinctions and divisions.

Community is a key concept. Virtual communities build up quickly around shared interests such as science fiction or film criticism or health support (Fox, 1996). This community metaphor is often extended to suggest a global commons. While it is far-fetched to talk of the Internet as a community rather than a collection of disparate communities and while it certainly is not global in the true sense of the word, the Internet does accommodate many different sets of interests and some believe that there is at least a community ethic or 'Netiquette' that pervades the Internet; the popular concept here is 'information wants to be free'. As Sobchak (1994) pointed out, there are shades of neo-libertarian individualism here. Nonetheless, rebuilding a community and renegotiating the rules of social life are attractive propositions for those who have been alienated and disadvantaged by the current rules. Turkle (1995: 239) drew on her studies of Internet participation to argue that downwardly mobile young middle-class people in the USA are using MUDS (Multiple User Dungeons, text-based virtual reality) as 'a vehicle for virtual social mobility', feeling that as 'they have no political voice they look to cyberspace to help them find one' (Turkle, 1995: 241).

Others see political opportunities in the possible anonymity of the Internet and the fluid identity games people can and often do play on it which allow a great deal of 'gender-bending' and 'cross-dressing'. People can live parallel lives, use nicknames or false names, conceal their identity and have multiple identities – including multiple gender and sexual identities. This is a matter of fascination for some scholars who are interested in exploring the construction of humanity, gender, sexuality and the reconstituted subject in cyberspace and there is some intriguing literature on this topic (see Hayles (1993), Morse (1994) and particularly Turkle (1995) for some empirical studies of 'life on the screen'). Stone (1995), a leading theoretician of identity/bodies/machines, explored this issue through some telling tales of the Nets which make problematic the notion of identity itself. The suggestion is not that there is no identity 'masked under the virtual persona', but rather that the disembodiment of the Internet allows repressed and multiple persona to come into play and that it encourages a 'radical rewriting . . . of the bounded individual as the standard social unit and validated social actant' (Stone, 1995: 43) and indeed challenges much psychoanalytic theory. As Stone (1995: 36) said, networks are social environments where

> Some of the interactions are racially differentiated and gendered, stereotypical and Cartesian, reifying old power differentials whose workings are familiar and whose effects are understood. But some of the interactions are novel, strange, perhaps transformative, and certainly disruptive of many traditional attempts at categorization.

Disembodiment allows much to happen that otherwise may not. As Stone (1995: 36) suggested 'new collective structures (are) risking themselves in novel conditions' and as Turkle (1995: 214) said, drawing on her empirical studies of gender bending on the Internet, 'MUDS are proving grounds for an action-based philosophical practice that can serve as a form of consciousness raising about gender issues'. The broad point to be made is that Internet communities and identities have the potential to provoke a new critical discourse about the 'real'.

There are many Internet activists who claim that the easy replication and distribution of digitized information provides a powerful resource for social justice activism. They see this technology as providing unprecedented opportunities both for resistance to forces of dominance and for the development of alliances across differences. There are many examples of this but here I will refer to the Human Rights Gopher set up in February 1995. As the promotion on the Internet points out:

> In an effort to increase access to human rights information, seven human rights monitoring organizations have begun to centralize their material on the Internet. Amnesty International (AI), Committee to Protect Journalists (CPJ), Human Rights in China (HRIC), Human Rights Watch (HRW), Lawyers Committee for Human Rights, PEN, and Physicians for Human Rights (PHR) have created a "Human Rights Gopher". . . . The human rights organizations hope to broaden the distribution of their information and speed up their ability to communicate . . . Internet users will be able to read and download the text of action alerts press releases, executive summaries of reports, letters to government officials, newsletters, and select reports the same day that they are issued . . . NEWNIRL%ITOCSIVM.BITNET@vm.cnuce.cnr.it

In Turkle's view, 'the Internet carries a political message about the importance of direct, immediate action and interest-group mobilisation. It is the symbol and tool of a postmodern politics' (Turkle, 1995: 243).

Dystopian perspectives

Dystopian themes largely emphasize the 'informatics of domination' (Haraway, 1987). A panopticon and surveillance theme is common and relates to the growth of sophisticated watching, listening, storing, sifting and intrusive devices and to the eventual capacity of full service networks to track the behaviour of individuals and to develop digital profiles for various state or market purposes (Ratcliffe, 1994). Chaum (in Levy, 1994) calls this a 'panopticon nightmare' saying 'Everything you do could be known to anyone else, could be recorded forever. It's antithetical to the basic principle underlying the mechanisms of democracy'. Let us take two examples. Interactive digital marketing (targeted or customized marketing based on digitized, cross-indexed advertising and databases on consumption habits) has potentially insidious effects which are not just about privacy and fair play but also about manipulation. The more you buy the more you give away about your personal preferences and yourself and thus the easier it becomes to sell to you. A key question here is 'How will the differences between the classes, races, ages and sexes be manipulated and with what effects?' Both within and outside the USA fears abound about digital 'wire tapping' by government and law enforcement agencies, particularly the CIA and FBI. The use of 'intelligent agents' capable of surveillance is likely to lead to the forms of self-surveillance of which Foucault talks.

Matters of national sovereignty and security are pertinent here. But the matter does not stop there for as Poster (1994: 78) observed 'nation states are at a loss when faced by a global communications network'. Their 'institutions, laws and habits' were developed for another media age. The Internet, for instance, pays no attention to national boundaries and it is not subject to government regulations. Governments are not only at a loss about how to deal with privacy and surveillance issues but also with matters of regulation, property rights, copyright, export laws, defamation and much more. Other government worries relate to questions of national identity. This issue is of particular pertinence to countries outside the USA and is expressed in concerns about cultural deregulation, further Americanization and the implications these will have for an individual country's unique cultural identity and for its culture industries and their export potential. The USA's cultural imperialism and its ambition now to be the information and entertainment superpower through the export of digital goods and services would seem to justify these concerns. Invented to point to the problem of access, when inverted the 'information rich/information poor' slogan points to the problem of being 'rich in poor information' and encompasses enduring social and gender justice questions about 'access to what?' What will the quality and nature of the content and interactions be and how will social relationships and individual and group identities be constructed within them? What sort of knowledge is offered? Whose knowledge is it and what does it say to users about who they are, how they should behave and what they should value?

Cross-national issues arise here too with regard to cross-cultural sensitivity, rights and responsibilities on the Internet. For example, what is considered perfectly acceptable in one country may be considered deeply offensive in another. No less sensitive are cross-cultural differences associated with matters of authorship and ownership.

A further concern relates to the implications of the commercialization of the Internet for its proclaimed current democratic practices and communities. It is clear that the information superhighway is being seen by business more as the marketing superhighway and as a result the fear is that the inclusionary ideals and vocabulary of the Internet cannot be sustained now that markets have recognized its immense potential. But of course there are wider implications.

The rise of the market on the Internet combined with the technologies of surveillance noted above raises serious issues about the further commodification of people's lives. The principal battlefield of the technology war is the home or more specifically the integrated telephone, computer and TV within the home. Networked homes have the capacity to undermine the industrial conditions of workers, to reinscribe the traditional version of femininity and overall to create new pressures on households. It is likely that the networked home will increasingly become the networked workplace. Already telecommuting is dramatically changing the nature of work and particularly homework. According to Burstein and Kline (1995: 262), in the USA, 7 million people work for their employer from home, 20 million are involved in home-based business and up to 40 million do at least some of their work from home. While all of these may not necessarily be involved in networked work, there is no doubt that the home is where secondary or peripheral labour markets flourish and where, for women, paid work is conducted at the same time as unpaid household and child care work. Further, 'new communications tools add time pressure, stress, and complexity to people's lives as home and work and work and leisure become increasingly difficult to distinguish' (Burstein & Kline, 1995: 263).

Other issues arise with regard to the further commodification of people's lives as a result of the networked home and the provision of infinitely more accessible home services. Home shopping with its ever-changing flow of seductive commodities and images is likely to position women even more as subjects for the endless array of gendered images and identities offered by the advertizing industry which will extend its reach into more and more aspects of life. While it may offer convenience it will also privatize and individualize consumers and further lock them into market forms of exchange and the social relationships which accompany them. Markets require a shift in focus from the collective and the community to the individual and redefine the meaning of such terms as rights, citizenship and democracy. Civil and welfare rights and civic responsibility give way to market rights in consumer democracy. The decline of the welfare state is what accompanies the rise of market forms. This next stage in the development of technologized consumer culture does not auger well for those who depend on welfare or for those who need unions to help them to gain some rights as outworkers. Neither does the rise of the amoral, selfish, anarchic individualism produced by an increasingly consumption-driven economy.

Many fears have been expressed about the psychological fallout of the information superhighway – that it will breed a cop-out society by feeding fantasy, escapism and nostalgia. Media critic, Postman (1986, 1993) argued that the information superhighway is unnecessary because we already have an overabundance of information. He wrote about the loss of meaning and the trivialization associated with the media age, the feelings of alienation, confusion and inertia that it produces, information glut and information junkies. Apparently some players of MUDS play for up to 40 hours a week, have trouble slipping back into real life and 'pinch time from work . . . and sleep' (Stewart, 1994: 11). In Postman's view, as the home increasingly becomes the site for accessing shopping, entertainment and work, 'cocooned and isolated individuals will be produced who find it difficult to distinguish between reality and simulation' (cited in Stewart, 1994: 11). The possibility of alienation from public life looms large here and with it questions arise about community and social responsibility in real life as well as life on the screen. However, again, there are other further issues worth canvassing.

New mass media forms in the 'networked home' raise important issues about identity, gender and household leisure. For some time analysts from cultural studies have speculated about the implications for the constitution of the identity of a televisual lifestyle about the subjective implications of the fragmentary, superficial, hyperactive and impressionistic offerings of the TV screen. Some express concern that these will have negative implications for the ways in which viewers come to experience and understand the world and that the problems will be magnified in the more complex and confusing environment of the converged technologies. Further matters of concern arise in relation to the individually tailored information processing program (intelligent agents) which are likely to be developed to assist people to handle the information surplus. In contrast, these will block out the benefits of the haphazard and serendipitous and lock people into their own limitations. To take another tack, pay TV, with its popular sports and pornography channels, is unlikely to rewrite masculinity in a positive way. Indeed, as many feminists have argued, sport and pornography are prime sites for the construction of aggressive and oppressive forms of masculinity. Video games, both those in arcades and homes, are renowned for their violence and broad banding will add considerably to the availability of such games and to opportunities for interactive violence. How boys construct their masculinity through these games is a matter of concern. In an attempt to lure girls into the market, creators have produced games around such toy characters as 'Barbie' and the 'Little Mermaid'. The demography of the Internet points to its main participants as young, White, well-educated US males. Indeed, the most common feminist line of argument about the Internet is that it is an outcome and expression of male culture. However, as I have argued elsewhere (Kenway, 1996) the gender issues are more complicated than that.

Of course many of the benefits and the problems alluded to so far have implications mainly for those with access to these new media forms. In order to get these debates into perspective, it should be remembered that this constitutes a privileged minority of the world's population. In the USA for example, only the affluent third of the population own a home computer and, according to the Australian Bureau of Statistics in Australia 1994, only 20% of households owned a home computer. Further, there are approximately seven million households in the USA without a telephone. Access in the USA invariably 'breaks down along traditional class lines' as Turkle (1995: 244) said and she went on rather chillingly to speculate that 'Perhaps people are being even more excluded from participation, privilege and responsibility in the information society than they have been from the dominant groups in the past'. In the so-called Third World, it is probable that many of the population have never made a phone call.

Access is a baseline issue and includes matters of cost, availability and competence and indeed the quality of access. As Holderness (1994: 24) pointed out, there is high- and low-end Internet access and this can mean significant differences in what it is possible to do, for example 'down loading a book in a couple of seconds' compared to spending 'all day running up bills to do the same'. He went on to explain that the costs in certain countries of the world in relation to income are prohibitive and that in the less-developed countries the capital is not there to purchase or attract (depending on which way you look at it) such 'capital intensive goods and services' and that therefore some countries are unlikely to gain Internet access and the developments which will flow from it. The path from having no access to having a computer, a modem, advanced communications software, an online service account and the knowledge necessary to use them all is not likely to be travelled easily by the information poor. Matters of language (most Internet communication is in English), poverty, social and geographic isolation, disability, gender, generation, and First and Third World/North and South location as they overlap and intersect are particularly pertinent here.

This points to the limitations of any mode of analysis which does not attend to broader patterns of production and consumption and clearly one must also consider the implications of new information and communications media for such broader patterns.

The Bigger Picture – Again

There can be little doubt that new technologies are helping to bring into effect a new economic order, call it what you will. Burstein and Kline (1995: 10) observed that this involves a

> shift from brawn to brain power, from manufacturing to services, from mainframe to micro processor, and from big smoke-stack belching heavy industries, vertically integrated under hierarchical management structures to the lighter, cleaner, more decentralised technology industries, horizontally networked into matrices of 'virtual organisations'.

All this connects to major trends in business and government organization where decentralizing, downsizing, outsourcing and customizing have become the dominant discourses while at the same time new communications technologies offer new management technologies of control. The feature of these changes which is most pertinent here is the rise of what has come to be called the knowledge or information economy and the rise of the knowledge worker (Drucker, 1995).

These times have seen the decline of manufacturing, the expansion of the service sector and the birth of the information sector which is of increasing importance as a source of output, growth and wealth creation. Moving 'bits rather than atoms' (Negroponte, 1995, *passim*) costs much less and therefore this represents the highest value-added sector. The talk in this sector is less of human capital and more of intellectual capital (Burstein & Kline, 1995: 274). What is needed here is people's knowledge and creativity with regard to applications and content, their capacity to manipulate, understand and make productive (commercial, exportable, transferable and licensable) use of symbols for the abstracted worlds of information, finance, content and entertainment. According to Burstein and Kline, (1995: 334) such symbolic analysts constitute 20% of those involved in the information sector.

They are the glitterati set of the digerati set and they are led by the men at the electronic frontier – the digital entrepreneurs. Clearly these men hold many of the current levers of cultural and economic production. Rushkoff (1994) implied this is 'the revenge of the nerds'. They lead what Kroker and Weinstein (1994) called the new virtual class. In an era when all things digital capture increasing media coverage, their corporate battles and values have a particularly high profile and are constantly offered to us by the press as models of entrepreneurial inspiration. For such digital entrepreneurs particularly in the USA, Europe and Japan and to a lesser extent in other parts of Asia, Latin America, Canada and Australia all the world is a potential source of labour, custom and profit. They are creating a new digital world order based on information flows. As Hennessy (1993: 10) pointed out,

> As the terms of economic power veer more and more towards control over information, knowledge is being stripped of its traditional value as product of the mind, making it a commodity in its own right whose exchange and circulation helps multiply new divisions of Labor and fractured identities. Politically, 'the ruling class' is being reconfigured as a conglomerate of corporate leaders, high level administrators and heads of professional organisations. An accompanying reinscription of the bourgeois 'self' as a more complex and mobile subjectivity inextricably bound up in myriad circuits of communication is unfolding in multiple cultural registers.

Sassen (1991) used the network metaphor to point to the decentralization of production and the continued central ownership and control in what she calls global cities. In these global cities, the banking, accounting, law and other services are provided to enable 'complex organisations to manage spatially dispersed networks of factories, offices and services'. Further, as (Probert, 1993: 20) pointed out, drawing from Reich, the 'enterprise web' is a more apt metaphor, as 'the centre provides the strategic insight that binds the threads together. The threads of the global web are computers, facsimile machines, satellites, high resolution monitors and models'. As she observed,

> producer services involve significant numbers of high wage professionals and technical employees, but even greater numbers of low wage clerical workers, usually women, and nothing much in between . . . the increase in low wage jobs and casual employment is linked with the growth of the knowledge industries, the growth of high income professional jobs and the resulting gentrification of global cities.
>
> (Probert, 1993: 20)

This class, she explained, has a lifestyle which has moved away from the consumption of mass-produced goods to the consumption of leisure and craft goods and these both employ labour which tends to be sweated work and outwork and involves a vast increase in part-time and casual work.

New technologies have many other implications for patterns of employment and class and other relations of inequality:

> Computer technology has . . . speeding up shifts in production and refining divisions of labour. The accompanying fragmentation and dislocation of communities and the increasingly anonymous corporate structure have made the operations of exploitation in the age of information ever more insidious even as inequalities between women and men, minorities and dominant racial and ethnic groups have intensified.
>
> (Hennessy, 1993: 10)

The digital revolution has contributed to the high degree of redundancy and job obsolescence in the manufacturing and increasingly in the service sector, to the decline of middle management and the middle classes, to mass and ongoing unemployment and to the rise of a permanent underclass. The information revolution makes promises about social and cultural riches and opportunities. However, it can only keep these promises to a fortunate few. For many it spells disaster. And, for global and national societies as a whole, it points the way to dangerous economic and social polarization and accelerating disenfranchizement of major sections of the population.

These are but some of many arguments about the ways in which new communications technologies contribute to the stratification of the workforce. The easy movement of information across dispersed locations and communities also allows for 'remote management' and for the dispersal of production across the globe. As Burstein and Kline (1995: 308) pointed out:

> the division of labour in creating information products and services is constantly changing and highly flexible. High speed communication links make it possible to shift data entry work and laborious computer coding to many sites around the world. 'Back offices' . . . are moving to Ireland, Jamaica, China, the Phillipines and India.

Simply put, 'Jobs in the productive sector are down loaded around the globe' (Kroker & Weinstein, 1994: 86). Kroker and Weinstein (1994: 79) argued that arranging free trade zones such as the North American Free Trade Agreement (NAFTA) and the European Community or most favoured nation status

> free up the speed of the virtual economy from the gravitational pressure of local regulatory 'circuit breakers' and allow for the 'endless repositioning of manufacturing nearest to the cheapest sources of labour'. No longer is labour value in search for a market . . . now a virtualised market for coordinating global market positioning is in search of stay-at-home labour.

In turn, this sort of thing allows for new international divisions of labour which intensify the control of workers at the same time as wage competition is increased.

While the digital entrepreneurs may well be creating a new digital world order and new capital formations, many of the conventional laws of capitalism remain. Capital will flow where it can productively find new business and build new markets and parts of the so-called less-developed world are seen as a vast emerging market for new telecommunications services. Indeed, telephony is regarded as one of the biggest worldwide growth businesses. Apparently personal computer ownership doubles every two years in China (Burstein & Kline, 1995: 297) and Singapore is pumping money into becoming a 'wired island', 'middle-office', connecting the corporate North to its manufacturing plants in the less-developed South (Holderness, 1994: 24). For the moment though, according to Burstein and Kline (1995: 308), in the emerging markets of Mexico, Brazil, Indonesia and China it is the local élites who are providing the markets for such things as satellite dishes, cellular phones and cable TV. The rich in these high-growth emerging markets are using digital technology to maintain their class location and the poorer are becoming poorer as a result of their additional information poverty. Of course, despite what the digital entrepreneurs may say, getting 'wired' is not going to solve basic problems associated with economics or education in the poverty-stricken households of those who Negroponte calls the 'digitally homeless'.

Of life on-line, Turkle (1995: 232) said

> The issues raised are difficult and painful because they strike at the heart of our most complex and intransigent social problems: problems of community, identity, governance, equity and values. There is no simple good or bad news.

Her remarks are apt for the off-line world as well. Predictably what will happen on and around the information superhighway will be a complex interplay between the Utopian/dystopian themes I have outlined and probably much more besides.

Conclusion

Given that technological competence is a new basic of education, equal access and equal competence must be a basic concern for educators. Such competence will have an impact on students' quality of education and their access to jobs and retraining, to government information and to learning about critical issues which affect their lives. A consideration of the manner in which all basic needs can be met is crucial. However, as I have shown, it is commonly expected that as new technologies converge and the information superhighway develops, they will have an ever-increasing impact on our work, leisure, health, lifestyles and national and cultural identities and social relationships. Nonetheless, little educational attention is being paid to the manner in which we produce and consume such technologies and to associated issues of politics and justice. We must encourage students to consider the social and cultural issues that are implicated in these possible transformations to the ways in which we 'live, work and play'. Be it in the workplace, the home or elsewhere, students need to be in a position to assess the costs and benefits of the new communications media and to make wise choices which maximize the economic, social and cultural benefits and minimize the risks and costs. Teaching students about technology is just as important as teaching them to use it. For, in the words of Mitch Kapor from the Electronic Frontier Foundation.

> We are not just consumers, we are also citizens. With all this talk about markets and profits in the new digital world-order perhaps it's time to start thinking about what kind of world we want it to be.
>
> (Burstein & Kline, 1995: 17).

References

(Note: articles published on the Internet do not have page numbers.)

Agre, P. (1995) Introduction, in: D. Schuler & P. Agre (eds) *Computing as Social Practice*. ALBEX. Published on the Internet. Permission to quote granted.

Bigum, C. & Green, B. (1995) *Managing Machines: educational administration – and information technology* (Geelong, Australia, Deakin University Press).

Brand, S. (1987) *The Media Lab* (New York, Penguin Books).

Burstein, D. & Kline, D. (1995) *Road Warriors: dreams and nightmares along the information highway* (New York, Penguin Books).

Cummins, J. & Sayers, D. (1995) *Brave New Schools: challenging cultural illiteracy through global learning network*, (Ontario, OISE Press).

Dion, D. (1995) Evocations of empire in a Transnational Corporate age: tracking the sign of saturn, in: *Postmodern Culture* (Oxford, Oxford University Press), HTTP.//JEFFERSON.VILLAGE.VIRGINIA,EDU/PMC/ CONTENTS.ALL.HTML.

Drucker, P. (1993) *Post Capitalist Society* (New York, Harper Business).

Drucker, P. (1995) *Managing in a Time of Change* (New York, Truman Talley Books/Dutton).

Fox, E. (1996) *Electronic Support Groups* (Geelong, Australia: Deakin Centre for Education and Change).

Haraway, D. (1987) A manifesto for cyborgs: science, technology and socialist feminism in the 1980s, *Australian Feminist Studies*, 4: 42.

Hayles, K. (1993) The seductions of cyberspace in: V. A. Conley (ed.) *Rethinking Technologies* (Minneapolis, University of Minnesota Press).

Hennessy, R. (1993) *Materialist Feminism and the Politics of Discourse* (New York, Routledge).

Holderness, M. (1994) Falling through the net, *New Statesman and Society*, 13 October, p. 24.

Kenway, J. (1995) Reality bytes: education, markets and the information superhighway, *Educational Researcher*, 22(1): 35–65.

Kenway, J. (1996) Backlash in cyberspace and 'why girls need modems', in: L. Roman & L. Eyre (eds) *Dangerous Territories* (New York, Routledge).

Kroker, A. & Weinstein, M. (1994) *Data Trash: the theory of the virtual class* (Montreal, New Word Perspectives).

Levidow, L. (1990) Foreclosing the future, *Science as Culture*, No. 8: 59–79.

Levy, S. (1994) *Money: that's what we want* (Wired Ventures Ltd). All rights reserved.

Morse, M. (1994) What do cyborgs eat: Oral logic in an information society, in: G. Bender, & T. Pruchrey (eds) *Culture on the Brink: ideologies of technology* (Seattle, Bay Press).

Negroponte, N. (1995) *On Being Digital* (New York, Knopf).

Poster, M. (1994) A second media age?, *Arena Journal*, 3(49).

Postman, N. (1986) *Amusing Ourselves to Death* (London, Heinemann).

Postman, N. (1993) *Technopoly: the surrender of culture to technology* (New York, Vintage).

Probert, B. (1993) Restructuring and globalization: what do they mean?, *Arena Magazine*, 18.

Ratcliffe, M. (1994) A red line in cyberspace, *Digital Media Perspective*, 23 December, p. 1.

Reingold, H. (1994) *The Virtual Community: finding connection in a computerised world* (London, Secker and Warburg).

Rundle, G. (1992) New ways of being human, *Arena Magazine*, October–November, p. 3.

Rushkoff, D. (1994) *Cyberia: life in the trenches of hyperspace* (London, Flamingo).

Sassen, S. (1991) *The Global City* (Princeton, Princeton University Press).

Sobchak, V. (1994) Reading mondo 2000, in M. Perry (ed.) *Flamewars: the discourse of cyberculture* (Durham, Duke University Press).

Stewart, M. (1994) If you can turn on your telly, you can turn on to the information superhighway, *The West Magazine*, 24 September, pp. 10–12.

Stone, A. R. (1995) *The War of Desire and Technology at the Close of the Mechanical Age* (Cambridge, MIT Press).

Turkle, S. (1995) *Life on the Screen: identity in the age of the Internet* (New York, Simon and Schuster).

Weston, J. (1994) Old Freedoms and New Technologies: the evolution of community networking, paper given at the *Free Speech and Privacy in the Information Age Symposium*, University of Waterloo, Canada, 26 November.

Wheelright, T. (1994) Futures, markets . . . , *Arena Magazine*, February–March, pp. 24–26.

12

Schooling and the Ownership of Knowledge

Carrie Paechter

There has been an increasing awareness in the last 30 years of the import-ance of issues of power-knowledge in classroom relationships. Attempts to alter the balance of power in classrooms, to set up micro-resistances to the prevailing order, often focus on the idea of student ownership of knowledge (Rogers, 1983; Resnick, 1987; Giroux, 1988a; Timpson, 1988; Taylor, 1989). This chapter explores concepts of school and owned know-ledge with a view to making the relationship clearer and the power-knowledge relations involved in developing students' owned knowledge more explicit.

An important aspect of power-knowledge relations in schools is the imbalance between teacher and learner in terms of whose knowledge is given legitimation and importance. In general, it is only the teacher's which matters, while students are often expected to discount or put to one side what they have learned outside the school (McNeil, 1986). Under what Freire terms the 'banking' model of education, knowledge is seen as being possessed by the teacher and transmitted more or less intact to the learner.

> Education therefore becomes an act of depositing, in which the students are the depositories and the teacher is the depositor. Instead of communicating, the teacher issues communiqués and 'makes deposits' which the students patiently receive, memorize, and repeat.
>
> (Freire, 1972: 46–47)

While this caricatures a complex and not entirely oppressive relationship, it does point to the asymmetry of the situation: teachers hold all the know-ledge, which is transmitted to students at the teacher's pace and discretion. Of course, it is not the case that students are ignorant; it is rather that they are ignorant of that which is considered important by the school. Such knowledge constitutes a special category, generally referred to as 'school knowledge', and counterposed to 'owned', 'really useful' or, simply, 'non-school' knowledge.

It might be asssumed that one way we might undercut the power-knowledge imbalance in the classroom could be through the inclusion and validation, within school, of more student-owned knowledge. Bernstein, for example, suggests that the weakening of boundaries, including that between school and non-school knowledge:

involves a change in what counts as having knowledge, in what counts as a valid transmission of knowledge, in what counts as a valid realization of knowledge . . . and so changes in the structure and distribution of power and in principles of control.

(Bernstein, 1971: 63)

The relationship between school and non-school knowledge is thus central to the interaction between knowledge and power within the school context. This chapter examines the boundary between these two kinds of knowledge and considers the potential for change in power-knowledge relationships that might arise as a result of negotiation across that boundary.

School Knowledge

In a sense, educational knowledge is uncommonsense knowledge. It is knowledge freed from the particular, the local, through the various languages of the sciences or forms of reflexiveness of the arts which make possible either the creation or the discovery of new realities. Now this immediately raises the question of the relationship between the uncommonsense knowledge of the school and the commonsense knowledge, everyday community knowledge, of the pupil, his family and his peer group.

(Bernstein, 1971: 58)

Despite recent rhetoric regarding lifelong learning, it seems to be generally accepted both by educationalists and by the general public, that school knowledge is in some way different from that found and used in the world outside. Wherein this difference lies, however, has often been either left blurred or defined in accordance with the various political beliefs and/or programmes of the writer concerned. Thus, for example, Bernstein's characterization, while emphasizing the abstract nature of educational knowledge, ignores its precision, a feature that is important from a psychological perspective (Novak, 1977). The distinction has also been made in terms of class, an argument being put forward that school knowledge is that valued by the middle or upper classes and hence a means of exclusion of working-class students from an education that would give them more power (Bourdieu & Passeron, 1977; Giroux, 1988b; Wright, 1989; Apple, 1990; Nash, 1990; Datnow, 1998). In parallel with this is a further suggestion that the inclusion of non-school knowledge into the school world may have revolutionary potential (Freire, 1972; Fitzclarence & Giroux, 1984; Giroux, 1985; Frankenstein, 1989). Others point to the way that the uncommonsense nature of school knowledge is used to differentiate between curricula and between students. It has been suggested, for instance, that one reason why so many students seem to be unable to engage with school is the difficulty (for cultural or other reasons) that they have with adapting to its particular knowledge codes, and that educational success is specifically to do with the ability to enter into this different knowledge-world (Keddie, 1971; Walkerdine, 1988). It is also noted that students may be classified and curricula differentiated according to the degrees to which non-school knowledge has to be incorporated into the learning situation, measured on a scale according to which the more non-school knowledge a student requires, the less 'able' he or she is perceived to be (Young, 1977).

At the same time there is enough consensus about what constitutes school knowledge to enable us to recognize it when we see it, and to have at least a commonsense idea of what differentiates it from that which does not have a place within school. A major feature is its high status. School knowledge is, among other things, that which is valued by the dominant groups in a particular society. Although what this is at any specific time may vary (an example being the demise of classics, and the rise of mathematics and science over the last 150 years), the function of education partly as a mechanism for progressive differentiation between and exclusion of students (Bourdieu & Passeron, 1977; Foucault, 1978; Markus, 1996) means that such value stems at least in part from its esoteric nature and its non-possession by the majority. This, in its turn, leads to a tendency for high-status knowledge to have comparatively little utility except as a credentializing system (if it were directly useful, more people would be likely to acquire it, simply out of necessity). Young, for example, characterizes the education of the Confucian literati (as described by Weber) as having three characteristics which act together to ensure that a particular definition of 'educated' supports the preservation of an administrative elite.

1 An emphasis of propriety and 'bookishness' with a curriculum largely restricted to the learning and memorizing of classical texts.
2 This curriculum was a very narrow selection from the available knowledge in a society where mathematicians, astronomers, scientists, and geographers were not uncommon. However, all these fields of knowledge were classified as 'vulgar', or perhaps in more contemporary terms, 'non-academic'.
3 Entry into the administrative elite was controlled by examinations on this narrow curriculum, so that the 'non-bookish' were for the purposes of the Chinese society of the time 'not educated'.

(Young, 1971: 30)

According to this characterization, school knowledge represents a narrow selection from wider possibilities, that selection being more influenced by the preservation of an elite group than by its usefulness to life in general. It is thus a subsection of the totality of the knowledge available, and chosen mainly in order to preserve a particular social system, though this is of course rarely made explicit. In his ensuing discussion, however, Young treats those knowledge areas that are, in fact, included as if they were necessary features of such a selection, describing this as 'the organizing principles underlying academic curricula'. In doing this he hypothesizes that those factors that, at the time he wrote, were empirically found to be features of high-status knowledge, will always remain key elements.

These are literacy, or an emphasis on written as opposed to oral presentation; individualism (or avoidance of group work or co-operativeness, which focuses on how academic work is assessed and is a characteristic of both the 'process' of knowing and the way the 'product' is presented; abstractness of the knowledge and its structuring and compartmentalizing independently of the knowledge of the learner; finally and linked to the former is what I have called the unrelatedness of academic curricula, which refers to the extent to which they are 'at odds' with daily life and common experience.

(Young, 1971: 38; closing bracket missing in original)

This has not always, however, proved to be the case. During the 1980s and early 1990s there was a burgeoning in the United Kingdom of legitimated knowledges that took other forms. Oral work, for example, became far more important, particularly in English, and one GCSE[1] mathematics examination included an assessment of the candidate's ability to work in a group (Southern Examining Group and Association of Teachers of Mathematics, 1989). More recently, nevertheless, there has been a move back towards the position characterized by Young. Notwithstanding the introduction of supposedly equivalent vocational and pre-vocational qualifications, governments of both Left and Right have continued to refer to the 'gold standard' of the academic A-level[2] examination.

It should perhaps be noted at this point that a tendency towards the reflection of particular configurations is in itself a feature of the academic curriculum, with what were once contingent features being treated, in time, as if they were important independent of the original reasons for their inclusion. Monaghan and Saul (1987), for example, point out that the continued priority given to reading over writing in early childhood education in the USA originally arose at the time of the early settlers, when most people had little reason to write, but it was considered essential that all should be able to read the Bible. Although such conditions no longer pertain, this imbalance remains a feature of the power relationships between specialists in reading and in writing. At the same time, Young is correct to point to the historical tendency to accord lower status to those aspects of schooling that have obvious relevance to the requirements of everyday life. These are often given the designation 'skills' and seen as peripheral to the education of the 'whole person' (Griffiths, 1965; Peters, 1965). As the elders of Benjamin's imaginary prehistoric tribe explain to the radicals who want to change their curriculum to one that teaches children to catch and kill the animals actually present in their hunting area rather than those which were around when the curriculum was devised:

> We don't teach fish-grabbing to grab fish; we teach it to develop a generalized agility which can never be developed by mere training. We don't teach horse-clubbing to club horses; we teach it to develop a strength in the learner which he can never get from so prosaic and specialized a thing as antelope-snare-setting. We don't teach tiger-scaring to scare tigers; we teach it for the purpose of giving that noble courage which carries over into all the affairs of life and which can never come from so base an activity as bear-killing.

(Benjamin, 1971: 15)

High-status school knowledge is thus seen as being distinctly and explicitly non-vocational, although as Keddie points out, the meaning of such terms as 'vocational' and 'relevant' depend upon one's reference group.

> Teachers express regret that a problem in motivating C stream pupils is their tendency to see education in vocational terms. It was never made explicit (if

realised at all by some teachers) that the educational aims of a course like this one [i.e. to encourage rational thinking and the perception and evaluation of alternatives] also fulfil the vocational purposes of the more successful pupils. A stream pupils have been told, and they told me, that learning to work independently (of teacher and textbook) will help them 'in the sixth form and at university'.

(Keddie, 1971: 138)

School knowledge as elite, esoteric, irrelevant to everyday life and serving the interests of a narrow elite; these were certainly characteristics of the selective and academic grammar school curriculum to which most of these writers are referring, and it remains the case that it is, by and large, the academic fields of mathematics, English and science, in their non-vocational aspects, that have highest status in school systems, a situation reinforced, for example, by the focus on these subjects in the English and Welsh National Curriculum. It should be noted, however, that when we consider the particular components of school knowledge we discover that what we are examining is constantly changing, at least at the micro level; 'mathematics' may remain on the timetable, but what is taught as high-status mathematics has come in a wide variety of guises in the last 30 years. The collection of facts and procedures that are empirically found to be legitimated by the school system is far from static, and the tendency of commentators to treat the currently valued areas automatically as this society's version of school knowledge is somewhat puzzling.

Such reflection of a particular configuration of school knowledge may partly be due to the possibilitarian outlook of many writers (Whitty, 1977, 1985; Wright, 1989). While those whose analysis stems from a Marxist or neo-Marxist perspectives (for example, Bowles & Gintis, 1976; Bourdieu & Passeron, 1977) tend to see change as dependent on a preceding revolution, other theorists (for the understandable reason that they want to promote radical and if possible rapid change) have had a tendency to seize on whatever is currently legitimated by the schooling system and suggest that if that were different, then the power-knowledge relations themselves might be amenable to alteration. Young, for example, regards academic curricula as:

> Social definitions of educational value, [which] thus become problematic in the sense that if they persist it is not because knowledge is in any meaningful way best made available according to the criteria they represent, but because they are conscious or unconscious cultural choices which accord with the values and beliefs of dominant groups at a particular time.

(Young, 1971: 38)

By tying the content of school knowledge to particular cultural choices, Young is able to make the rather simplistic prediction that:

> any very different cultural choices, or the granting of equal status to sets of cultural choices that reflect variations in terms of the suggested characteristics, would involve a massive redistribution of the labels 'educational' 'success' and 'failure', and thus also a parallel redistribution of rewards in terms of wealth, prestige and power.

(Young, 1971: 38)

As was indicated earlier, in the nearly 30 years since the above was written, at least some of the curricular emphases have changed, several, superficially at least, in the way Young implies, yet the distribution of 'wealth, prestige and power' has not, or at least not in the direction that he anticipated.

This lack of correspondence between what might have been expected to happen in theory and what has occurred in practice points to a failure in the theory fully to take account of the complexities embedded in the concept of school knowledge. In particular there is a failure to grasp that it is not merely high-status knowledge that is at issue, but *school* knowledge, specifically, that which pertains to schooling. To discuss knowledge alone is to tell only half of the story; we have to consider what happens to it in school.

An alternative way to look at school knowledge which takes into account the special function of the school itself is to consider its differences from the world outside. Dewey is an early example of a writer for whom these were of particular concern.

> These apparent deviations and differences between child and curriculum might be almost indefinitely widened. But we have here sufficiently fundamental divergences: first, the narrow but personal world of the child against the impersonal but infinitely extended world of space and time; second, the unity, the single wholeheartedness of the child's life, and the specializations and divisions of the curriculum; third, an abstract principle of logical classification and arrangement, and the practical and emotional bonds of child life.
>
> (Dewey, 1902: 7)

This separation between school and the outside world is inevitable up to a point, if only for administrative reasons, but it means that children, as they progress through the school, have to learn an increasingly different way of being, thinking and reacting (Öhrn, 1993). This positions students as strangers in the school world, faced with the task of incorporating its operational systems, norms and values into their thinking-as-usual if they are to succeed (Schutz, 1964). Keddie points out that it is precisely the ability of work solely within the school knowledge-world, ignoring what would be salient features of a situation according to common sense, that marked out successful students ('A pupils') in her study:

> There is between teachers and A pupils a reciprocity of perspective which allows teachers to define, unchallenged by A pupils, as they may be challenged by C pupils, the nature and boundaries of what is to count as knowledge. It would seem to be the failure of high-ability pupils to question what they are taught in schools that contributes in large measure to their educational achievement.
>
> (Keddie, 1971: 155–156)

Young points to the way in which secondary teachers, particularly of high-status subjects, may explicitly emphasize this difference, underlining for students that they have entered a special world, with its own rules and norms. He quotes a science teacher introducing the laboratory (a special arena in itself) to a group of first year secondary (Year 7) students:

It may well be the first time you've done science and there are a whole lot of different things about working in a lab than there are in all the other classrooms in the school . . . you have to work with certain kinds of rules which are different . . . later we'll give you a list of them which you can put in your folder . . . there are things that are potentially dangerous . . . we've got gas taps here . . . those of you who've been in a kitchen do not need to be told this (so abstracted from the real world is the teacher that he can even imagine that some kids may never have been in a kitchen!).

(Young, 1976: 53–54)

In secondary schools the difference between the school and the outside world may often be explicitly stressed as, for example, the necessity to learn special, subject-based meanings of certain words (similar, base, generalization) is pointed out to students. In infant schools, by contrast, there may be an overt attempt to connect the world of the school with that encountered outside it, partly to ameliorate the child's 'strangerness' in the classroom. However, because there is indeed such a separation between the purposes of the home and that of the school, such attempts may in practice unwittingly emphasize and reinforce these differences rather than play them down. Walkerdine (1988), for example, describes an infant classroom in which a group of children are asked to 'play' a 'shopping game'. Each child has 10 pence and they take it in turns to turn up cards from a pile, each card having a picture of what they can buy and its price. They then have to write down the sum to be carried out and work out the answer (their change from ten pence). As the children play, it becomes clear that the game bears only a minimal resemblance to shopping, and that it is some of the most salient features of real shopping that have been changed. Although some of the children make up their initial 10p with a variety of coins, they are told that for this game they must use 10 single pennies. The goods to be bought are all priced at less than 10p, although (as the children are well aware) they are substantial items that would have cost much more. The teacher lays great stress on the writing down of the sum (after all, the game is *really* an exercise in the subtraction of numbers from 10). Finally, the only child who attempts to preserve one central feature of 'real' shopping, that when you have spent your money there is no more, is told that in this game you get a new 10p each time.

In this instance the labelling of the activity as 'shopping' only serves to highlight the separation of the school and the non-school worlds. As one of the children points out (having just 'purchased' such items as a yacht for 4p and a teddy bear for 9p), 'Two pence, that's not rich. It's not enough to buy bubble gum and a bazooka' (Walkerdine, 1988: 158). Thus, partly because of attempts on the part of teachers to relate the school and non-school worlds, children learn from an early age that school knowledge is different from home knowledge, in many and varied ways, and that when they enter the classroom they must leave much of what they already know behind them. Failure to grasp this is likely to lead to failure in school, and, indeed, the group discussed by Walkerdine were described by their teacher as 'slow learners' (Walkerdine & The Girls and Mathematics Unit, 1989).

A further separation between home and school knowledge occurs in the primary, and particularly the infant classroom, where some ways of learning are given more value than others; thus, school knowledge is not only about what you know, but how you came to learn it (Walkerdine & The Girls and Mathematics Unit, 1989). In particular, there is a view, derived from an interpretation of the work of Piaget, that only experience and activity foster understanding (Walkerdine, 1988). The words found at the front of the first teachers' guide to the Nuffield Mathematics Project sum this up:

> I hear and I forget
> I see and I remember
> I do and I understand
>
> (Quoted in Walkerdine, 1988: p. 155)

This emphasis on doing is combined with a contraposition between work and play, with work seen as negative:

> Work is bad, because it relates to sitting in rows, regurgitating 'facts to be stored', not 'concepts to be acquired' through active exploration of the environment. Work, then, forms a metaphoric relation with *rote-learning* and *rule-following*. Each decribes a practice, a mode of learning, which is opposite and antithetical to the 'joy of discovery'. Play is fun.
>
> (Walkerdine & The Girls and Mathematics Unit, 1989: 33)

This leads to an undervaluing of learning accomplished through work and a belief that activity is in itself a sign of understanding. As Young (1976) points out in the context of secondary science, 'all too easily *doing* becomes equated with following instructions *for* doing' (p. 51). At the same time those students who do not learn best in the active Piagetian mode are considered to have learned less well, and even to be less 'able' (Walden & Walkerdine, 1985).

At the same time, it is argued, some parents, especially those who are working-class, are perceived by teachers as lacking the ability to prepare their children to learn properly. In particular, they are considered to inhibit learning by doing things the wrong way. This is surely because their teaching is geared to a different, more instruction-oriented discourse (Merttens & Vass, 1990).

> Primary schools hold that working-class parents 'get it wrong'. They do not 'understand children's needs' and are blamed either for not helping their children or for doing it in the wrong way. They teach them sums instead of letting them explore concepts; they buy the wrong books and toys.
>
> (Walkerdine, 1988: 54)

What is interesting here is that the working-class parents explicitly teach their children high-status knowledge, or at least what they see as high status, the ability to do sums. Pedagogic emphases have changed, however, and what counts as legitimated knowledge is now that which is acquired, at least in part, through independent discovery. School knowledge in this case is less formal than that provided in the home by a conscientious working-class parent. This again suggests that the key issue is not the content of knowledge, but how it is framed within the discourses of the school. It also points up another shift to be made by the child entering school. She or he has to come to understand that the learning work carried out there is often very different from the learning work done at home, and that it may well be pretended that it is not work at all, but play.

This is not to argue that open learning is of itself a feature of school knowledge. Indeed, one might well argue that non-school knowledge is typically learned through the exploration of particular contexts. It is important, however, to understand that the relationship between school and non-school knowledge is philosophical and sociological, and that as such it is not amenable to interventions based in psychological theories of learning alone. School knowledge is not necessarily that which is learned by rote, and conceptual understanding does not in all cases imply that a student will gain access to the 'power' contained in that which is understood. To explore this further, however, it is necessary to have a change of emphasis and to consider what I am going to refer to as 'owned knowledge'.

Owned Knowledge

The characterization of owned knowledge is problematic, if only because it has generally been defined solely in terms of what is usually seen as its opposite, that pertaining to the school. There has also been a tendency for writers to cite each others' implicit definitions, thus avoiding the need to be precise themselves; I intend, at least to start with, to follow this tradition. This failure should not, I think, be ascribed to laziness on our communal part, but is connected with the constant comparison and contraposition between owned and school knowledge; the definition of each seems to be implied in the other. However, this contraposition is also partly a heuristic device; the two terms are not strictly opposites, but rather the extreme ends of a socially constructed continuum. At the same time I am using the specific term 'owned' rather than 'non-school' to indicate my distance from an emphasis on school knowledge that is implied by the use of a descriptor that amounts to 'everything else'; by this I mean to suggest that we are concerned with a subset of what has previously been referred to as 'non-school knowledge', having its own particular characteristics. It then remains for us to tease out what these are.

Given that one aspect of school knowledge is its institutionally-legitimated character, we need to start our consideration of owned knowledge outside of the school. In this we are following the nineteenth-century radicals, who similarly considered that 'really useful knowledge' was not to be found (at least, not solely) within the schooling system. Johnson describes these groups as conducting:

a running critique of all forms of 'provided' education. This covered the whole gamut of schooling enterprises from clerically dominated Anglican Sunday schools, through Cobbett's 'Bell and Lancaster work', to the state-aided (and usually Anglican) public day schools of the mid century. It also embraced all the institutes, clubs and media designed to influence the older pupil – everything from tracts to mechanics institutes.

(Johnson, 1979: 76)

The radicals were concerned to break down the boundary between 'education' (i.e. school) and 'not-education-at-all (everything outside school)' (Johnson, 1979: 79). In doing this, they rejected that which was provided by such organizations as the Society for the Diffusion of Useful Knowledge, who they saw as serving the interests of dominant social groups, and demanded *really* useful knowledge in its place:

It was a way of distancing working-class aims from some immediate (Capitalist) conception of utility and from recreational or diversionary notions. It expressed the conviction that real knowledge served practical ends, ends, that is, for the knower.

(Johnson, 1979: 84)

Although the nineteenth-century radicals were prepared to use the schooling system when it suited them, they retained the right to decide what was important in what it offered, making it clear that the legitimation of what was and was not 'really useful' lay outside the school. At the same time, the oppositional nature of their characterizations means that the positive definition also contains a negative: owned, or 'really useful' knowledge is, precisely, that which is not controlled, legitimated or learned within the school system (although the latter may be able to provide some of its components). Similarly, Keddie's (1971) implied definition of school knowledge depends in part on an internal contraposition with 'commonsense'. We thus have a virtuous circularity of definition. It remains virtuous because the content of each end of the school/owned continuum is continually changing. It also points to a problem. What was owned knowledge 100, or 50 or even 10 years ago, is often found to be school knowledge today, and vice versa. Furthermore, as teachers, particularly those working in vocational areas or of a liberal or radical persuasion, continue to attempt to incorporate really useful knowledge into schools, such knowledge seems to lose its student-owned status and become yet another part of the school knowledge system, subject to the legitimating discipline of the examination.

It may be possible to approach the definition of owned knowledge by looking at the way it is acquired. At the minimum, it would seem sensible to assume that a necessary condition for knowledge to be owned would be that it be fully understood, and thus, one might say, truly possessed. Rote-learning alone, then, would not qualify, although something initially learned by rote, such as words in a foreign language, or a mathematical formula, might come to be owned at a later stage, through use or further understanding. It is important here to ensure that we do not fall into the trap, noted earlier, of specifying too closely how such understanding may be reached. 'I think about and I understand', 'I have it explained to me and I understood' or 'I discuss and I understand' are surely as likely to be true as 'I do and I understand'. We might also want to include some sort of criterion connected with the desire to learn a particular 'piece' of knowledge;[3] it is a characteristic of commonsense, real-world knowledge that it is learned in a context and for a purpose. This is reflected, for example, in the intentions of the English and Welsh national curriculum Working Group on technology, who were at pains to emphasize what they refer to as 'action knowledge', a term which points to the purposefulness involved in learning within design and technology activities:

> What is crucial here is that knowledge is not possessed only in propositional form ('knowing that') but that it becomes active by being integrated into the imagining, decision making, modelling, making, evaluating and other processes which constitute design and technological activity. Understanding (in the sense of the ability to use and apply knowledge in different situations), rather than knowledge (with its connotation of inert information) describes better what is important for design and technology.
>
> (National Curriculum Technology Working Group, 1988: 30)

Considerations of context and purpose, furthermore, make sense in terms of psychological theories of meaningful learning, which are concerned with the means whereby students can be helped to acquire concepts in such a way that they are able to understand and use them. One example of this is to be found in the writings of Novak (1977) whose ideas are based on the work of Ausubel. He is interested not in the content of school knowledge, but in how it is learned, and describes meaningful learning as:

> a process in which new information is related to an existing relevant aspect of an individual's knowledge structure.
>
> (Novak, 1977: 74)

Meaningful learning occurs when new information is linked to existing concepts. Consequently, the most important single factor in learning is what the individual already knows; the aim of the teacher should be to relate new material to this. In itself this is unproblematic. Confusion arises, however, when it is assumed that 'starting from where the learner is' necessarily means starting in the non-school context, and that, in doing this, the teacher will automatically bridge the divide between school and non-school knowledge. The argument seems to go like this; students will bring their own purposes and values to practical activity which may well precede and introduce them to high-status knowledge (such as school physics). Via a direct experience of activities made meaningful through their relationship to their real concerns, students will be better able to learn such higher status knowledge. This is made explicit in the final report of the English and Welsh technology working group, which, while considering the new subject to have equal status to the traditional 'academic' curriculum, makes a clear distinction between the use of knowledge and skills in design and technology and in other subjects:

> Their function in relation to design and technology is different, being to service the development of design and technological capability through their application and use in activities. They may therefore be associated in design and technology at levels different from those in other subjects and a pupil's first experience of, for example, a scientific concept or a mathematical relationship may come through practical experience in a design and technological activity.
>
> (Department of Education and Science/Welsh Office, 1989 paragraph 2.1)

This represents an attempt to root students' conceptual understanding to contextualized activities. Such concerns with meaningfulness for students are also to be found in work on student-generated problems in mathematics (Brown & Walter, 1983; Brown, 1986) and in the humanist education movement, as exemplified by the writings of Rogers (1983). Rogers stresses that it is important for learners to have control over the learning process, to learn things because they want to or because they perceive for themselves that they need to. He suggests that teachers should become facilitators of learning, providing support and resources, but allowing students to direct and evaluate their own learning. Although he recognizes the difficulties in putting this into practice, particularly due to teachers' reluctance to relinquish their power in the classroom, he suggests that by changing the structure of teacher-student relationships in this way students (and teachers) may be enabled to become 'fully functioning persons', open to experience and continually learning how to learn.

It is Rogers' reservations about the possibilities for changes in practice which point to what is probably the key issue here. It seems likely that central to ownership of knowledge is having the power contained within that which one knows. This incorporates all the aspects outlined above and at the same time explains why it is that a simple inclusion of real-world aspects into school life is insufficient; it remains possible for the school to take over such knowledge, rendering it powerless and no longer owned, stripping it, in the process, of its connection with its original context, so that 'in school, nothing is "for real", not even in the workshops' (Young, 1971: 40). Hextall and Sarup, writing from a Marxist perspective, consider this takeover to be an aspect of the alienation of labour and argue that in submitting their work to external examination students give up control of their knowledge and therefore the power contained within it (Hextall & Sarup, 1977). Similarly, Keddie notes that:

> The school may be seen as maintaining the social order through the taken for granted categories of its superordinates who process pupils and knowledge in mutually confirming ways. The ability to maintain these categories as consensual, when there are among the clients in school conflicting definitions of the situation, resides in the unequal distribution of power. There is a need to show how this enters into and shapes the interactional situation in the classroom.
>
> (Keddie, 1971: 156)

If power is central to the conception of owned knowledge, it becomes clear that students will be able to retain ownership of their non-school knowledge only if they continue to have access to the power that it contains. Owned knowledge is not simply something that is learned well, it is that which contains within it the potential for effective individual and group action. It positions its possessor as an acting subject, able to use her or his knowledge in a dynamic way. The question now arises, how can we bring about a situation in which owned knowledge is given sufficient legitimacy in the schooling system for ownership to continue within the classroom? How can we cross the barrier between owned and school knowledge?

Notes

1 General Certificate of Education, an examination usually taken at age 16 and constituting the main school-leaving qualification.
2 An academically-focused university-entrance examination, generally taken at age 18.
3 This is not meant to reify knowledge, but there seems to be no better expression.

References

Apple, M. W. (1990) *Ideology and Curriculum*. London: Routledge.
Apple, M. W. (1993) *Official Knowledge: democratic education in a conservative age*. London: Routledge.
Benjamin, H. (1971) The saber-tooth curriculum, in R. Hooper (ed.) *The Curriculum*. Edinburgh: Oliver & Boyd.
Bernstein, B. (1971) On the classification and framing of educational knowledge, in M. F. D. Young (ed.) *Knowledge and Control*. West Drayton: Macmillan.
Bourdieu, P. & Passeron, J-C. (1977) *Reproduction in Education, Society and Culture*. Beverly Hills: Sage Publications.
Bowles, S. & Gintis, H. (1976) *Schooling in Capitalist America*. London: Routledge & Kegan Paul.
Brown, S. I. (1986) The logic of problem generation: from morality and solving to de-posing and rebellion, in L. Burton (ed.) *Girls into Maths Can Go*. Eastbourne: Holt, Rhinehart & Winston.
Bown, S. I. & Walter, M. (1983) *The Art of Problem Posing*. New Jersey: Lawrence Erlbaum Associates.
Datnow, A. (1998) *The Gender Politics of Educational Change*. London: Falmer Press.
Department of Education and Science/Welsh Office (1989) *Design and Technology for Ages 5 to 16, Proposals of the Secretary of State for Education and Science and the Secretary of State for Wales (Final Report of the Working Group)*. London: Department of Education and Science.
Dewey, J. (1902) *The Child and the Curriculum*. Chicago: University of Chicago Press.
Fitzclarence, L. & Girous, H. (1984) The paradox of power in educational theory and practice, *Language Arts*, 61: 462–477.
Foucault, M. (1978) *The History of Sexuality Volume One*. London: Penguin.
Frankenstein, M. (1989) *Relearning Mathematics*. London: Free Association Books.
Freire, P. (1972) *Pedagogy of the Oppressed*. Harmondsworth: Penguin.
Giroux, H. A. (1985) Critical pedagogy, cultural politics and the discourse of experience, *Journal of Education*, 167(2): 23–41.

Giroux, H. A. (1988a) Border pedagogy in the age of postmodernism, *Journal of Education*, 170(3): 162–181.
Giroux, H. A. (1988b) *Schooling for Democracy*. London: Routledge.
Griffiths, A. P. (1965) A deduction of universities, in R. D. Archambault (ed.) *Philosophical Analysis and Education*. London: Routledge & Kegan Paul.
Hextall, I. & Sarup, M. (1977) School knowledge, evaluation and alienation, in M. Young & G. Whitty (eds) *Society, State and Schooling*. Ringmer: Falmer Press.
Johnson, R. (1979) Really useful knowledge: radical education and working class culture 1790–1848, in J. Clarke, C. Critcher & R. Johnson (eds) *Working Class Culture*. London: Hutchinson.
Keddie, N. (1971) Classroom knowledge, in M. F. D. Young (ed.) *Knowledge and Control*. West Drayton: Macmillan.
Markus, T. A. (1996) Early nineteenth century school space and ideology, *Pedagogic History*, 32: 9–50.
McNeil, L. (1986) *Contradictions of Control*. New York: Routledge & Kegan Paul.
Merttens, R. & Vass, J. (1990) *Sharing Maths Cultures*. Basingstoke: Falmer Press.
Monaghan, E. J. & Saul, E. W. (1987) The reader, the scribe, the thinker: a critical look at the history of American reading and writing instruction, in T. S. Popkewitz (ed.) *The Formation of School Subjects*. London: Falmer Press.
Nash, R. (1990) Bourdieu on education and social and cultural reproduction, *British Journal of Sociology of Education*, 11: 431–447.
National Curriculum Technology Working Group (1988) *Interim Report*. York: National Curriculum Council.
Novak, J. D. (1977) *A Theory of Education*. Ithaca: Cornell University Press.
Öhrn, E. (1993) Gender, influence and resistance in school, *British Journal of Sociology of Education*, 14: 147–158.
Peters, R. S. (1965) Education as initiation, in R. D. Archambault (ed.) *Philosophical Analysis and Education*. London: Routledge & Kegan Paul.
Resnick, L. B. (1987) Learning in school and out, *Educational Researcher*, 16(12): 13–20.
Rogers, C. (1983) *Freedom to Learn for the 80s*. Columbus: Charles E. Merrill.
Schutz, A. (1964) The stranger, in B. R. Cosin, I. R. Dale, G. M. Esland, D. MacKinnon & D. F. Swift (eds) *School and Society*. London: Routledge & Kegan Paul.
Southern Examining Group and Association of Teachers of Mathematics (1989) *Mathematics GCSE Mode 3 1990*. Tunbridge Wells: Southern Examining Group.
Taylor, S. (1989) Empowering girls and young women: the challenge of the gender-inclusive curriculum, *Curriculum Studies*, 2: 441–456.
Timpson, W. M. (1988) Paulo Freire: advocate of literacy through liberation, *Education Leadership*, 45(5): 62–66.
Walden, R. & Walkerdine, V. (1985) *Girls and Mathematics: from primary to secondary schooling*. London: Heinemann.
Walkerdine, V. (1988) *The Mastery of Reason*. London: Routledge & Kegan Paul.
Walkerdine, V. & The Girls and Mathematics Unit (1989) *Counting Girls Out*. London: Virago.
Whitty, G. (1977) *School Knowledge and Social Control, Units 14/15 of Schooling and Society*. Buckingham: Open University Press.
Whitty, G. 1985) *Sociology and School Knowledge*. London: Methuen.
Wright, N. (1989) *Assessing Radical Education*. Buckingham: Open University Press.
Young, M. (1976) The schooling of science, in G. Whitty & M. Young (eds) *Explorations in the Politics of School Knowledge*. Driffield: Nafferton Books.
Young, M. (1977) Curriculum change: limits and possibilities, in M. Young & G. Whitty (eds) *Society, State and Schooling*. Ringmer: Falmer Press.
Young, M. F. D. (1971) An approach to the study of curricula as socially organised knowledge, in M. F. D. Young (ed.) *Knowledge and Control*. West Drayton: Macmillan.

Index

181